THE

AUSTRALIAN CAPTIVE;

OR,

AN AUTHENTIC NARRATIVE

OF FIFTEEN YEARS IN THE LIFE OF

WILLIAM JACKMAN.

IN WHICH, AMONG VARIOUS OTHER ADVENTURES, IS INCLUDED A FORCED
RESIDENCE OF A YEAR AND A HALF AMONG THE CANNIBALS OF
NUYTS' LAND, ON THE COAST OF THE GREAT AUSTRALIAN BIGHT.

ALSO INCLUDING, WITH OTHER APPENDICES,

AUSTRALIA AND ITS GOLD,

FROM THE LATEST AND BEST AUTHORITIES.

With various Illustrations.

EDITED BY

REV. I. CHAMBERLAYNE.

NEW YORK:

C. M. SAXTON, 25 PARK ROW.

1859.

AUBURN:
MILLER, ORTON AND MULLIGAN,
Stereotypers and Printers.

WILLIAM JACKMAN.

WILLIAM JACKMAN, THE CAPTIVE.

EDITOR'S PREFACE.

THE editor is in such relations to the public, that, though they will hardly hold him to answer for the truth of the following history, they have a right to demand that his agency in its publication should proceed on the ground of his personal satisfaction that, in patronizing the "Australian Captive" as an authentic narrative, they are the subjects of no imposition. He accepts this issue. He will not endorse the statements put forth in the subsequent pages,—they are on the authority of the adventurer; but, on the other hand, did he not believe them entitled to the reader's credit, no consideration would engage him to bear a hand in palming them upon the public. From personal acquaintance, as well as from various collateral circumstances, to say nothing of internal evidence, which nevertheless is striking, he has no hesitation in professing his conviction that the adventurer aims at a plain and true relation of facts, from beginning to end.

"Of facts." At a few points the editor has taken the liberty of elucidating the subject by introducing some statistic and other kindred matters. And when the reader is aware that the relator, though strikingly shrewd, of quick perception and a strongly retentive memory, is quite uneducated, he will hardly need a suggestion as to the authorship of an occasional reflection on a moral, or a speculation on some philosophic subject : much less will the style and general structure of this unpretending production appear to him of doubtful origin.

But for the deficiency referred to, the " Captive" would have returned from the *terra incognita*—the interior of New Holland —with material for an invaluable addition to the confessedly meagre stores of knowledge touching the geography of the third continent. Even as it is, the editor indulges the hope, that the following unlettered sketches of Australia and of the aboriginal Australians, will not be found entirely void of interest, even to persons of science.

Its extent considered—2000 miles north and south by 2600 east and west*—there is, probably, no country on the globe, not even Africa, of which so little is known, and of which that little is liable to juster imputations of inaccuracy. When all this is considered, and that it is a state of things which, from the natural and invincible causes producing it,† is likely to be of indefinite continuance, the scientific, instead of waiting the report of some topographical exploring expedition, or some narrative of a more favored " Captive" from the *quarter-deck*, will, mayhap, accept the offering contained in these pages, furnished though it be by a castaway and a captive from the *forecastle*.

Life in the Australian bush, as the reader will find it depicted, is under more constraint, and wears less the air of

* Murray: his miles are English.
† These causes are the want of navigable rivers, the difficulty of the mountain passes, and the marshy state of the level country.

naturalness, by reason of the loss of a sheet that was to have supplied the blank names of various persons and things in that part of the narrative : a loss the more regretted, as it has been found impossible to repair it.

Among the mistakes, inseparable, more or less, from the recital of such multitudinous details, some will doubtless be found in foreign names, both of persons and other objects. Many, it is true, have been corrected ; while enough remain to furnish ample exercise for the reader's forbearance; it having been found impossible to bring them to the test of any known authorities.

After much effort to *civilize* the subsequent descriptions of scenes in savage life, some of them have proved impracticable on any emendatory principles known to the editor. His only option, therefore, seemed to lie between their utter exclusion, on the one hand, and a faithful adherence to, at least, the sense of the original matter-of-fact memoranda, on the other. The latter alternative has been adopted. Whoever would contemplate man as he is, must look for him in darkness as well as light ; as grovelling and ferocious, on the one hand, as he is elevated and godlike on the other.

This history of personal adventures goes to the public with admitted and great deficiencies. When the reader, however, finds it silent on topics which would readily have suggested themselves to the literary adventurer, and that the interest of the subject suffers in consequence, he will do well to reflect that it is one of the cases in which the editorship is not responsible, and for which it possesses no honorable remedy. Had the writer entered on his humble labor with the license of the fictionist; had he even felt at liberty to *mend* the record, it had certainly issued in a very different, and, possibly, a much more engaging relation. A governing aim has been, at all events, to leave the story a true one, in whatever graces of a more captivating character it may be found defective.

The " Australian Captive" is believed to be a new character. If any other civilized man has returned from a forced and lengthened residence among the Anthropophagi of New Holland, and told the story of what he saw and suffered among them, the writer of this book has no knowledge of it.

—————◆•◆•◆—————

Note.—The two portraits are Daguerreotypes of the original—the best that could be procured in that part of the far West to which he had removed before the satisfactory completion of the narrative. The frontispiece, if the artist prove successful, will exhibit him in his sailor's guise; the second, as he may be supposed to have appeared after his escape and lavation, on board the British brig. Both, however, are to be taken with an allowance of ten years in the age of the subject; that being the time between his metamorphosis from savage to civilized life, and the date of the two Daguerreographs.

CONTENTS.

CHAPTER I.

Nativity and early boyhood.—Short apprenticeship.—Ships in a troller—First cruise.—Unwelcome meeting.—A difficulty settled.—The North Seas.—Harsh treatment.—Runs away from his ship.—Found by a kinsman, and restored to his friends.—Reënters his apprenticeship.—Second escape.—Ships in the May Flower.—Malaga.—The burning ship.—A gale.—Boy lost. —Belfast and breakfast.—London, ... 17

CHAPTER II.

Under weigh for Australia.—Cargo of convicts.—Teneriffe.—Traffic.—Punishment of a cheat.—The Runimede.—Heavy gale. —Alarm and insurrection of convicts.—Fishing, and the fisher fished.—Prisoner overboard.—The rescue.—The shark.—Punishment.—Confession of a convict, with its occasion and consequence.—Mutiny; how detected, and how punished.—End of a long voyage, ... 28

CHAPTER III.

Leaves his ship, and how.—Ships in the Siren.—The drunken steward.—The irritated skipper, and the oily accident which befell him.—Narrow escape from the cat.—A bad scrape.—Launceston.—George's Town.—George's River, and back to Launceston.—Runs away, and takes to the bush.—First night, and first constable.—Constable second.—Night with a shepherd.—Ivory Bight, with an unlucky antecedent.—Turns cook to a rich settler.—Quarrels and quits, ... 41

CHAPTER IV.

PAGE

Sojourns at Ben Lomond.—"Looking after horses."—A wild
colt.—Scene at the smithery.—Advertised as a runaway.—
Dives deeper into the bush.—The bush-rangers.—Plunder.—
Impressment.—Discharge.—Leaves for parts unknown.—Betrayed.—Constable takes a prisoner.—Prisoner takes the constable.—The parting scene, ...   57

CHAPTER V.

The old shepherd: his hospitality.—Catecheticality.—Tragical
story of a bush-ranger.—Domesticates with farmer Raymond.—
Short acquaintance with another constable.—Cuts him.—Digression.—A night in the woods.—Surprised and taken.—
Launceston.—Justice Mulgrave, ...   68

CHAPTER VI.

Ships for London.—Runs away.—Is arrested.—Three months on
a tread-mill.—A flare-up.—Scene changes to a dungeon.—Rechanges to the mill.—Prisoners decide on subjecting the machine to certain repairs, and what they gained by it.—Observations and instances relating to the severity of the penal code, .   79

CHAPTER VII.

On board the Carib, a whaler.—Early success.—Visits the coast
of New Holland for supplies.—Is wrecked and cast away on an
uninhabited part of the coast.—Numbers of the lost and
saved.—Shifts to which the latter were driven after reaching
shore, as well as the shifts by which they reached it, ...   89

CHAPTER VIII.

The stroll.—The surprise.—The capture.—Prisoner denuded.—
Captors, with their prisoner, plunge into the forest.—Painful

PAGE

march.—Joins a large body of the tribe.—Native surprise, and
first impression.—First night among savages.—First morning,
including the kangaroo hunt.—Some account of that curious
animal, ... 96

CHAPTER IX.

Native implements.—The knife.—The battle-axe.—War and hunting spears.—How made.—Breaks a three-days' fast.—Sickness
consequent.—A forced cure.—Uncertainty of the chase, and its
consequences.—Servile and abject state of females.—Frequency
of wife-killing, with the trivial occasions upon which it is practised.—An instance, ... 108

CHAPTER X.

Warned to a general training.—Enters the ranks.—The sham-
fight, which is not all a sham.—Cadets of the chase.—Feats in
target shooting.—Puts himself upon the acquisition of both
arts—the art of hunting, and the art of war.—Acquires both,
and is respected.—Long drouth, and its effect upon the chase.—
These visitations imputed to him, as a dealer in wizardism.—
Tribe demands his death.—Chief's resistance—triumph—vigilance, ... 119

CHAPTER XI.

Temptation to attempt an escape.—Yields to the temptation, and
makes the attempt.—Strikes for the coast.—Is unprovisioned.—
Miseries of hunger and thirst.—A night among native dogs.—
Some account of those formidable animals.—Fruitless chase of
an opossum.—Lies down to sleep, invoking the sleep of death.—
Uncaught kangaroo.—High mountain, affording a wide prospect, but no ocean in it.—Another night, which proves terribly
terraqueous.—Lightning and the mahogany-tree.—Eighth day ;
discovered and taken in tow by errant fellows of his clan.—Returns to his master.—Good-natured reception.—Offer and refusal of human flesh.—More " land-eel."—Private lecture from

A*

the chief.—Narrow escape of danger from that quarter.—
Further account of female vassalage.—The lagoon station, with
doings there, which suddenly change from gay to grave, . . . 129

CHAPTER XII.

The nocturnal surprise.—An obstinate fight.—The author's share
in it.—Is wounded, and rendered insensible.—Hospital remedy.
—The enemy beaten.—Killed on both sides.—Desperate mode
of fighting.—The ten prisoners.—Two of them old offenders.—
Are sentenced to death.—Execution, with various savage tortures.—Defiant and unflinching conduct of sufferers.—Degradation of remaining prisoners.—Their dismissal.—Chapter concludes with the causes of the war, ... 142

CHAPTER XIII.

Author's recovery.—Social elevation.—Success in the chase, and
consequent carnival.—Master and man in a kangaroo adventure.—Ditto in dogmatics; i. e. in a dangerous dispute with
dogs.—How it ends, and the trophies borne to the encampment.—Royal entertainment.—Royal oration in honor of the
adopted member of the body politic.—Large gastronomy.—
Songs, the chorus, and the dance.—Author in high favor.—
Matrimony as a measure of state policy.—A proposal on that
subject is declined; is repeated, and redeclined.—Offer renewed
under highly seductive circumstances, and still unaccepted.—
Consequent ticklishness of the author's position, ... 152

CHAPTER XIV.

On the coast.—Mistakes corrected, touching (1) the piscatory
habits of the natives; (2) their African descent.—Their Asian
origin.—Extent of exceptions to this derivation, and how accounted for.—High living.—Subject of matrimony resumed.—
Surrenders to destiny, with reasons for so doing.—Marital ceremony.—General usages in regard to betrothals and marriages.—
Elopements.—The amende honorable.—Frequency of homicides.—Fratricide and his paramour overtaken by a fearful
retribution.—Acuteness of external native sense, ... 164

CHAPTER XV.

Three murders and two murderers.—The latter are surprised.—
Both fly ; are pursued; one taken.—His confession and execution.—More extensive retaliation resolved on.—Spies.—Short
preparation.—Further traits of native character.—All on the
war path.—A forced march.—A division of forces.—The midnight reconnoissance.—The ambush.—The surprise.—The onslaught.—Heroic, but ineffectual resistance.—Touching incident.—Revolting allusion.—Brief homiletic "on the state of
nature," 179

CHAPTER XVI.

Return to camp.—Superfamished.—Resort to the chase.—Quest
of a private adventure.—Finds it in a Miss Emu.—How she is
struck, and how she strikes.—Adventurer finds himself in a
twofold misadventure.—Is extricated.—Hostile encroachments.
—Opposing forces meet.—Parley between chiefs.—The enemy's champion, and his challenge.—A pitched battle.—Rout and
loss of the enemy.—Brief cessation of hostilities.—Capture and
execution of a spy.—Descent to the coast.—The stranded whale,
and a "whaling" feast.—Harassed by the enemy.—"Heir apparent" and his attendant slain.—A princely funeral, ... 189

CHAPTER XVII.

Retaliatory war.—Deaths on both sides.—The surprise.—The
flight.—The pursuit.—The rescue.—Rescuers rescued.—Two
prisoners.—One escapes death by dying.—The other dies by
being put to death.—Final visit to the coast.—Fishing ; in
which the fisher, by being fished, has a narrow escape of becoming food for fishes.—Finally, the adventurer gives his mahogany-colored friends and relations the slip, by escaping on shipboard; and how, ... 205

CHAPTER XVIII.

Curiosity and surprise on shipboard.—Kind reception.—Metamorphosis.—Final shore-scene.—Exeunt omnes.—Whaling cruise off

PAGE

the coast.—King George's Sound.—Ships for Canton.—Renewed
kindness of Capt. T.—Arrival at Canton.—Protracted opportunity for observation.—Notes on the Chinese.—Anecdote illustrative of character.—Return voyage.—Succession of disasters.
—Arrival in Swan River, ... 218

CHAPTER XIX.

Five months in an American whaler.—Again at King George's
Sound.—Three months as an *attaché* of a surveying party in
the back-woods.—Despatched for supplies.—Lost, famished,
tricked by natives.—Regains the settlement.—Delivers despatches, and declines the service.—Ships in a whaler.—How
the whalers whaled the whales, and the whales whaled the
whalers.—Returns to the Sound.—Four months in Harvest.—On
a lee-shore.—Wrecked.—Desperate struggle *for*, and narrow
escape *with*, life.—Portuguese sailors.—Once more in the Sound.
—Articles for another whaling cruise, ... 226

CHAPTER XX.

Cape Rich, on the east coast, for supplies.—Sails for Australian
gulf.—Success there.—The Fejee islands.—Off and on at Rotuma.—Trade with the natives.—Their friendliness, with other
characteristics.—Ashore on liberty.—Absconds.—Is concealed.
—Betrayed.—Discovered.—Reclaimed.—Moral.—Four months
in Otaheite.—Otaheite and the Otaheitans, ... 239

CHAPTER XXI.

Otaheite, and the Otaheitans, continued; wherein is contained an
account of the author's twofold captivity, by the captivating
islanders; as first, how he ran away, because he was captivated;
and, secondly, how he was captivated because he had run
away—the latter branch of the subject being unfolded to the
reader in various captivating details, which end the chapter, . 250

CHAPTER XXII.

Touches at the Sandwich Islands.—Their volcanic origin.—Soil and climate.—Spontaneous productions.—General state of cultivation.—Hawaii and its fire-crowned mountain.—Oahu with its capital and royal city.—The islands indebted, for their rescue from savagism, to the gospel.—Their progress in civilization and the arts.—Cruise on the N.W. coast.—Success there.—The two unfortunate ships.—Return to the Sandwich group.—Cruise off New Zealand.—Doubling the Horn.—Touches at Tristran da Cunha for water.—Notice of the place.—Quarrel between the captain and mate.—Sails for Brazil.—Stops at Trinidade.—Enters the harbor at Bahia.—Sale of cargo.—Tranships to a Brazilian man-of-war.—Regulations of Brazilian and Argentine naval service.—Incidents of a six months' service, . 262

CHAPTER XXIII.

Sins against his English conscience, by joining the crew of a slave ship.—Reach the coast.—The slave factor.—The live cargo.—The home passage.—Chased by a British man-of-war.—Narrow escape of being boarded by one of his boats.—Make the coast of Brazil.—Another escape, though not without a scratch for it, which proves a little sanguinary.—Land the cargo.—Leaves the slaver, with fair promises never to give his countrymen another chance of hanging him to the yard-arm for a pirate, . 274

CHAPTER XXIV.

A cruise in the British brig Racer.—Detailed to the pinnace, which captures an American slaver.—Capture of a Sardinian brig.—The Bonavistean ; how she was boarded and overhauled ; evidence on which a prize crew was put aboard of her ; how the captain slipped through our fingers, with several *et ceteras*.—An English brig boarded, and how she hoaxed us out of a rich prize.—Montevideo, and the court-martial.—Moldonado and the alcalde.—The tender, with various *et ceteras*, varying from " grave to gay," 283

CHAPTER XXV.

PAGE

The schooner ashore.—The pinnace and her crew sent to get her off.—The *cogniac* found on board of her.—Officer imbibes it during the day.—Rule by which its use was admitted at night.—Expedient by which the officer strove to preserve the men from overdosing, and what befell him in consequence.—Hard labor, the next day, and its success; together with hard headache and no brandy to cure it.—Night brings a fresh supply, which entails *divers* and *diverse* consequences, natural and accidental.—Lieutenant of the schooner who had furnished the *five gallons*, returns to Montevideo, to report its two-fold effect.—Affairs growing no better very fast.—Third night associates us with uncomfortable bed-fellows.—Return to Montevideo, leaving the schooner worse than when we found it.—Narrow escape of punishment, and large allowance, for a month, of "twelve-water grog."—What this substitute for *punishment* amounts to in a British ship-of-war.—Concomitant consequences of the *two nights.*—Some addenda touching the regulations of an English war-ship, ... 293

CHAPTER XXVI.

Painful intelligence from home.—Desires, but is unable to effect an escape.—Precautions against occurrences of that character.—Pinnace is sent ashore for provisions.—Some of the men manage to get to the beach, and return, "half-seas over."—Pinnace benighted in consequence.—Men mistake themselves for admirals.—Midshipman in danger.—Lose their mast.—Wind rises, and boat unable to return to the brig.—Picked up by a Dutch ship.—Loss of provisions, including the captain's wine.—How that gentleman makes us pay for it the next day.—Author decides on *making*, if he cannot find, an opportunity to quit.—Makes it out of the *missing* of the middy.—Finds concealment.—Leaves the town for the interior, ... 302

CHAPTER XXVII.

ongs for salt-water life.—Tempting offer.—Embraces it, and is a Buenos Ayrean man-of-war's man.—Large bounty, and what be-

PAGE

came of it.—Joins the squadron before Montevideo.—Compliment to English and American seamen.—Quality of native marines.—Plan of attack.—Preparations for action.—Elevation of the author.—*I and the admiral.*—Success of the naval attack.—Repulse of the land forces.—Fleet hauls off.—Killed and wounded.—Brush with the Montevidean fleet.—Capture of a pirate.—French interference.—Quarrel growing out of it.—How ended.—Our fleet captures the Isle of Rhette.—It is claimed by Admiral P.—Almost a quarrel between the two English admirals.—How obviated.—Cost of the fruitless acquisition.—Conspiracy in our own ship.—How detected and suppressed, ... 314

CHAPTER XXVIII.

Sinister influence of English agents in protracting the war.—They are superseded with a view of pacifying the belligerents.—Buenos Ayres declines the overture to that effect.—Admiral Brown's fleet blockaded by English and French forces.—Admiral Brown attempts an escape, but is taken.—Ordered into Montevideo, where his crew is disbanded.—Author ships in a Brazilian man-of-war.—State of the service illustrated by various incidents.—Trouble at Montevideo.—Ordered home to the Rio.—Gale.—Damage.—Loss of life.—Protracted passage, . . 328

CHAPTER XXIX.

Ships in an English merchantman for the coast of China.—Dismasted in a gale, with loss of lives.—Doubles the Cape, and reaches Valparaiso.—Taken sick at the latter place, where his ship leaves him.—Notice of Valparaiso, the Chilians, et cet.—Six months in a Chilian trader, in which he visits Santiago, Lima, and other places on the coast.—Sees Denmark.—Revisits Bahia.—Voyage to Mayo, one of the Cape Verde islands.—Sterility.—Manufacture of salt.—Half-day on shore.—Donkey-back procession to the "salt pans," with the accompaniment of a driver.—In passing a church, author's *asinus* carries him, *nolens volens*, into the vestibule, there giving great scandal by guzzling the "holy water."—Short ceremony of expulsion, fol-

PAGE

lowed by a short and sharp discussion, and how it ended.—Rio
Janeiro.—New Orleans.—Liverpool.—New Orleans again.—
Again at Liverpool.—Ships for St. Johns, N. B.—Pleasant adventure among the passengers.—Follows it ashore at New
York.—Attends it into the west of the Empire State, where it
matures into matrimony.—Whereupon the author apologizeth
to the reader, and endeth his story, ... 343

APPENDIX.

A —Van Diemen's Land, ... 359
B.—The Bumrum, vel Boomering, ... 361
C.—A Sixth Continent, ... 362
D.—State of Agriculture, ... 362
E.— Gossip of Sea Travel, ... 363
F.—The Lasso and Bolas among the Gauchos, ... 365
AUSTRALIA AND ITS GOLD, ... 367
THE HARVEST OF GOLD, ... 374
THE AUSTRALIA GOLD DIGGINGS, ... 384

THE AUSTRALIAN CAPTIVE.

CHAPTER I.

Nativity and early boyhood.—Short apprenticeship.—Ships in a troller.
—First cruise.—Unwelcome meeting.—A difficulty settled.—The
North Seas.—Harsh treatment.—Runs away from his ship.—Found
by a kinsman, and restored to his friends.—Reënters his appren-
ticeship.—Second escape.—Ships in the May Flower.—Malaga.—
The burning ship.—A gale.—Boy lost.—Belfast and breakfast.—
London.

MY nativity dates Dec. 19, 1821, in that part of
Old England yclept Detsom, in the neighborhood of
Dartmouth, in the county of Devonshire. Of my
father, I can say but little, as he followed the sea, and
as I followed him to that element, at an early period,
to return no more. Unlike most sea-faring men, however, he ended his days, as I was happy to learn, at
home, and in the bosom of his family. He died Nov.
1842.

Whether inherited from him, I am unable to say,
but, from my earliest recollection, I was beset by a
strong penchant for a life on the ocean. Aware of
this, and, at the same time, determined to over-rule

2

it, he apprenticed me, when in my eleventh year, to an honest miller in the neighborhood. In a twelve-month, however, acting under the blind impulse of an increasing passion for sea-life, I left him clandestinely for Brixham, and shipped in a troller, *The Friends*, Capt. Griswold, belonging to that place. I was now a little less than twelve years of age. After disposing of her cargo of fish at Portsmouth, our ship returned to Brixham to refit for Ramsgate, from whence she was to proceed to the North Seas.

In the mean time, a young man of my acquaint-ance having met me on shore and carried tidings of my whereabouts to my mother, she, with a neighbor-ing woman, intercepted me in the nick of time, when I was setting the captain on shore for the last time. Here she told the captain, what I dare say he had suspected before, that I was a runaway, and added, what, probably, he had not so much reason for sus-pecting, that I had a master who would not allow me to go to sea, without making my abductor trouble. As I was unwilling to return, however, the captain told my mother that, being ready to go to sea that afternoon, if I were permitted to accompany him, and should be satisfied to continue in his service, he would, on his return from that voyage, see my master, and arrange matters with him to his satisfaction. To this, as the best terms she could effect, my poor mother assented; when she returned home, and her unheed-

ing boy, once more aboard ship, stood away for Ramsgate.

Dec. 19, 1833, we arrived at the place last mentioned, and thence, after two days, made sail for the
North Seas, where we trolled successfully for three
months.

Here my captain, who had allured me into his service by promises of kind treatment, soon showed
himself in his true character of a tyrant. When
heaving up the troll, I was required to stand down in
the hold, and coil away the nine-inch hawser. Failing to suit the time and manner of this and various
other operations, equally unadapted to my juvenile
capacity, to his caprice, a thwack on the head with a
handspike was the almost certain hint for the necessary improvement. At other times, after I had spent
the night with a lantern at mast-head, I was sent below for the brandy, with orders to serve a glass to
each of the men; which done, I was ordered to carry
it below, and all without intimating permission to
appropriate a drop to my own benefit. On one of
these occasions, after the brandy and I were below, I
thought, "If the skipper will not ask me, I will even
ask myself to take a glass;" and, thoughtless of the
watching eye which had followed me down the companion, suited the action to the word. On reaching
the deck, he seized me by the collar, and demanded,
"Who authorized you to drink my grog?" Of course

I could quote no authority on that head which would
have been likely to satisfy my interrogator. The
next part of the ceremony was performed by means
of the tiller rope, in the shape of a sound thrashing,
and the whole was concluded with something intended
for wit, which went off on the idea of my double
warming, by way of brandy and the hemp. This state
of things continued, without interruption, till one of
the men, in whose presence he gave me a brutal blow,
interfered by saying: "If you strike that boy again, I
will strike you." The consequence of this was anything but a pleasant state of feeling between the
twain. To me, however, as kicks and cuffs came with
a sensibly diminished frequency, the effect amounted
to a clear gain.

April, 1834. We anchored at Ramsgate. On putting the captain ashore and returning to the ship, I
found that another boy and myself were left, for the
time, in sole charge. Predetermined, as I had been
for some time, to take myself off upon the first opportunity, I thought to myself, "Now is my time." On
going ashore, I found myself a perfect stranger, and
without a farthing in my pocket. At Brixham, where
the cruise would have been up, I should have been
entitled to my wages. Instead of submitting to present inconvenience, for a few days, which a wiser head
would have done, I chose to sacrifice all other considerations to the gratification of a longing for imme-

diate release from an irksome bondage. Unable to
pay for lodgings, I went to the steamhouse, and took
them in comfortable proximity to the boilers, alongside of which I slept till morning. At daylight, I
was among the shipping, in quest of a passage to
Brixham. Presently I lighted on a ship bound to
that place, loaded with oranges, from St. Michael's.
On application to the captain, he replied that he
could not afford to pay me wages, but would allow
me to work my passage. The reader will readily
imagine that, situated as I was, this offer was readily
embraced. The next afternoon, as we were hauling
out of the basin, I saw my old skipper looking from
the pier-head to see if I was on board of any of the
ships that went out with that tide; and having very
little notion of being towed back to the troller, I went
below, where I stayed till we were fairly out of the
basin, when I went to the deck and to my work.

May 7. We arrived at Brixham. On landing,
whom should I meet but the wife of my late captain.
By some means she knew me, and asked where her
husband was, and whether I had not left him. To
the latter part of her question, I replied in the affir-
mative; and added, that I did not mean to return.
She said, if I would not return, she would have me
taken up and sent back; alleging, that I was under
engagement to be apprenticed to him at the end of
the voyage. While words were running high between

us, a gentleman came up, to whom, upon being questioned, I gave a true statement of the matter in dispute. Farther questions elicited mine and my father's name, as well as the place to which we both belonged; when he said, that his name was Henry Jackman, and that he was my uncle; adding, "It is many years since I have seen your father; but I am very happy to see you here." Then, turning to the skipperess, he advised her to give herself no farther trouble about me, as he should see me properly taken care of; at which we bade her ladyship good-bye, and he conducted me to his boarding-house. On the way he told me, what I could not deny, that he supposed I was a runaway from home; that I was too young to be knocking about alone at this rate, and advised me to go home and stay there; adding, that he was going there, and would take me with him, at all events.

Accordingly, the next morning we started. I need not say, that my dear mother was overjoyed to see me, nor that she strongly supported my uncle's advice to return to my old master, the milier, and serve out my time. To this, though my inclination to wander was scarcely less strong than ever, I at last assented. My kind uncle accompanied me to my master. I gave him what satisfaction I could, as to the probability of my being able to resist my propensity to the life of a rover; upon which, at my uncle's pressing instance, he reinstated me in my *mill*-itary position.

My master was uniformly kind, as, indeed, he ever had been, and things went on smoothly for about ten months; when, my evil destiny prompting with renewed force, I determined to leave, for *good.* My master's nephew, about my own age, agreed to be my companion in the venture, and we started on the last day, or rather *night,* of February, 1835. The next day, on seeing a man riding towards us on the way from Detsom, our guilty imaginations instantly metamorphosed him into our pursuing master, of the mill; when, like two of Bloomfield's frightened pigs, we both

"—— decamped with more than swinish speed,
And, snorting, dash'd through sedge, and rush, and reed."

Having gained a covert in a neighboring wood, we kept whist and lay close, till the fainter sounds of the horse's hoofs told us that the danger was past. Here *Chauncy* bolted outright, declaring that he would go no farther, and he strongly plead with me to adopt the same conclusion. I told him I had been back once, already, and that I was now determined to "lose the horse or win the saddle." So we parted. He put *back* for home, and I put *on* for Plymouth, where I arrived that night.

The next day, after several unsuccessful applications, I fell in with a sea captain who said he would ship me, and I found myself on board the May Flower, captain Cummings, of Plymouth, bound to Cardiff, thence to Gibraltar, and thence to Malaga. We were ready for sea, March 15, arrived at Cardiff on the 19th, where, after taking in a cargo of coal, we made sail for Gibraltar on the 30th, at which place we arrived, April 17. Here we discharged cargo, took in ballast, and then made sail for Malaga, at which place we anchored, May 2. Here we took in a cargo of raisins, oranges, lemons, sumach, wine, and lead.

While lying here, I witnessed the grand and awful spectacle of a burning ship. It was a Spanish brig, loaded with brandy and olive oil. A Spanish man-of-war was lying there, the captain of which manned his boats, and strove, by firing into her, to sink her, in order to prevent her from firing the other shipping. But with such a cargo, in a state of rapid combustion, the tendency was to any other than the downward direction; so that sinking was out of the question. She took fire at 7 in the evening, and burned till 9 A.M. of the next day. The account we obtained from one of her own men, who was in the forecastle at the time, was, that three men went into the hold with a candle and bucket to draw some brandy. They were never seen afterwards. The captain and mate were on shore, and in less than fifteen minutes after the fire was discovered, the ill-fated ship was wrapped in flames.

May 29. Our cargo was shipped, and we made sail for Liverpool; but were forced by head winds to put into Gibraltar, where we lay five days. June 7. When we were nine days out, we encountered a heavy gale, which lasted three days. A heavy sea which struck us, carried away the galley, and a boy, who happened to be in it at the moment. We lost sight of him immediately after the poor fellow went over. Our longboat was also carried away, together with our bulwarks, foretop-gallant-mast, foretop-mast, and flying jib-boom. Our sails were blown from the yards like coach-whips, and we sprung our mainmast. When the gale was over, we fished our mainmast, got up another foretop-mast, bent some sails, and were once more on our homebound way.

June 28. We arrived at Liverpool, discharged our cargo, and I received my wages. Here I shipped on board the Sybil, captain MacFarlane, of Belfast, for which place, after taking in a cargo of salt, we sailed July 7, and arrived there on the 12th. The captain, whose family were here, and who very naturally wished to be as free from the ship as possible in order to enjoy their society, told us that, while we were discharging freight, he would allow us for our board, and that we might get it where we pleased. This was early in the morning, and the whole posse of us bore away for a boarding-house. The keeper of the first we came to, on being hailed, said he would take us.

"And what," we demanded, "will you charge us?"

"Fifteen shillings a week," was his answer, "if you

B

have meat three times a day; but if you take *stirabout* twice a day, I will board you for ten."

With no son of Erin to tell us what was the precise difference between the two proposals, we declared for the latter, and turned in, wondering not a little what the *stirabout* was, and what shape it was coming in. After waiting till hunger, as well as wonder had rendered us a little impatient, the landlady placed on the table two large dishes, one containing milk, and the other, what appeared to be a thick pudding. Upon this we took our eating positions, and, after waiting a while, asked our hostess if she was going to give us any breakfast. She replied: "That is your break-fast." "And what the — do you call that?" "Why, stirabout, to be sure." Having bargained for stirabout, we were bound, in honor, to waive the *verbal* for a *practical* discussion, or rather, *application*, of the subject. Unlucky dogs that we were! we thought of nothing but the necessity of stowing away the rations in the empty holds of our stomachs in the double quick time in which a hungry sailor is accustomed to perform that part of his duty. The consequence was, that the stirabout—not exactly boiling, to be sure, but at the point which Fahrenheit, if immersed in it, would have pronounced the boiling heat—the consequence was, I say, that the stirabout went *in* and *out;* in *quick*, and out *quicker*, leaving nothing behind but skinless mouths, and the taste of fire. The reader may imagine, as best suits his humor, whether the sputter, the clatter, and the general uproar that followed, and in the middle of which we took leave of our landlord and his stirabout, contained wishes for more *good*, or *ill* luck, to *it* and *him*.

In our next quarters, which we entered with an express article against stirabout, we remained until we had unloaded ship, and reloaded with beef and pork, when we made sail for London. Springing a leak, when we were three days out, called for hard and constant labor at the pumps, day and night, till we reached our destination, which was July 29. Our voyage up, cargo discharged, and wages paid, I took leave of captain McFarlane, and shipped in the John Berry, captain Forwith, of London, but then from Deptford, bound to Sidney, New Holland.

CHAPTER II.

Under weigh for Australia.—Cargo of convicts.—Teneriffe.—Traffic.—Punishment of a cheat.—The Runimede.—Heavy gale.—Alarm and insurrection of convicts.—Fishing, and the fisher fished.—Prisoner overboard.—The rescue.—The shark.—Punishment.—Confession of a convict, with its occasion and consequence.—Mutiny; how detected, and how punished.—End of a long voyage.

Aug. 17, 1835. We got under weigh, sailed down the Thames, and stood out upon our long voyage. I say long, the distance from London to Sidney being reckoned, in round numbers, at 14,000 miles. The John Berry was a government vessel, and freighted with male convicts. Their exact number was unknown to the writer; but it must have been not far from three hundred. The ship's crew, including officers and common sailors, was about thirty, beside which, we had on board not far from an equal number of marines. The ship, like all others in this kind of service, was in charge of the captain, only so far as related to the mere matter of *sailing* her; and this remark will enable the reader to understand why he is so slightly noticed in the subsequent narrative of this voyage. The acting commandant was the personage

known as the "*Doctor.*" All sanitary and municipal
matters, relative to the prisoners, were under his exclusive jurisdiction; the practical effect of which was,
that nearly all authority on board the ship was exercised by him. In short, as "*Surgeon Superintendant*"
—I think that the proper designation—he had absolute control of the cargo, which involved a corresponding control of officers and men, except, as intimated
above, the mere matter of sailing the ship.

The first land we made was Teneriffe, where we
took in three bullocks, and thirty pipes of water.
Here the people of the island, who are principally
Spanish, came off to the ship with various productions
of the place, such as oranges, grapes, and wine, for
the purpose of trafficking with us. My mouth watering for the tempting fruit, I offered the Spaniard a
new silk handkerchief, as an exchange for a stipulated
quantity of it; but when the knave had received, he
refused to deliver; so that I was minus more than
half the promised oranges and grapes; whereupon I
contrived to punish him, in manner following. Under
the bows, where none could see us, I showed him a
crow-bar, offering to exchange it for four bottles of
wine, and a certain quantity of oranges and grapes, to
which he eagerly assented. On lowering the end of
the bar, for the fellow stood in his boat, he handed up
the exchange articles, and seized the iron. Now it so
happened that *his* end of the thing was decidedly *hot*,

which rendered it so much less tenable than mine, that the pulling match which followed, very soon declared in my favor. With blistered fingers and blistering curses, he appealed to the mate for redress of grievances. But that gentleman, not choosing to understand the grounds and reasons of his complaint, could only say, that though he was sorry, he had no time to attend to him, and that he was so very busy, that he could not so much as stop to cry, just then. This I thought a capital thing at the time; but have since concluded that, for a generous tar, to say nothing of a Christian, there was a little too much malice in it for a genuine joke.

We had lain here but a short time, when the Runimede arrived with another cargo of convicts for Hobart Town, Van Dieman's Land, which made it necessary for us to proceed upon our voyage; as the Admiralty forbids two convict ships to lie together in a foreign port, unless a man-of-war be there at the time. That saving circumstance not existing in the present case, we were obliged, though in the night, to get up our anchor and proceed on our voyage, without having completed our supplies. This was Aug. 19th. When off the Canary Islands—it was about 10 at night—we were struck by a sudden squall, which threw us on our beam-ends, and nearly drove us ashore. Such, indeed, was our dangerous proximity to the rocks, at one moment, that we could have reached them by the throw of a biscuit. True, our ship soon righted; but, our topmast went by the board, our jib went to shivers, and our foresail was taken clean from the rovings. At this crisis, though our ship had regained an even keel, the prisoners were under the panic of apprehension that she was going down. This produced a loud uproar, and a general rush upon the hatches, for the purpose of gaining the deck and possessing themselves of the boats. The sentinel, who was over the hatchway, fired an alarm, and the marines were ordered to stand to their arms, and shoot the first man who made his appearance. This had the salutary effect of subduing one great fear, by another still greater. The insurrection ceased. For their greater comfort, poor fellows! the captain told them, that, if the ship went down, they would all —officers, crew, and convicts—go together, and be buried in one coffin. The blow was soon over; so that, with what little sail we could make, under favor of a gracious Providence, daylight showed that we were clear of the islands. The blast had gone by; but it left us a nice little piece of work. Happily, however, we had two good carpenters on board, and plenty of spare spars; and by the time, which was not long, that the spars were ready to go aloft, a new suit of sails was ready to be bent on to them. In two days, to be brief, we were all *atant*, and bearing away once more for the South Pacific.

When about a week out from Teneriffe, we found ourselves passing through a shoal of that kind of fish which sailors call *albocores*. One of its habits is to prey upon the flying-fish, and it is taken by a bait made in imitation of that unique object. By seizing a hook into the artificial fish, and giving it a motion similar to the original, the decoy is complete, and success is answerable. The two hundred which we succeeded in taking, weighed from ten to twenty pounds apiece. But I must needs make a piscatory adventure on my own *hook*. It fell out on this wise. Two large *pene-toes*, with some sword-fish, hove alongside, and as it was my forenoon watch below, I determined to try my hand with one of the former. The first thing to be done, was to put a strong hook into a large wooden fish; then to bend a hand lead-line on to the hook; and then, *laying out*, as the phrase is, on the martingale, to bend the other end of the line on to that outstanding object. When all this was done, and I had got my proper balance, I was ready, with several coils of the line in hand, for the operation of *bobbing*. Presently, one of the fish, having satisfied himself that all was right, leaped to the surface on which the lure floated, and seized it. Good! But I was naturally excited, and—I am ashamed to own it—but, happening just at that moment to hold *myself* a little less firmly than the floundering *fish*, instead of pulling the rascal *out*,

"*He* pulled the rascal *in*."

This was certainly against me; but, at the same time,
several circumstances were in my favor. I held on to
the line; the ship was under easy motion; a man happened to see my sudden plunge, and sung out accordingly; the boat was lowered, and I was picked up;
finally—and this was the most favorable of all the
propitious coincidences—I was not drowned. The
fact is, however, I was but a little short of it. For,
though I was attached to the line, and the line to the
vessel, and thus prevented from parting company
with the latter; there was another *attaché* to the same
line, who was much stronger than I, and more at
home in the same element, who compelled me to pass
an uncomfortable part of my time on that side of the
surface where it was not nearly as natural for me to
breathe as it was for him. In short, when my shipmates overhauled me, I was very near what the poet
Saxe calls,

          "A stiff cold water man."

When taken up and got on deck, I was insensible,
and remained so till the fish, by means of the tackle,
had also been hoisted on board. Before this latter
object had been accomplished, the fish had stove one
of the boats into which he had been taken, and drove
the men after me into the water, who were picked up
by another boat, which towed the wrecked craft, still
containing the fish, alongside of the ship, from whence

B*   3

the latter had been raised to the deck, as already related. After some heavy bets among the officers, as
to his weight, it was ascertained to be two hundred
and fifteen pounds. He was cut up and divided
among the prisoners.

Beside losing a sailor by sickness, we came very
near losing a prisoner by drowning, in the following
manner. For bathing purposes, the prisoners were
restricted, by the regulations of the ship, to a large
tub, which served for their exclusive accommodation.
One of their number, however, determined, one calm
day, to have the luxury of a sea bath, out and out;
and over he went, accordingly. He had calculated
on being able to keep up with the ship, but was out
in his reckoning, as she was under rapid motion, and
he fell fast astern. The prisoners sung out, that a
man was overboard; but the mate, who was walking
the poop at the time, coolly said: "Let him go, for
an example to the rest." The "Doctor," who was in
the cabin, heard the alarm, and, immediately making
his appearance on deck, demanded of the mate, why
he did not lower a boat, and pick that man up. The
latter gave, for answer, that he did not think it worth
his while to do that for a convict. The supercargo
ordered him to lower and send off a boat immediately,
adding, that if he ever acted in that manner again, he
would confine him to his cabin. The boat was lowered;
but, by the time we reached the poor fellow, he was

a long way astern, and could have kept his head
above water but a very little longer. At any rate,
we found he had been spoken for; for we had scarcely
got him into the boat, and begun pulling for the ship,
when a large blue shark came alongside of us, and
looked disappointed. The rascal dogged us to the
ship. The first thing done, upon gaining her deck,
was to put the prisoner in irons. The next was to
take advantage of the longing of the *lawyer* for a
client and a brief, by briefly ushering him amid a
large lot of longing clients at once. Twice the wary
villain possessed himself of the large piece of pork
that baited him, without appropriating the hook. To
obviate that sort of recurrence, we took some *spun-
yarn*, and tied the hook and bait so firmly together,
that one could not be had without the other, any
how. This little bit of legal artifice threw the gentleman off his guard; for, by this time, the pork had
begun to set so well on his stomach, that he was
willing to risk its digestion of the metal rather than
defraud it of the meat. So down they both went, and
up, under the stern, came his sharkship. While hanging here for about an hour, the gentry of the cabin,
who wanted to try their pistols, threw not far from
twenty balls into him from the windows. Thence he
was raised to the poop, where a few strokes of his tail
soon scattered his customers, and smashed the sky-
light; beside which, he came within a little of making

the entertaining addition of himself to the coterie of
the cabin. His next theatre was the quarter-deck,
where all, including thirty marines, came up missing
in less than a couple of minutes. Luckily, however,
for the peace and safety of the ship, the black cook
had seen a shark before, and when he thought that
the present incumbent had acted lord paramount about
long enough, the frizzly-headed old wag issued from
the cully, axe in hand, and very grinningly and know-
ingly whipped off the fish's tail. The game was up.
The jaws of the monster, armed with five rows of
teeth, respectively, opened wide enough to fall over
a man's shoulders. His length was fifteen feet, five
inches.

The next day the marines were ordered to stand to
their arms. The ship's crew were also called on deck,
and every man armed with a pistol and cutlass. None
of us knew to what all this tended, till the prisoners
were marched out, the boatswain ordered to rig the
gratings, and the picked-up convict of the day before
was brought aft on to the quarter-deck. Then it was
plain that the poor fellow, in default of having been
caught by the shark, was to catch the cat. In his
long lecture, the Doctor told him, that, as he was the
first man who had been brought up for punishment,
he intended to make him an example; and that he
should now give him four dozen for the benefit of his
health. Then followed the seizing up, and the inflic-

tion of the four dozen on the culprit's bare back, which was cut up in a manner which I will not pain the reader by attempting to describe. The display of force was doubtless well-timed in its effect upon the prisoners. They saw that resistance or a rescue was impracticable, and stood out the scene in silence; immediately after which they were all turned forward, and every man went his way.

Three days after this, it came on to blow a good stiff breeze, when near the end of the first night-watch, all hands were called to reef the topsails and splice the main brace. When this had been done, the steward and third mate were sent below to draw the men some grog, where they found a man lying along-side of a rum cask with plenty of raisins and biscuit around him. The fellow was dead drunk. A rope's end was bent on to him, and he was hauled on deck, where, upon overhauling him, he was found to be a prisoner. The consequence was, that he was double ironed, and the next day reported to the Doctor, whose sovereign bidding brought all hands to witness another punishment. The poor fellow took five dozen manfully, but without a word of the required confession, as to the means by which he had found his way into the ship's stores. Upon this, however, with the Doctor's threat to flog him to death if he did not confess, he owned up, by saying that he had cut a hole through the deck, under his bunk, by which he got what provisions he wanted; adding, that it was because he was almost starved to death. The passage was found, accordingly, and so neatly done, that one might have walked over it a hundred times without discovering it. So, with another dozen, making six in all, the poor wretch was released, with fifteen days in irons.

Such are the incidents of life in a transport ship; such the scenes that give it diversity, or rather—for they amount to that, in their ultimate effect—that invest it with its irksome monotony. With one more, and but one, shall I tax the reader's patience. It is one but too nearly resembling those most recently related; and the reader will probably think, with the writer, that, while it resembles them, it naturally resulted from them. It was a mutiny among the convicts. The plan was that, on nearing the Bassy Straits, which lie a little south-west of New Holland,* they would rise upon the ship's crew, put the officers to death, land the rest of the people belonging to the ship, and then make their escape to some of the islands in the South Seas. This, at all events, was the story of the informant, and corroborated by the extorted confession of the principal mutineer. The informer was an Irishman, of the name of Murphy, himself a convict, and one of those who, for the greater order and security of the rest, enjoyed a kind

* That is, from Sidney, the ship's destination.

of overseership among his fellows in crime and condemnation. According to him, he overheard a consultation one night, while lying in his hammock, in which the above indicated plan was fixed on. Among those whom he professed himself able to identify by their voices—and he offered to swear it—was the picked-up prisoner, who had been treated to the four dozen. He was James Shaw, from Liverpool, and represented by Murphy as having assumed the peril and responsibility of leading the forlorn hope of his fellow-convicts.

He and they were once more guarded to the quarter-deck, where they were charged with the mutiny. This they point-blank denied. Perceiving that he was not likely to be made any wiser in this way, the Doctor ordered up the gratings, and again all hands were summoned to the edifying spectacle of another punishment. By this time the alleged principal in the mutiny is stripped and seized up, and Scott, the boatswain, cat in hand, is waiting for the word. The Doctor, premising that, if they had taken the ship, they would have shown no mercy to *him*, says to the cat-o'-nine-tail man, "Do your duty." And well does he understand, and faithfully perform it, till the whole five dozen are well laid on; and all before there is a word or a sign of the prescribed confession. Flesh and blood, however, can now endure no more, for both are falling; one in pieces, and the other in

streams. He begs for mercy, and is told to tell the
truth, and he shall be forgiven. And he tells, what
is admitted to be, and very likely is, the truth; for
convicts are desperate fellows. And he is taken
down and forgiven, by being put in double irons,
and kept on bread and water till he reaches his Australian prison.

Though this occurrence bred some natural fears for
the rest of the voyage, and made it to be the order
for every man to sleep, when he could sleep, with a
brace of pistols under his head, and a cutlass by his
side, yet we passed the dubious *Straits* in safety, and
finally landed all our prisoners and ourselves in Sidney, Nov. 29, in the short time of one hundred and
two days from London.

CHAPTER III.

Leaves his ship and how.—Ships in the Siren.—The drunken steward.—The irritated skipper, and the oily accident which befel him. —Narrow escape from the cat.—A bad scrape.—Launceston.— George's Town.—George's River, and back to Launceston.—Runs away, and takes to the bush.—First night, and first constable.— Constable second.—Night with a shepherd.—Ivory Bight, with an unlucky antecedent.—Turns cook to a rich settler.—Quarrels and quits.

AFTER discharging our live cargo, we lay in Sidney Cove five weeks, in which time the Berry was stripped to a gantline, and painted inside and out. Then proceeding to Port Philip, on the southern extremity of the island, we landed passengers, and prepared for the intended voyage to Bombay in the East Indies. But I ran away. This proved my misfortune as well as my fault, as the reader will soon perceive, and as I was soon, and for a long time, forced to feel. As to the fault, a part of it was mine, while the other and larger portion of it belonged to him whose superior cunning made me his dupe. It was thus. One morning, while we were lying at Port Philip, as I was on my way up to market after fresh meat and vegetables for our voyage, I was accosted by a man who asked the name of my ship, and the amount of my wages, which having ascertained, he told me that he was captain of the government brig Siren, employed in cruising about different parts of the coast, and carrying provisions to the troops; and then asked me if I would not like to leave my ship, and join his. I told him that my captain, to whom I was engaged for that voyage, would not allow me to leave. He said: "Never mind that. If you smuggle your clothes on shore by the next boat, my boat shall be in readiness to take you on board the brig." I told him I would let him know when I returned from market. Accordingly, on my return, he met me on the wharf, and I told him I would do it. That night I returned with my effects to shore, and the Siren's boat, which I found waiting for the purpose, put me on board that ominously named craft, where I soon found that I had escaped Scylla, to be stranded on Charybdis. The first thing about which I was enlightened, was, what I very unwillingly learned, that my time in the Siren was for nothing less than twelve months; that being, the captain said, the shortest time for which any one could be shipped in that service. The next information he gave me, for my comfort, was, that no sailor could travel in the country without a pass from his captain; that taken up without one, he would be thrown into prison; and that, finally, if, in that case, his ship had sailed without

him, they would give him a month on the *tread-mill.*
I was beautifully duped; that was clear enough; but
these amiable hints, especially the last one, left me no
choice but that of making the best of, what, by this
time, was clearly a bad bargain.

Jan. 17, 1836.   The above little preliminaries having been settled, and some English troops having
been taken on board for Launceston, Van Dieman's
Land, we set sail for that place.   The fourth day out,
in the morning, our steward came up missing.   He
had been shipped in Sidney.   The ship was searched
fore and aft, below and aloft.   No one had seen him
since the night before; and as we were double-reefed
and under a stiff breeze, it was concluded that the
poor fellow had gone over in the night.   But four
days after, when some of the people were in the hold
for provisions, one of them thought he heard a snor-
ing, as of some one asleep.   On calling for a lantern
who should they find between rum-casks, the bung
out of one of them and a pump *in*, and a gallon measure, half full of rum, alongside of him, but the poor
steward !   The *handy-billy* raised him to the fresh air
of the deck; but it was twenty-four hours before anything could rouse him from his *unspeakable* ecstasy.
The captain put and kept him in irons till we arrived
in Launceston.

This affair so annoyed the skipper, that, for want
of more legitimate objects, he sought all sorts of occa-

sion for annoying all the rest of us in turn. As an instance; one evening in the dog-watch, *when I was not on duty*, I received his orders to take a bucket of grease and *slush* down the main-top-gallant, and main-mast. Knowing that it was a *work-up job*, I determined to make the captain pay for it. The brig was tossing about like a dolphin in a wash-deck-tub. The weather was warm, and the grease as thin as oil. The captain was walking the quarter-deck, and when I thought his position was about *right*, the bucket— accidents will happen—the bucket capsized. Unwilling to *hurt* any one, however, I threw the empty vessel against the top-mast rigging, and, in the same moment, sung out with all my might: "Stand from under." But the contents—it was unlucky for the skipper; but, happening to be exactly right for it, and looking up for the purpose of wondering what it was—the heavy mass of ointment struck him full in the face. He staggered like a soldier in fits, and his hair curled like a pound of candles.

I was immediately called down, though, for that matter, I was coming, having no more to do there just then, for want of grease. In the meantime, the same occasion which brought me from aloft had sent the skipper to his cabin, for the double purpose of discharging the redundant unction, and rearranging his general toilet. His reappearance on the quarter-deck, and my appearance before him to answer for

my alleged malfeasance, were simultaneous. The
brief indictment was briefly answered, by pleading,
that it was not my fault that the lanyard had parted.
The hearing ended with—"I will give you something
that will not part so easy;" followed with an order
to the boatswain to seize me up, and give me the
benefit of a couple of dozen. The former part of the
order was obeyed, with due promptness. In the
pause which preceded the execution of the latter, and
more material part of it, however, I took occasion to
remark to the captain, that he could do as he pleased
about the flogging, provided he was willing to stand
by the consequences, and hinted something about
Launceston and law. He said the law was in his own
hands. I reminded him that, not being captain of a
man-of-war, he had no right to flog me, nor any man
on board the brig. Upon this he inclined to haul off
a little, remarking: "If I thought the lanyard parted
accidentally, I would not flog you." To which, however, I only answered, that he could please himself as
to that, for I should make no apology. Upon this,
with a volley of the hard words, so well known in a
sailor's vocabulary, including a threat as to what I
might expect if I did not *toe the line*, I was let off,
and sent forward.

The next day, while it was my watch below, I was
sent to scrape down the fore royal-mast and the top-
gallant. Of course I knew that, like the other, it was

a work-up job; *i. e.* work prescribed for mere punish·
ment. I went up, and, seating myself on the fore
royal-yard, kept scraping the mast in *one place,* till
seven bells. On coming down, the mate inquired if
I had done, and was answered that I had not. Upon
this, he went aloft to see how matters stood, and immediately informed the skipper that I had spoiled the
mast. "If you have spoiled the mast," said the skipper, addressing himself to me, "I will spoil your
back;" and suiting the action to the word, seized the
end of the fore-brace, and though he did not quite
spoil it, it was not because he did not make a very
snug application of the rope. This done, he said he
would make me pay for the mast, and take "twelve-
water-grog" for a month. The latter award implied
that, when the men had their grog, which was every ·
day at noon, I was to stand on the quarter-deck, and
drink from a basin, one glass of Jamaica in twelve
glasses of salt water, in presence of the captain, and,
of course, with no chance of giving it a passage overboard.

Jan. 27, we arrived at Launceston, where, after dis-
embarking the troops, we took on board another
squad of the same sort of gentry, and, Feb. 7, sailed
down the river forty miles to George's Town, where
we landed a part of them, and thence proceeded to
George's River, lying still farther below, where we
disembarked the rest. It was now Feb. 10. When

this was done, we were allowed a day on shore, which we improved in shooting a large number of wild geese, which very much abound in these waters; after which, aided by some dogs, which were borrowed for the purpose of an accommodating settler, we returned to our ship with three fine kangaroos. The next day we made sail for Launceston, where we arrived Feb. 17. By this time, being very much inclined to let the captain pay for the mast himself, and, at the same time, strongly disrelishing the idea of any more of his salt-water-grog, I determined to try my land legs, and a cruise on shore. This hazardous, and, as it proved, rather disastrous experiment, was put in execution.

Feb. 18. Launceston is near the south end of Van Dieman's Land, and is only second in importance to Hobart Town, the capital of the island, situated at its southern extremity, and distant from the former place some 130 or 140 miles. To avoid a recapture, I struck off into the interior, in the direction of the latter place. On leaving the town, which I did, not far from sunset, I was overtaken by a man who asked me where I was going. I told him to Hobart Town; and farther, in answer to his various questions, that I was a sailor, and a perfect stranger in the country. He said: "I would inform you, as a friend, that if you are going to travel in the country, you ought to have a passport; as, to prevent the escape of con-

victs, there is a penalty of £50 for harboring or entertaining any person who proves to be one." I told
him I was not a prisoner, and had no passport. He
added that, under such circumstances, I would find it
a hard matter to get a night's lodging, or anything to
eat. When we came to a turn in the road where we
were to part, I asked him if he would direct me to
some house that would be likely to entertain me. He
said there was a public house about four miles ahead,
and gave directions for finding it; but expressed himself, as before, as very doubtful as to the matter of
entertainment. By this time it was pitch dark. At
last, though with no little difficulty, however, I
brought to at the tavern, and like a true Jack Tar,
called for something to drink—a habit, by the way,
which I am happy to inform my reader, I have since
entirely discontinued. Boniface demanded who I
was and where I was from. I told him I was a
sailor, had left my ship at Launceston, and was
bound to Hobart Town. Upon this, suspicions were
so far obviated that he consented to keep me, and I
walked into another room. Here I found a number
of men belonging to the house and neighborhood,
with whom, after they had put me through the colonial catechism, I entered into general conversation,
and finding them a generous set of fellows, I called
in liquor, and treated them as long as they would
drink. While I was at supper another customer was

ushered into the room—a regular six-footer—and presently took his seat at the same table. It did not long escape him that I was a stranger, and he made my acquaintance by asking me for my passport. I answered that I had none; and, in turn, demanded his authority for asking it. He replied that he was a constable, and patrolled the road between that place and Perth. Then, after various other queries squinting that way, put it to me directly: "Are you not a prisoner?" My answer was: "I came into the country free and of my own free will; and that is more than many who live here can say"—most of the *settlers*, including the *bush-constables*, belong to that class of patriots who "left their country for their country's good." To this rather provoking taunt I coolly added: "I calculate to go out of it as I came." Repeating his suspicion that I was a runaway prisoner, he said he should take me back to Perth with him. At this critical juncture, one of the men who had honored my liquor, interposed by saying: "I know he is not a prisoner, for I saw him at Launceston discharging a cargo." "Very well," said the patrol, "I am coming this way to-morrow, and will call again and see you; in the meantime I will take this man's word that everything is right."

Of course, I took smart care that he should have no more trouble on my account, by leaving at day-dawn the next morning. Before I did this, my new friends advised me that, if I kept the main road, I might be sure of an overhauling at Perth; at Campbell Town; at Oatlands; at Green Pond, and every . settlement through to Hobart Town; in a word, that I would meet as many constables as milestones. Availing myself of this friendly information, I took to the . pathless woods, through which I made my way, till I struck into a by-path leading toward a mountain called Ben Lomond. Soon after this, I met a footman, whereupon ensued the following colloquy:

I. Good morning.

He. Where are you going?

I. It is more than I know myself.

He. Where is your passport?

I. Where is your commission?

He. I am a constable, and authorized to overhaul any suspicious-looking craft.

I. I have as much reason for overhauling you, as you me, for you look more like a grave-yard deserter than a constable. Good morning.

Upon this I left him standing still in the road. Presently, however, another man passed me, when, looking back, I saw the twain, apparently in earnest consultation. Judging they would soon be after me, I dashed into the woods again, and saw them no more.

At about 12 M., I found myself on the top of the mountain, at the foot of which flowed a beautiful river. At the brink of this, I fell into a pleasant

path, which, in a couple of hours, brought me to the
door of a shepherd's hut, in which a man was standing, who very courteously invited me to walk in and
rest myself. I entered. In a few minutes the tea-
kettle was on; some mutton was fried; and I was
treated to a good dinner. Of course I must treat in
turn; that is, if money would procure the means, for
custom, in that country, includes a glass of grog
among the indispensables. I handed *mine host* a dollar. The dollar brought a bottle of rum from an adjoining shanty; and the rum made my good friend
and me very sociable for the afternoon and evening.
Among other things, I learned that Mrs. McNally
lived at Ivory Bight, distant about twelve miles, and
that she wanted to hire.

In the morning, then, though not till after I had
once more partaken of the kind shepherd's fare, I was
off for the Bight. As there was no road, and as the
settlers live a long way apart, I was obliged to use
great care in following such directions as I could find
upon my way. When near my journey's end, I met
a man who told me *where* and *how* to cross a river, I
was to find in my way, which was some twenty rods
over. Before leaving, he told me, if the old lady did
not hire me, he would be glad to; and I promised,
that, in that case, I would return and see him on the
subject. Within half a mile of the Bight, I came to
the ford of the river It was *not* very deep, but it

was very *swift*, and the bottom rough with rocks and stones. The case was a bad one; but what made it worse, was, that when about half-way over, my foot slipped; I was on my beam-ends, and it was not possible to right ship, till I had been carried clear over the rapids into the deep water below. Here the swimming art was in high request; but, unluckily for me, I had never realized that accomplishment, and it was too late to learn. Providentially, however, I brought to, at last, against a large log which lay transversely in the bed of the stream,* by means of which, as the water was comparatively still, and afforded soundings, at the same time and place, I managed so as to reach the shore.

But I had been half drowned for nothing. The place in Mrs. McNally's service had just then ceased to be vacant. Accordingly, recrossing the river—and the reader must allow me to boast, that I did it without recapsizing—I made my way to Mr. Brimmingham's, the person mentioned above, who wished to employ me. He said he would give me £25 to cook for his family twelve months. The wages would do, but,

> "To cook, or not to cook?
> That was the question."

I told him the honest truth, and that was, that I knew

* All the timber in that country, like the mahogany, which makes no inconsiderable part of it, is so heavy that, when in the water, it sinks like a stone.

just nothing at all about it. He insisted that I would soon learn. I hesitated. He urged. In fine, I yielded, and was duly installed in my new office. I ought to inform my reader, that my immediate predecessor in the department, was the family schoolmaster; for in that country, school privileges can rarely be enjoyed by any, but those who are able to make a monopoly of the business, as was the case with my employer, who had a large family, and wealth in proportion. The former, however, was principally composed of hired men, and these, again, were principally prisoners; it being the practice of the government to let out the convicts to all responsible applicants, at given wages. These not disposed of in that way, are employed on the public works, such as the construction of roads, and other improvements for the benefit of the country. It happens here, as in all other penal institutions, that male subjects largely preponderate over those of the opposite sex. Owing to this circumstance, much of the work which custom, in other countries, assigns to women, must here be performed by men, or not at all. This last remark explains the matter of my induction to a domestic office, in which the family pedagogue had figured before me. It may be as well to add in this place, what may be less convenient at any other, and notwithstanding that it is not immediately pertinent to my story, that one fourth of the population here, as well as in New Holland, are convicts;

and perhaps rather more, if we include the bush-ran
gers; that is, convicts who have escaped to the woods,
and live by plunder. Of these gentry, however, we
shall have occasion to speak hereafter. I will also
add, that, while the climate is highly salubrious, and
free from sudden changes, it is so mild as to enable
the natives to dispense with clothing through the year,
and to allow the agriculturalist to raise, and reap two
annual harvests. The soil is endued with a medium
degree of fertility. Most kinds of grain and other
productions, common to the temperate zones, are cultivated with success. Wool, however, and it is of a
very fine quality, is the great staple.

The first lesson from the schoolmaster was on the
subject of bread-making. The large oven was heated;
and the dough, duly yeasted, kneaded and moulded
into loaves, was put in; but, judge of my consternation when, on taking them out, I found them masses
of cinder! The next thing was to put off after the
schoolmaster, by whose second lecture I profited so
much that the bread came out uncharred. The next
day the mistress told me I was to make some *dough-
boys* and a *Yorkshire pudding* for the men's dinners.
I told her I could make her a duff—a name for a
sailor's pudding—if she wanted; but that, as to dough-
boys and Yorkshire pudding, I knew nothing about
either. But she would show me. So off I was sent
for eggs, milk, and butter. The butter was to be *run;*

the eggs *battered;* then the three ingredients mixed
with each *other*, and all with the *flour*. This, which
was to be the Yorkshire pudding, with a spare-rib,
and a leg of mutton, was left to *do* by the fire. But
the mistress, coming in soon after, told me that more
wood was wanting to make it do well, and then left
me to regulate the quantity by my own discretion.
Here I failed again; for, the fact was, I *piled* it on.
It waxed hot. With such a fire, I knew not which
of the many irons I had in it to take out first. As to
the wooden mantletree, when *all* things were on fire,
it ought not to have been expected that I should notice that. And I did not, till, with the superincum-
bent mass of chimney material, down it came, and the
rib, the leg, and the pudding, were all knocked into
pi. The effect of the housequake, blended as it was
with so many other elements of kindred interest, was
awful; especially, when among the rest who felt the
shock and hastened to the scene, the master entered,
cursing and swearing like a trooper.

While repairing damages, and getting up another
dinner, I began to think that, as cook under captain
Brimmingham, my cruise was nearly up. And so it
proved, as my next short yarn will tell. The next
day, the chimney having undergone repairs in the
mean time, the mistress, who acted in quality of chief
mate, and, consequently, distributed the necessary
orders, directed me to go into the garden and fetch

some cabbage for dinner. When there, after surveying the whole ground, I could see nothing of the cabbage kind, save some headless stumps, with a few
sprouts thereon; and, supposing that these were the
true objects, I eradicated and brought them to the
kitchen, sprouts and all, including one which I could
but notice as the finest of the collection. When the
mistress, who happened to be there, saw the marked
object just referred to, she said: "The master will
pray when he comes in; for that is a cabbage he had
saved for seed." Well, he came, accordingly; and
the sight of his seed cabbage produced the precise
moral effect that the mistress had intended to predict,
unless indeed, the event exceeded the augury. The
way he did it was awful. So I told him, that I did
not care anything for his cabbage, nor him either;
and that, if that was the way he prayed for people, I
did not want him to make me a subject any longer.

CHAPTER IV.

Sojourns at Ben Lomond.—"Looking after horses."—A wild colt.—
Scene at the smithery.—Advertised as a runaway.—Dives deeper
into the bush.—The bush-rangers.—Plunder.—Impressment.—Discharge.—Leaves for parts unknown.—Betrayed.—Constable takes
a prisoner.—Prisoner takes the constable.—The parting scene.

HAVING honorably quarrelled, as shown by the
sequel of the last chapter, I was honorably bound to
quit. The consequence was, that, the first morning
following this conjuncture of affairs, I was once more
a traveller in quest of another situation, without knowing exactly which way to go in order to find it. It
was nearly sundown when I came to the house of a
settler, at which I was hospitably entertained till
morning. Then, continuing my way, till I had
reached the foot of Ben Lomond, I fell in with four
or five settlers, to whom I made known my object.
One of them asked me if I understood looking after
horses. The anglicism of *looking after*, not importing
as my Yankee reader would have been likely to *guess*
it did, the idea of *hunting*, or *looking up*, but *taking
care* of the animals, I could only answer in the nega-

c*

tive. However, as he thought I could soon learn the business, and as there was a feeling of mutual interest in the object, we struck a bargain on the spot, and I was taken at once to see the "*orses.*" There were eight of them, and fine fellows at that. One of the number —intended for stock—but three years old, stood seventeen and a half hands. On walking up to him, the better to observe his huge proportions, he took me by the shoulder as familiarly as an old acquaintance, or as if he had been one of those ever-attentive friends of mine—the constables. It struck me as rather unceremonious; and, *certes*, it *did hurt;* but I laid up nothing against him at that time, imputing it, as Paddy did the kick from the donkey, to the "crathur's ignorance." At night, however, I was alone. All the animals had been fed, and all but Caractacus had been bedded. I had stooped down to do the same kind office for him, when the ungrateful dog snapped at the small of my back, and fairly *seized me up.* This I looked upon as an outrage, and applied the whip as an expression of suitable resentment. It was soon apparent, however, that the game was such that more than one of us could play at it, for, as I whipped, he kicked, and when the whipping ceased so also did the kicking—gradually—but not till the whole broadside of the stable was completely stove out. The racket raised the owner of the colt, of course, and then— whew! However, I told him how the war began,

and that, if the lubber came down upon me again in
that way, I should defend myself as long as there was
a shot in the locker. To all of which my master, more
reasonable than might have been anticipated, only
replied by saying, that, if any flogging was necessary,
I must take him out into the stack-yard and do it
there.

The next morning he was as saucy as ever, and,
remembering the general order as to the scene of
future action, I led him out accordingly, where, early
in the ensuing scuffle, his bridle broke. The next
dash he made was to clear the fence; which brought
him among the cattle in the adjoining yard. There
his principal exploit consisted of staving in the ribs
of a four-year-old ox, so that we had to kill him. As
to the hero of the day, when once more in tow, he was
minus a shoe, and that made it necessary to send him,
in charge of a couple of us, to the neighboring smithery. Our way was through a field containing other
horses, and as the colt inclined to have a frolic, so did
we, presuming that he would be less troublesome at
the shop in consequence of blowing off some of his
steam. So bending a long rope on to the bit of his
bridle, we let him act in his own way for half an hour,
when he sweat finely, and was rather worried. On
our arrival at the shop, which was about noon, the
smith told us to ride him about till he got his dinner.
Though he had never been backed, the chap who was

with me thought himself jockey enough to manage
him. So I unbent the rope, and assisted the smith in
getting the cavalier under weigh. The colt went off,
gently enough, till he disappeared, for a few moments,
among the trees at the head of the valley. On reappearing, however, we saw him put his head between
his fore-legs, and the next moment his heels and rider
were in the air. Finding himself a free horse, he
swept over the only fence that stood in his way, and
broke for the woods. I was taking my turn at a
sweat by this time; for, while in hot pursuit of the
runaway, I could not help thinking what would be
the upshot, in case we lost him, as he was valued at
£140. It fell out, however, that, while the heated
and thirsty animal was taking a long drink at an intervening stream, we succeeded in retaking him. By
this time every foot was shoeless. So much the more
necessity was there for an overhaul at the smithery.—
I will make a short yarn of the way things were done
there.—The cautious artisan had just lifted the first
bare foot from the ground, when he found that he
had, in fact, even a harder customer than he had
feared. The horse pitched right on to him, tooth and
nail, and, but for the interference of a third party,
was in a fair way, not only of killing, but eating the
son of Vulcan on the spot. Of course, the poor fellow
owned beat, and told us to take him back as soon as
we liked. By the time we had him moored again, in

the stable, he began to show that he had had a hard
"*day on shore.*" The heavy pull at the cold water
threw him into a high fever. He refused his rations,
and for three days took nothing but medicine. After
that he was quiet enough.

I had been here about two months, when the Launceston Gazette displayed an advertisement of a runaway sailor from the brig Siren, with a *Two pounds
reward.* The name and description both pointing at
me, I was strongly suspected at once. To settle the
question of which I had now become the subject,
Adams, the cook, bolted to the barn, where I was at
work, and told me the news, with the false addition,
that two constables were in the house, in pursuit of
me. This took me all aback, and what to do I did
not know. In the midst of my quandary, the mistress
came out, and told me that I was not safe in stopping
there; and that my doing so would be equally unsafe
for them, as it exposed them to a heavy fine; that I
had better settle with the master, and leave immediately. Acting on this friendly counsel, and nettled,
at the same time, with the officiousness of the Gazette,
I started, determining not to stop till I had got outside of its circulation.

When near the backside of the island, where I
thought they did not *take the papers,* I found myself
in communication with a settler—his name was Griffith—who had then recently established himself in

that location. As the main point with me was exemption from the cause of my late displacement, and as the present object appeared as promising in that respect as could be reasonably demanded, I agreed with the proprietor to enter his service for a month. Little did I dream that, in eluding one danger, I had thrown myself into the teeth of another, and a much greater! " The bush-rangers." The contents of this chapter imply a pledge on that subject. I hasten to redeem it. The reader will understand, then, that one evening, before I was scarcely nested in my new retreat, a rap at the door induced me, who happened to be nearest, to open it, to see who was there. The first thing I met was the butt of a rifle, which laid me senseless on the floor. This was instantly followed by the entrance of the whole gang, who, with levelled arms, threatened death to the first person who offered to stir or make a noise. Then, ordering every man to kneel before the fire, they further ordered Griffith to tie their hands behind their backs, and then still further ordered him to take a candle, and show them where he kept his provisions. They were ten in all. Three guarded the door; three guarded the prisoners; while the remaining four attended the master in search of plunder. This consisted of tea, sugar, beef, pork, flour, powder, shot, and balls, together with the contents of a small library. The firearms found, were all destroyed. By the time they had gathered and

packed their plunder, I had recovered, when one of
them—probably the leader—said they must have a
couple of us to help carry their stuff through the
woods. A tap on my shoulder was followed with—
"My young fellow, we will take you for one." Then,
looking over the rest, he picked another, and added:
"These two will do. We stand a better chance of
escaping, with *them*, than we should with a *horse*."
Then, tying the master's hands behind his back,
they told him—"Your house will be watched by
some of us for two hours. If, within that time, you
offer to stir, or raise an alarm, or suffer any one else
to do it, we will return and shoot you like a dog."
Upon this, we two, who had been selected as carriers,
were unbound and loaded with the spoils. When we
had got a short distance from the house, the party
halted. Both of us were then blindfolded, each being
subsequently led by one of the banditti. In this way
we travelled through the woods till near daylight.
Then our hands were again tied behind us, our heavy
burdens were removed, and we were turned adrift.
They told us, however, in parting, that they should
not be a great way off before daylight, and that, if we
removed our bandages, or made any noise before that
time, they would be sure to return and shoot us.
Seated on a log, we waited for day. It was not long,
however, before we ventured so far as to unbandage
our eyes; and then we succeeded, though with much

more difficulty, in recovering the use of our hands.
It was now day. Once more at liberty, we collected
our scattered senses as fast as possible, and struck for
home. But so utterly were we bewildered, that we
were knocking about in the bush three days before
we found it.

Thoroughly satisfied with frontier life, and the
gentry of the bush, I was now willing to risk constables and consequences, by putting back among the
settlers. Accordingly, leaving the vicinity of Ben
Lomond, I shaped my course for a place called White
Hills. Here I found, and engaged myself to, a man
known as Patrick Welch. Still, I was the runaway
sailor, from the brig Siren, and the two pounds reward
was sufficient to put half the people of Van Diemen's
in pursuit of me. What threw the odds against me,
though I did not know it till it was too late, was, that
the unlucky Gazette was extant at the Hills, and that
my new master was reckoned in its list of patrons.

One day my worthy employer asked me a number
of questions in a seemingly careless manner, and but
too well calculated to prevent suspicion, by which, as
I afterward inferred, he satisfied himself as to my
identity with the advertised fugitive of the brig. I
afterward inferred, also—and, by this time, the reader
need not be told that I would not have been likely to
do the thing *before*—I *afterward* inferred that this careless questioning had been prompted by the fresh sight

of the *two pound proposition*, afore mentioned. At all·
events, the day following, after I had gone to my
work in the field, my master saddled his horse, and
rode away in the direction of the Malben river, the
residence of a magistrate. He was still absent, when
I came to dinner. He returned alone; but, in a
couple of hours, I saw him and another person crossing the field in my direction. Nor did *this* awaken
apprehension, till, coming up, I found the stranger a
constable, and myself his prisoner.

I was taken to Malben, and put in prison. Thus
ended the first day. The next, I was brought before
the magistrate for examination; but he had it all to
himself. When he found that he was growing no
wiser "very fast," he ordered the constable to take
me to Launceston, to be further dealt with in the
premises. About half-way to that place, between
two pieces of woods, I satisfied my attendant, who
carried a loaded musket, that the use of my hands for
a few moments would be imperatively necessary. He
objected that it would be contrary to law to unhand-
cuff me, under the circumstances. After some hesitation, however, he consented, and in a few moments
was, doubtless, more comfortable when, presenting
myself before him, I held up my two hands to take
on the irons. His own were raised in the act of slip-
ping them on, when a heavy blow in his bread-basket
dropped him. While he was falling, I snatched his

musket, and, by the time he was fairly down, he found the heavy end of it hanging rather dangerously over his head; and what I said about knocking something *out* of it, in case the owner stirred, I dare say helped to keep him quiet, *nolens volens.*

When I found I had the advantage of my late convoy, I thought that good manners did not require me to hold any long parley with him, and I bolted for the woods. But, on arriving at the next opening, and looking round, I saw him in hot pursuit. Stopping short, and levelling the musket, I gave him to understand that he was a dead man if he advanced another step. He stood. At this moment it occurred to me that ammunition would be necessary, and that what was in the gun ought to avail for procuring it. Walking up to him, I ordered him to deliver. He had none. I told him there was no use in trying to put me off with that story, as I knew he was not there without the supplies. I made him pull off, and throw me his coat, from the pockets of which I drew a dozen balls and a pound of powder. Then, telling him I had all I wanted, and throwing him his coat, I told him to take it and be off. He asked me for his musket. I told him to start, or he should have its contents. Then, with still more of the suppliant, he said that he was a crown prisoner, and, if he went back without his musket, they would give him seven years at Port Arthur — a penal settlement, much dreaded by convicts. I told him he might go to Norfolk Island—which is ten times worse—for all me: that if he could have got the two pounds, I might have gone to the —— for all he would have cared. Whereat I " left him alone with his glory."

CHAPTER V.

The old shepherd : his hospitality.—Catecheticality.—Tragical story of a bush-ranger.—Domesticates with farmer Raymond.—Short acquaintance with another constable.—Cuts him.—Digression.—A night in the woods.—Surprised and taken.—Launceston.—Justice Mulgrave.

WHEN overtaken by the night, I discharged my arms, kindled two fires, laid myself down, with my musket for a pillow, and slept till morning. At 3 P.M. I came to a shepherd's lodge, and hungry enough, having fasted nearly two days. The solitary inmate, with the natural inquisitiveness of age—for he was an old man—began to ask me questions. On intimating my situation, however, he kindly suppressed his curiosity, till he and I were the better for a good dinner. Then he put me through the following course.

He. What part of the world are you from?

I. Old England.

He. Where are you going?

I. To look for work.

He. Have you not followed the sea?

I. Yes.

He. I was about sure of that, from the cut of your jib. I am an old sailor myself, and was discharged with a pension from a British man-of-war, and I don't like to see a brother sailor in distress.

I. I am not exactly in distress, but am box-hauling about, like a ship without a rudder.

He. Have you a passport?

I. No.

He. Don't the constables trouble you?

This point I evaded, and he resumed:

They will overhaul you. A pirate can as easily get away from John Bull, after he gets his grappling irons on him, as a man without a passport can escape the clutches of a constable. Such numbers of convicts escape to the woods, that the heavy penalty of fifty pounds hangs over the head of any citizen who harbors one. (And he went on.) I advise you, as a friend, to part with your musket; for if a stranger is found with one, he is liable to be taken up as a bush-ranger; and, in that case, if he cannot give a satisfactory account of himself, he will be sent to Norfolk Island.

And then my venerable host delivered himself of the following account of

THE SHEPHERD AND THE BUSH-RANGER.

A short time ago, there was a shepherd of my acquaintance, whose hut used to be visited by a bush-

ranger. The bush-ranger, whose name was Michael
Howe, had a faithful dog, on which he made great
dependence, and which would have saved him, as we
shall see; but his hour had come. The large price of
£200, set upon his head by the governor, transformed
the previous friend of the fugitive into a treacherous
and deadly foe. The shepherd, who had a son a soldier, at Hobart Town, the capital of the island, wrote
to the governor, that if he would send him, he thought
he would be able to capture the fugitive. The soldier
was sent, accordingly, and nothing remained but to
wait till the hungry convict should return to share
the hospitality of his *friend.* He came; but, as he
neared the house, the unusual conduct of his dog induced him to hesitate. Instead of quietly following
his master to the house as formerly, he stopped, and
barked; and started back, and barked, and barked
again. When the shepherd was drawn to the door,
the convict, who was standing on a little eminence
some distance off, asked him what could be the meaning of this strange behavior in his dog; whether
some person was not in the house; and, finally, whether
he—the shepherd—was going to betray him. To all
this his old host replied with so many and strong assurances of fidelity, that the poor fellow cautiously
approached the door, and finally entered. At the
moment he did so, the soldier fired from his concealment, but was in such a *flurry* as not to hit. The

convict levelled his rifle at his unseen enemy, fired, but without effect, and turned and fled. His enemies, armed respectively with axe and musket, pursued him—overtook him. The musket felled him, and the axe severed from its shoulders the thousand dollar head. But when they had got it to Hobart Town, they found it above par. It secured the discharge of the son, and the *pardon* of the father; for the old villain was himself a convict. And they both took ship for England, free, and as happy as the governor's reward, and the consciousness of so much good desert could make them.

Parting with my old friend, and with my musket, I laid my course once more for Hobart Town. Though a stranger, in travelling on the island, especially if destitute of that *sine qua non* of a passport, as I was, must pay a heavy tax to the popular virtue of inquisitiveness, I must do the settlers the justice to say, that hospitality is scarcely less a common virtue. Thus annoyed, and thus befriended, I travelled on till it was my hap to fall in with farmer Raymond, to whom I engaged myself for a month.

But my old enemies were crossing my path at every turn. Scarcely was I settled in my new situation, when the following little affair occurred. Entering the house, one day, I found a stranger seated by the fire.—It was about the last of July, and, of course, winter in that hemisphere.—After eyeing me for a

moment, he said: "Young man, I perceive you are a
stranger in these parts. I would like to know where
you are from." My reply was: "I am an Englishman, from Dartmouth, in Devonshire." "What is
your name?" "Edward Johns." Then the master
of the house, being questioned, replied, that I came
there looking for work; that he had hired me; and
that was all he knew. "Have you a passport?"
"No." "Then you have no business here. Have
you never had one?" "No: and another thing; I
don't want any." "We will see about that, without
going any further." So saying, he rose from his
chair, thrust his hand into his pocket, and pulled out
a pair of hand-irons. By the time his colors were up,
I had raised mine, in the shape of a stick of firewood;
and, the better to explain its import, added: "If you
offer to lay a hand on me, I will lay the weight of
this stick over your head." The word and the sign
were understood, and to explain his peaceable inten-
tions, the worthy remarked: "I have no wish to injure you; all I want is, to take you to a magistrate,
that, if a free man, you may be provided with a passport." My answer was: "I have my freedom, and
mean to maintain it, while I hold this stick, and am
able to use it." While uttering this belligerent speech,
I was stepping backward for the door, with my unarmed hand extended by way of feeler, when, what
should it grasp, but the tipstaff's *musket!* I need not

say that it bore me company as, with a bound, I
cleared the door. "Does this belong to you?" "Yes."
Discharging it, I pulled out my jack-knife—my eye
on the officer, to keep a safe distance between us—and
deliberately unscrewed the cock, and took it off. By
this time Tip was a little nearer than I liked. Of
course I was not slow in giving him notice—raising
the musket, in the mean time, to render it impressive
—that he was to keep the proper distance, unless he
wished to bite the dust. The poor fellow! he was in
a beautiful perspiration by this time. When my job
on the musket was done, I hove it as far as I could,
and took to my heels. My man had to find it before
he was armed for the chase, so that I was fairly in the
woods before he was under weigh. Whether he ever
entered the bush, or what *did* become of him, I have
no means of knowing; which circumstance must apol-
ogize, at once to the reader and him, for the ensuing
silence of this history on the subject of that redoubt-
able personage. ————————

The reader, who carries along in his mind's locker
the idea of my age at the time of these passing adventures, may think his credulity too largely taxed, unless,
at some point, I digress into a little explanation. I
could never claim kin with the race of pigmies, on the
one hand, nor, on the other, are there any records, or
even authentic *tradition*, by which I could ever estab-
lish my lineal descent from a certain king of Bashan.

D

But when the reader finds me, at the time of this
writing, but little less than a six-footer, with bone and
muscle to match; and when he is farther advised,
that I rose to these proportions when unusually young,
he will cease to wonder that, at the age of sixteen, I
should have been able to do and bear what few of my
full-grown contemporaries would have willingly haz-
arded. And then he should remember, that I was
thrown, from early boyhood, into scenes of peril and
hardships. So that, what from being impetuous and
fearless, hardy and strong, and a *little* overgrown;
accustomed to self-dependence, and bred, withal, among
reckless and desperate men, I had ceased, at this
passing period of my history, to *feel* myself a boy,
or to *be* one. In a word—the reader must excuse the
egotism—I had a gnarled head, that carried a tongue
civil, or saucy, as occasion required; a brawny breast,
that knew no fear, and a brawny arm, with a fist at
the end of it, which no prudent antagonist would be
likely to provoke without looking at it more than once.

The night after I had so uncivilly declined the
handcuffs, and beaten off and distanced the lubber
that offered them—that night was passed in the woods.
It was like others, passed in the same way, only that
it was without a fire, and the weather was cold.
Quitting my bed of bushes in the morning, and obtaining the necessary refreshment and information of
an old settler at noon, I pushed for Hobart Town,

where I hoped to get a ship, heartily sick, as i was, of my land cruise. Standing away north, till about 3 P.M., I was suddenly met—the reader anticipates me, and it were useless to get up anything by way of surprise, on his part, however sorely it was felt on mine—by two constables, both armed, *a la Van Diemen's.* The usual questions were followed by the usual answers. The issue of the case seemed all but transparent from the outset. True, I could have fought or run; but, then, I did not care to be shot, as it might have proved fatal to the hope of fighting or running on some more inviting occasion. So I decided, under all the circumstances, to content myself, as well as I could, with being saucy, taking on a pair of handcuffs, and being marched back to Launceston. By the way, however, I was first examined by the Perth magistrate, to whom I gave my assumed name, and so much other satisfaction as induced him, with very little delay, to forward me to my original destination. The following day found me once more where I had taken my unceremonious leave of the Siren, six months before.

After two days in prison, I was brought before Justice Mulgrave, the highest judicial dignitary in South Van Diemen's. A glance told me that he was a hard character. With a look betokening the Bengal tiger, he interrogated me, and was answered as follows.

Magistrate "Where did you come from?"

Prisoner. "From the Jail."

Mag. "Do you not know better than to answer me in that manner?"

Pris, "I told you the truth."

Mag. "What brought you here?"

Pris. "I believe it was the constable."

Mag. (In a rage.) "Tell me, immediately, who you are, and where you came from, or I will put you where the dogs will not bark at you."

Pris. "Where is that?"

Mag. "I will soon let you know who you are talking to."

Pris. "My name is Edward Johns, of England; and I left the Pyramus, which came from Bristol with the general cargo."

Mag. (Looking over his book.) "There were men who ran away from the Pyramus; but I cannot find your name among them; I shall therefore send you back to jail, till I can write to Hobart Town, and ascertain if your name is there, or if they can find out who you are."

Upon this, the constable was ordered to take me back to prison, where I lay a fortnight. At the end of that time, I stood once more in the presence of this impersonation of English justice, who questioned me again, in various ways, and to whom I merely replied, that all I had to say had been given on my previous examination; adding: "You can lead the horse to water, but you cannot make him drink." After some words of threatening, which were answered with others of defiance, I was remanded to my place of durance; whence, after the lapse of ten days, I made my third appearance before the worshipful, who was supported, on this occasion, by Messrs. Wentworth and Franklin. After questioning, and cross-questioning me to their hearts' content, and eliciting nothing, they put their heads together for some time, when the following brief colloquy ensued.

Justices. "We must discharge you. You can go where you please; only take care not to come before us again."

Pris. "You have had the pleasure of keeping me in jail, and you may have the pleasure of paying me a dollar for every day you have kept me there."

Jus. "Quit the office immediately, or we will put you back there."

Pris. "You can bark pretty loud; but you may soon see that one can be found who can bark still louder."

Leaving the office, I proceeded directly to the house of the deputy governor. The servant hesitated as to admitting me, but offered to convey my message. As I insisted, however, on delivering it myself, he went to his master, and soon returned with an order to send me in. On entering, that gentleman kindly inquired my business; to whom I said: "I came to

the country about seven months ago, when I ran away
from my ship, and went into the country, where I remained till I was taken up, because I had no passport,
and brought before the magistrate, by whose order I
had been kept in jail nearly a month. That, when he
found I was a free man, he discharged me, without a
passport; and that, when I asked him to pay me for
the time of my false imprisonment, he ordered me
about my business, and not to let him see me there
again." "I will see about that," said the governor.
Then, sitting down, he wrote a note which he delivered
to me, saying; "Take that to Mr. Mulgrave, and if he
does not satisfy you, come back to me, and I will see
about it." My lord Justice received the note, shook
his head, and told me to come again the next day.
The next morning I was there again; all the justices
being present. After conferring apart, they cashed
over, and gave me a passport in the bargain. To restore their equanimity, I left them with—"Good-bye;
and I hope you will keep t'other eye open for the next
sailor that comes this way."

CHAPTER VI.

Ships for London.—Runs away.—Is arrested.—Three months on a tread-mill.—A flare-up.—Scene changes to a dungeon.—Rechanges to the mill.—Prisoners decide on subjecting the machine to certain repairs, and what they gained by it.—Observations and instances relating to the severity of the penal code.

Dec. 29, 1836, found me shipped for London, in the Caroline, belonging to that place. While descending the river to George Town, however, she was found to be leaking pretty freely, and while lying there at anchor, for the purpose of taking in wood, we were obliged to pump ship every half-hour. All the men agreed that we ought not to undertake so long a voyage with the vessel in that condition. The consequence was, that we of the forecastle went aft to the quarter-deck, and told the captain that we would not proceed on the voyage, unless the ship were overhauled before leaving George Town. The reply to this was, that she would have no repairs done to her before she got to London, if she ever did; and that if she did not, she would not need any. We insisted on going ashore. He swore that we should not leave the ship; and some of us did not do anything less than swear—though it was inside of our teeth—that we would do the thing, at all hazards.

Accordingly, during my watch on deck that night, four of us agreed to leave. For this purpose, we singled out and greased the boats' falls, so as to prevent a noise; lowered the boat, hauled her under the bows, got our chests and hammocks into her, and pulled ashore, where we remained on the beach till daylight. Then, leaving the boat on the beach, we carried our traps to a public house, where we intended to stop. By this time the mate was up, who, finding the boat gone, hailed another, belonging to the Wallaby, lying near the one we had left, and got the loan of it. No sooner was it fairly alongside, than the skipper and his man were in it—alike advised of the *escapade*— and pulling for the beach. The consequence was that we were scarcely comfortable in our new quarters, when two of the constabulary hove to, and hailed us. We gave them a short answer. They became saucy. We advised them to start, as, otherwise, we would help them to do so. Whereupon, attempting to arrest us, we gave them a good threshing, and hove them out into the street. Then, leaving our stuff in care of our landlord, we set off, overland, for Launceston.

The constables, however, had observed our direction, so that, being better acquainted with roads than we, they came up with us in about four miles.

In the meantime, instead of two, they now numbered six, having been reinforced by four soldiers, one of which latter, was a *ci-devant* Jack Tar. As soon as they found themselves within speaking distance, they ordered us to heave to, or they would fire on us. To this, however, we paid no attention, but made the best possible use of our sea legs, till, at length, we found them alongside. Then the salt one vociferated—"Back your mainstays, or we will do it for you." Beside outnumbering us, they were armed; we were not. To trifle longer, would have been to tempt our fall. Thus our headway was deadened; and, heaving about, as we were obliged to do, we stood on the other tack, till we dropped our anchor in the bottom of George Town jail, where we lay two days.

The captain then came, and demanded whether we would return to the ship, and make the voyage, as we had agreed. All of us agreed that it was disagreeable to us to agree to any such agreement, and that we were positively agreed not to do it. The skipper ended, for the present, this disagreeable disagreement, by turning on his heel, with—"Then I know what to do with you." Nor were we troubled with any long uncertainty, as to the object of the skipper's parting intimation, as we presently found ourselves in presence of the George Town justice, and on our trial for non-fulfilment of contract. It was in vain that we urged, in justification of the admitted fact,

D*   6

that the ship was leaky and unseaworthy, and that
we did not think we ought to be put into our coffin
before we were dead. All this was vain, save that it
drew from the court the offer to us of two things—
namely: to join our ship, or take three months in
prison, at hard labor. To this we replied, that we
would not go back to the ship, any how. "Then I
must send you to the tread-mill, at Launceston, for
three months." And he was as good as his word—for,
after another week in our recent place of durance,
we had an opportunity of learning from the Launceston tread-mill what the "hard labor" clause of our
sentence stood for.

From five to eight in the morning we were on the
wheel, before breakfast. That meal consisted of half
a pound of bread, as black as a pot, together with a
pint of *skelly*—a very thin gruel, without salt. From
half-past eight, we were on the wheel again, till twelve,
when we knocked off to go to dinner. This was made
by the half pound of black bread, before mentioned,
and a quarter pound of meat. At one P.M., we were
turned on again, where we remained till six, when,
with another half pound of bread and the pint of
skelly, we were locked up for the night. This was the
routine, and this the fare of a day, and of every day,
unless for some misconduct, we were subjected to
some extra penalty.

The wheel is nearly forty feet in length; a little for-

ward of, and about three feet above which, is an iron
rod, horizontal, like the wheel, and of corresponding
length. Those on the wheel, have hold of this with
their two hands, and, by this means, are able, by
shifting their weight from hand to foot, and vice versa,
to retard or accelerate the motion of the machine,
which is employed in grinding wheat—unless, which
sometimes happens, there is none to grind. In that
case, as prisoners, whether convicts or otherwise, who
are connected with it, must never rest—its motion
continues for their sole benefit. This is called "*grinding wind.*" Over the wheel, and in sight of the ope-
ratives, an overseer has his seat, whose business, among
other things, is to see that the treading is duly done,
without any improper holding on to the horizontal
fixture, above described.

> " And hereby hangs a tale."

I was one day holding on to the fixture, afore-named,
a little harder than our vigilant overseer thought
necessary, when, " Start up!" was sung out, with its
customary tone of official harshness. I was irritated,
and, being inclined, if not to stand, at least to lean
upon my reserved rights, returned an answer denoting
a little obstinacy, and still more contempt. This
brought me back a threat of confinement, mingled
with something about "bread and water." Whereupon, one of my shipmates and I left the wheel, and,

going up to the chap, told him to be more civil, or we
would shut up his dead-lights for him. This was the
signal upon which he disappeared. Of course, our
triumph was short, and, as the reader anticipates,
dearly purchased. For, soon, the superintendent, duly
enlightened as to the flare-up, was upon us with but
little less than half a dozen of my old and very atten-
tive friends, the constables, who locked us in cells,
six feet by two, for two days, with the usual per diem
allowance of a pound of bread, and two pints of
water.

We twain had so much ill-desert in us, that it required the co-operation of three of her majesty's justices to get it out of us. How they succeeded, "it
boots not me to say;" but, at any rate, they *tried* us.
As for me, I was found to be an old customer; for
these chaps were the veritable trio who figured in the
preceding chapter, who got such, and so large sport out
of me, and who were obliged to pay for it, to the tune
of a dollar a-day. The loving looks which they, and
especially my dear friend Mulgrave, cast at me, showed, at once, that I was not unthankfully forgotten.
To let that gentleman know that recognition was likely to prove mutual, I asked if I were owing him anything. He replied, that he had a bit of an account to
settle with me; adding, that he thought he had seen
my face before. I admitted that he was probably
right, as to that, and considerably more than intimated

the opinion, that his face would not be greatly flattered by comparison with specimens that might be met with in a pig-market.

The superintendent, having been called upon to state his complaint, charged us, as he said, "with mutinous conduct, and threatening to shut up the. *dead-lights* of the overseer." Everything appeared plain enough, with the single exception of the *dead-lights;* but this, the learned jurist declared, was more than he was able to understand. Not knowing what false gloss might be supplied, nor how much it might make a bad matter worse, I volunteered to enlighten the court, by explaining, that *dead-lights* was a nautical metaphor for the eyes: and, by consequence, that our offer to the overseer was, that of merely closing his peepers. Upon this, and when the incumbents of the bench had conferred together for a few moments, they told the superintendent to bring the *triangle,* and that they would seize us up, and give us seventy-five apiece. I told them, that we were neither convicts nor crown prisoners, and that I would like to see them put a lash on my back; that they were welcome to try it, but might be assured that it would cost them more than their commissions were worth. These and other similar remarks induced a pause and another conference, the which ended in a mittimus to the dungeon, for one week, on bread and water.

At the end of that time, we found ourselves once

more among our old companions, and at our old station,
on the wheel. One morning, not long after, while
the overseer was at breakfast, we first resolved ourselves into a committee of the whole. Then we resolved, that it was high time the wheel had undergone repairs. In the next place, we resolved that we
would make a *united effort* to render the necessity of
such repairs as obvious to our employers, as it was
already to ourselves. To fifty-five of us; and that
should have been earlier stated as our whole number;
to fifty-five of us, the *will* to create that necessity was
only a little easier than the *deed*. It was done. The
overseer returned; the superintendent was summoned.
It was a very clear case; that is, a very broken one, and
which must needs be mended. Of course, our hope
was, that we were to gain by this state of things, in
some way. How we were to lose by it, we could not
well conceive. But we were soon enlightened, and it
was on this wise.

After marching us into the spacious yard of the
prison, which was enclosed by brick walls twenty feet
in height, they kindly furnished every man of us with
two heavy blocks of wood. These we were to take
one in either hand, and then, in this ignoble plight,
we were marched around the yard, and then again;
round, and round, and round. As already intimated,
the wooden weights were heavy, and hard to hold, in
the outset; and it were needless to add, that we found

them becoming more and more so very fast, till it
was past questioning, that "holding on" was a far
less easy operation, under present, than former circumstances. In a word, we were ripe for another—
any other—change, and willing rather to invite, than
to forego it. But I anticipate.

When we were "turned to," after dinner, some of
the men spoke to the overseer to say, that they wanted
to see the magistrate. The superintendent was called,
to whom the above-expressed wish was stated. Upon
this, he went away, and soon returned with a dozen
constables. Then he sent for a couple of magistrates;
and we were severally examined. By this time, it
became apparent that the affair was likely to be regarded in the light of another mutiny. The consequence was, that only sixteen of the whole number
could be induced to own that *they* wished to see the
magistrate, at all. From this number, five were selected as ringleaders in the business, and sentenced to
receive a hundred lashes apiece. They were convicts.
After keeping them in the watch-house till next morning, we were all called out to witness their ignominious punishment. Poor fellows. * * * * *

Passing a variety of incidents connected with the
remaining period of my tread-mill experience, I only
remark that, long before it ended, inadequate food,
together with other varieties of rigorous treatment,
had left me with scarcely strength to put one foot be-

fore the other. By rigorous treatment, as above, I
mean the entire punishments provided for various
minor offences; such as the clandestine possession of
any little matter of comfort, or luxury. For instance:
before turning in at night, we were searched with reference to all objects of that description; and a piece
of tobacco would send its possessor to the dungeon,
on bread and water, for a week. Of this I had super-
abundant evidence; evidence from observation and
from experience. At the same time, not being a convict, I escaped those extremes of severity to which
most of my fellow-prisoners were subject, as in the
few instances I have had occasion to notice before.
Some remarks on the penal code, and its practical operation on its wretched subjects, as related alike to
New South Wales and the other penal settlements,
together with Van Diemen's Land, I may take occasion to introduce in connection with observations to
be made hereafter on the former of these two islands.*

* See Appendix A.

CHAPTER VII.

On board the Carib, a whaler.—Early success.—Visits the coast of New Holland for supplies.—Is wrecked and cast away on an uninhabited part of the coast.—Numbers of the lost and saved.—Shifts to which the latter were driven after reaching shore, as well as the shifts by which they reached it.

WHEN our three months of punishment for desertion were ended, we spent three weeks at a boarding-house in town; partly for the purpose of waiting for another ship, and partly to recover the necessary strength for fulfilling its duties, when anything eligible in that shape should offer. My companions took a British home-bound vessel; shortly after which, I shipped in the Carib, a whale-ship, Capt. Thompson, belonging to Bricksom, England.

April 28, 1837, having sailed from Launceston to Hobart Town, we weighed anchor for the coast of New Holland, for the purpose of sperm-whaling. Arrived on the coast, we cruised from latitudes 28° to 35° south. We were here about three months. In the former half of that time, we had taken seven hundred barrels of sperm. When the three months were up, however, we were under the necessity of putting into a bay, on the south coast, for wood and water. It is called the Archipelago. This whole extent of coast, from Adelaide, on the east, to King George's sound, on the west, is totally uninhabited; a distance of about one thousand miles.* The Archipelago bay, so memorable in my humble history, is nearly equidistant from the two places last mentioned.

Little did we deem that our noble ship was destined to cast her hapless people, along with her shattered fragments, on this desolate and inhospitable shore. But so it was written; as, by the light of the next morning, we were compelled to read. This, however, is anticipation. We sailed into the bay; let go our anchor; furled our sail; sent down our top-gallant-yards, and made everything snug for the night, as well knowing the fickleness of the weather on this coast, which even then gave indications not altogether flattering. Early in the evening, the captain ordered the mate to turn the hands up to moor ship, which was no sooner done than it began to blow a heavy gale from the N.E. Our two anchors were out. The chain of the smaller one, of 180 fathoms, parted at about nine o'clock, nor did our best bower bring the ship's head to the wind before it also parted. It was my watch on deck, and I called the captain, telling him both cables were parted, and that the ship was

* "South Australia" is the name of a new colony, west of Adelaide, on the south coast.

drifting fast toward the shore. The captain sprang
from his berth, and the next moment all hands were
on deck. The fore-sail, and fore-top-mast stay-sail,
were loosed; the helm was hard up, and all hands
were at the windlass, heaving in chain. But there
was so much out, and the swell, which came rolling in
from the sea, was so heavy, and we were already in so
shoal water, that the ship would not pay off before
the wind. Before we had the chain all in, she struck
heavily on the beach. It was in vain that the captain sang out, "Heave away at the windlass, my lads;
for we will get her off as soon as the gale is over."
Poor ship! she had three or four planks knocked out
of the bottom at that very moment. When, therefore, she struck the second time, which she did much
harder than before, she began to settle in the sand,
and keel over on to her beam-ends. The consequence
was, that, being unable to work any longer at the
windlass, we were driven aft to the quarter-deck.

By this time, the surf, which was forty to fifty feet
high, was breaking over, fore and aft. Forward, it
swept everything. Aft, it took our bulwarks, try-
works, and bow-boat. At this crisis, as the ship was
laboring very heavily in the surf, we did not expect
that she would hold together for two hours. The
captain ordered the fore and main masts to be cut
away. The night was dark as pitch, and when the
sea broke over us, nothing but a firm hold saved a

man of us from being carried away with it. The skipper asked who would volunteer to go forward and cut away the fore-mast. The mate answered by taking the axe, and I by seizing the lantern. Each of us had a rope about his body, with the other end made fast to a ring-bolt in the deck, and as soon as a favorable moment offered, we got forward to the mast, and began to cut away. Hardly had we begun, however, before a heavy sea knocked us both senseless. When it left the deck, we recovered; but our lantern was gone. Watching the next opportunity, I went aft, brought the binnacle lamp, and the mast went by the board. Then we went aft, to cut away the main-mast. Just as we reached it, however, a tremendous sea broke over us, which carried away all our remaining boats—five in number—along with the companion-way; and with them five of the men, whose dead bodies we afterward found on the beach. All this while, the mate and myself clung fast to the fife-rail. Before the next breach, however, we succeeded in sending the main-mast also by the board, when the ship lay much easier, and began to sink pretty well into the sand. But she was a wreck, and could not hold together till daylight. And we were without a boat. The only chance of getting to the shore alive, was by means of the mast and yards, which, by some of the ropes, were kept from floating away from the ship's side. For myself, I got forward, where a spare

top-mast was lying, lashed to the ring-bolts. Cutting
it loose, and making myself fast to it with a rope, the
bulwarks being level with the deck, the next sea set
me and my life-preserver adrift. Presently, however,
I found myself entangled with the floating part of
the wreck.* Long time did I lie in that state, the surf
ever and anon breaking over me; so that, but for having lashed myself to the spar, I must inevitably have
perished before getting clear of the ship. But, as a
merciful Providence willed it, a violent sea drove me,
at length, from my moorings; and the next I knew I
was on the beach. It was in vain, however, that I
now strove to disengage myself from the top-mast;
and the flux and reflux of the surf tossed me alternately forward and backward till my senses left me.
At length, however, a huge swell hove me, spar and
all, high and dry upon the beach, where I lay till
some of my shipmates, who had gained the shore before me, came to my assistance. After cutting me
loose, they rolled me on a barrel, and stood me on
my head, till my senses returned; after which they
walked me to and fro on the beach till I was able to
take care of myself.

The first thing I did upon finding myself fairly
alive, was to offer up my thanks to God for his merciful preservation of me in so great a danger. True, I
was a sinner; but not a brute; nor, what is worse, an
infidel. I had a heart, and it felt thankful. Here,

then, we were, on a desert shore, many thousand
miles from home, and half a thousand from the nearest civilized settlement, and with the chance against
us of being found and massacred by the savages, before we could be able to repair our boats, and get out
of their reach; for we were totally unarmed, and, at
the same time, with no other than the scanty and wet
clothing in which we had made our narrow escape
from a watery grave. Daylight at length dawned on
us; but it only served to show us sights of woe,
among which was the unwelcome certainty that our
missing comrades were not among the living. For
when, at day-dawn, we were mustered by the captain,
who was among the surviving, it was found that our
number was reduced from thirty-two to twenty-seven.

The first thing to be done was to obtain fire. This
cost us much hard labor; for, as our powder and
matches were spoiled, we were forced to seek our object by the more primitive expedient of friction, by
means of dry pieces of wood. At last, after a deal
of fruitless effort, a shipmate and myself, who had
gone a distance by ourselves for the purpose of doing
the thing in our own way, returned with burning evidence of our superior ingenuity. Portions of the
wreck soon made us a large fire. Our bread was in-
edible; but we found a barrel of flour on the beach,
with plenty of beef and pork; so that, though destitute of kitchen utensils, yet, finding a stream of fresh

water in the neighborhood, we kneaded and baked some bread, which, with the salt meat, supplied us with a breakfast. The object next in importance, after this supply of our more immédiate wants, was the repair of our boats; the captain intending to coast our way round to King George's sound, distant, as formerly stated, some five hundred miles, that being the nearest English settlement on the coast. Subjects of repair, among the boats, were selected from those which were least damaged. The rest were to supply what these wanted, and especially the nails. Of boards the supply was ample; but the process, chiefly for want of tools, was likely to involve difficulty, and considerable time.

The second day after our great calamity, the wind in the mean time having died away, the ship—what there was left of it—was found fairly out of water, so that we could walk around it without wetting our feet. The people were divided into three parties, and the labor distributed accordingly. One of them was employed upon the boats; another in collecting valuables from the wreck; and the third in providing for the comfort of the rest. It was my bad fortune, as will presently appear, that I had been detailed on this last named service. A part of it consisted in collecting a sort of shell-fish, which, as they were rather numerous at different points along the beach, made a very agreeable as well as salutary addition to our salt provisions.

CHAPTER VIII.

The stroll.—The surprise.—The capture.—Prisoner denuded.—Captors, with their prisoner, plunge into the forest.—Painful march.—Joins a large body of the tribe.—Native surprise, and first impression.—First night among savages.—First morning, including the kangaroo hunt.—Some account of that curious animal.

THE order established in our forlorn community was briefly stated at the close of the preceding chapter; as, also, that I had found myself included in the corps of purveyors, and that an occasional service in that connection consisted in the collection of such animal food as is washed ashore by the sea. It was this occasional service which led to my sudden separation from my comrades, and from civilized society; and which subjected me to all the hazards and hardships of a long captivity among a race of cannibals. How it fell out, and what followed, will now be related.

It was on the third day following our nautical misadventure, that I took a stroll along the shore of the bay beyond my former limits. Collecting the bivalves and univalves into little heaps, as I proceeded, it was my intention to bag them on my return, and carry them to head-quarters. The reader has rightly inferred that I was alone. After having been out about two hours, and just as I was thinking that it was time I should return, my reverie was broken by an unearthly yell. I started. The hair rose upon my head,

"Like quills upon the fretted porcupine."

Seven naked savages stood before me, each armed with a spear. One wild glance revealed the utter hopelessness of my situation; for an intervening point hid me entirely from my shipmates, and any attempt at escape only promised to transform me into the figure of the man my readers may have seen in an old almanac. As I did not offer to stir, they drew close ᛫ ᛫und me, still poising their deadly weapons, as for ᛫ ᛫ ᛫tantaneous despatch, in case of the slightest in᛫ ᛫ ᛫ ᛫᛫ns of resistance or flight.

᛫ ᛫᛫ ūrst words that relieved the hideous pantomime, were᛫ ᛫he meaning was to come to me afterward— " Yaneki eru goli? Aman bockin coli?—Who are you? Where did you come from?" Then they told me—making signs by way of explanation—to pull off my clothes. To all this, I demurred, and hesitated as if it were unintelligible. But a red flannel shirt was an object of irresistible cupidity to a savage fancy, and they soon relieved me of more than half the trouble of compliance with their polite requirement. The transformation was no less sudden than complete; leaving my person as native and as nude as any of theirs, bating only the grease and a little paint.

The principal figure of the group was distinguished by a bunch of white cockatoo feathers behind each ear, together with a pair of something, like epaulettes, formed of the plumes of the emu, a large native bird, the congener of the ostrich. His long hair was tied up behind, somewhat after the common female fashion. This was the chief, and such the insignia of his authority. The native notions forbidding monopoly, the shirt, with the tempting red, was no sooner in their hands, than it was torn into as many parts as equalled the number of my captors, and appropriated by each as his own fancy prompted.

After amusing themselves at my expense for some time, with no other inconvenience to me than some petty annoyances, they were ready to decamp, and made signs to me, accordingly. Up to this moment, I had cherished the hope that some of my shipmates would make their appearance; but in vain. It was in vain, also, that I motioned my kidnappers to go toward the wreck. They headed directly toward the woods, which were distant only some forty rods. Two of the seven led the van; naked and barefoot, I formed the centre, and the remaining five brought up the rear.

In this order, our march continued for about ten miles. To me, they were long ones; for even the most painful of inward feelings could not render me entirely insensible to the sufferings incident to a jour-

ney, rapid, as this was, over a rough surface, and
through a tangled forest, and with feet and every part
of my person totally unprotected. This painful scene
continued, with little to disturb its sameness, save
that, ever and anon, a flock of kangaroo broke and
fled from before us in various directions, like frightened
sheep, till, all at once, as if by magic, two hundred
men, women, and children—nude, gentle reader, all
nude, as Adam and Eve in the garden—started up
before us. We were close upon them, before they saw
us. At sight of me, they raised a yell, sufficient to
frighten a youngster, as I was, out of a year's growth.
At the same moment, the women slung the smaller
children on their backs, and ran; the larger children
squealed, like so many guinea-pigs, and ran also; the
women vociferating: "Yenec jon ack: Yenec jon
ack—He is the devil: He is the devil." On arriving at the huts, though we found them minus the
women and children, the men presently gathered
around me, and appeared to be hugely inquisitive as
to who I was, and whence I came. At length, they
made signs to me to sit down by a fire, in front of one
of the wigwams. These people, when travelling, are
very wary of a large fire. This was scarcely larger
than a man's hat. The reason is, that fire, or even a
smoke, would endanger their discovery by an enemy;
an event that, in most cases, would prove equivalent
to their massacre; for the tribes, with few exceptions,

are in a state of unceasing war, in prosecuting which, it is a master stroke, by stealing upon a sleeping enemy, to put them to an indiscriminate slaughter—men, women and children.

After teasing me with numberless questions, till they were satisfied that I was so utterly *outre* as not to understand the first syllable of their elegant vernacular, they further tested my pretensions to polite society, by an offer of food, in quality and shape of raw oppossum. Alack, that it was so!—but so it was, that I was forced to decline it—whereupon they broke into a loud laugh, doubtless wondering how my education could have been so sadly neglected.

But night was drawing on, and different hunting parties, with more or less evidences of success, continued coming in, till all were assembled. The whole tribe, including women and children, numbered about fifteen hundred. By sunset, I found myself surrounded by several hundred men, who remained in deep, and occasionally angry consultation till nine o'clock. Nor had I any reason to doubt, that the question of this protracted and exciting debate, was the life or death of their prisoner, nor that the chances stood strongly in favor of the latter alternative. So fixed, indeed, were my apprehensions of death, at that time, that hope and fear were mainly busy with the mere question of its *mode.* Dying was not so much the object of dread as that, I knew not what roasting process

would go before it. On the other hand, I hoped—and
it was about all I could hope—that the wretches would
be kind enough to do the killing first, and be quick
about it, and roast and eat their suppers afterward.

When this grim court, however, adjourned and dispersed, I knew the question was settled otherwise, at
least for the present. Indeed, I was not without hope
that the chief, who obviously claimed me as his property, was predetermined to turn me to some better
account than that of feasting his liege subjects. Nor
was this hope unstrengthened, when, to make a safer
place for me, that dignitary sent away his wives—there
were only seven of them, with children in proportion
—to construct another lodge for themselves, putting
me into what was their part of the hut, and laying
himself down in the fore-part of it; and all, as I concluded, not only to obviate the escape of his prisoner,
but to obviate abduction or assassination.

But, to me, the night was sleepless, and from two
causes. I was surrounded by blood-thirsty miscreants,
and it was no great reach of night-fancy, under such
circumstances, that one of their spears might let the
life out of me before morning. But apart from mental uneasiness, I was suffering with cold. It was
about the last of September, and, of course, answered
to the same time in our month of March. True, I
was partially sheltered, but then I was totally un-
clothed, and on the naked earth. My teeth chattered,

and sleep was a stranger to my eyes the live-long night. Day dawned, but my new associates were still in their deepest slumber. Sound sleep never overtakes these people till after midnight. The men lie down by the fire, which is always in front of the huts, and there they sleep in all weather, winter as well as summer. The interior of their rude dwellings is always left to their women and children. At midnight, dew begins to fall. It is copious, like a drizzling rain. With this, the deep, native sleep begins, which holds till the sun is two hours above the horizon. So literally do these children of nature leave each day to take care of itself, that they eat no breakfast which a hunt of the same morning has not furnished. Of this, this first morning of my connection with them was to furnish a proof in point.

By the time the dew was dry on the grass and herbage—and they never hunt before—their spears were in readiness. Led by the chief, who took good care to keep me near him, they filed off into the scrub. A couple of miles brought us to a sudden halt. To my eye, there was nothing *visible*, absolutely *nothing*. The native eye, and ear, and smell, have a keenness of perception of which civilized man knows nothing. After a breathless pause of about two minutes, the chief raised his hand, making certain motions with its fingers, when the party flew off in different directions, while I remained where I was, an admiring spec-

tator of the strange manœuvre. Presently they had
formed a wide circle. Now they advanced a step or
two. Then they were motionless as statues. Then
they moved a few steps again; and again were still;
and all this while every eye seemed fixed on some
central object which, to my unpractised sight, remained
invisible. At length, however, I saw the game—two
hundred kangaroo, or more. The beautiful things
were grazing among the scrub. They fed; the hun·
ters advanced; they erected themselves to reconnoitre,
and they of the chase were still.

Thus the circle of spears gradually lessened, till, at
a signal from the leader, there was uttered a simultaneous scream, which sends the frightened herd to one
side of the circle. Another scream sends them still
more frightened to the other. Thus frightened and
repulsed, and repulsed and frightened, they become
desperate, and finally burst through the surrounding
hunters. This being the signal, whizz goes a whole
volley of spears. These weapons are barbed, and where
they strike they fix. He who throws with effect, is
prepared to follow his victim. This he does so closely
that, what with his being retarded by the shaft he carries in his side, and stopping frequently in vain to
disengage himself from it, by rubbing against a tree,
and what with faintness from loss of blood, the hunter
soon comes near enough to deal another spear. His
next expedient is a heavy two feet stick, which he hurls

with such dexterity and force, as to make sure of knocking the animal down at a distance of fifty yards. This done, the coup de grace is dealt by a tomahawk of stone; and finally, a stone knife skins and cuts him up. Then they strike a fire, and when the flesh has been on the blazing brush till it is fairly blackened, is fitted for food. This, with the skin, is then, carried to the wigwam, and then, gentle reader—then breakfast is ready.

Such a hunt as I have described always ends in the capture of more or less of these animals;* sometimes as many as eight or ten. On the occasion above described, I think our luck went no higher than seven.

Like nearly all the 'quadrupeds of Australia, these animals are marsupial. When full grown, their weight averages about two hundred pounds. The hind quarters, with the head, are the only part of the animal—save the blood and intestines—which are used for food. The other parts being almost entirely fleshless. The kangaroo is mouse-colored. Its habits are gregarious. I scarcely need to add, that it rather leaps than runs; a peculiarity of motion to which a strongly muscular tail, aiding, as it does, the action of the hinder legs, is no less singularly than happily adapted. Of the other animals of this country, I shall probably find occasion to speak hereafter.

* That is, with such exceptions as are noticed hereafter

CHAPTER IX.

Native implements.—The knife.—The battle-axe.—War and hunting spears.—How made.—Breaks a three-days' fast.—Sickness consequent.—A forced cure.—Uncertainty of the chase, and its consequences.—Servile and abject state of females.—Frequency of wife-killing, with the trivial occasions upon which it is practised.—An instance.

Unable to accommodate myself at once to the dietetic habits of my new associates, I was more at liberty to observe some other things, which, as the reader will be likely to be interested in them, I will set them down in this place, at least some of them. Casual reference has already been made to some of the implements of these rude people. They will naturally be imagined by the reader as rude, like the people who invented them; or who, at least, must have imported them in some former period from the people, whoever they were, whence themselves originated: a people not more elevated in their modes of life than themselves. In one point, the current notices of the aboriginal New-Hollander do his native or, at least, his *actual* invention no injustice. I refer to such accounts as deny him any knowledge of navigation. It is certainly corroborated by the whole

F*

course of my observation, while connected with these
people, that they discover no aptitude or inclination
in the nautical direction, whatever; not even so much
as to have originated the construction of a bark or
wooden canoe. This is the more remarkable, as their
country is intersected by large rivers, and surrounded
by the ocean, indenting it with numerous bays, and
as the people not only frequent these waters, in the
more ordinary way of a vagrant life, but as they are
compelled to resort to them for food, by a necessity
frequently following from the failure of the chase.
Still more will the circumstance, in question, appear
remarkable to the reader, when he comes to learn,
that the *general* ignorance of mechanical invention,
charged upon these people by superficial observers, is
far from being true; so far, indeed, that if successful
in his attempt, the author of this narrative will show,
that considering their total privation, in common
with most mere savages, of all metallic appliances, they
exhibit a cleverness in various handicraft matters
which educated men, under the same circumstances,
would find a little difficult of imitation, and which they
would be still less likely to have originated.

And first, as being, perhaps, of the first importance,
let us describe the hunting-knife; the only thing
under that general notion known to the natives. This
then, like the other articles to be described in this
place, is constituted of wood, which supplies the

handle; of stone, which substitutes the blade, and of
black-boy, which forms the medium of connection between them.   The stone is a highly vitreous kind of
white flint.   A mass of this is laid upon another mass
of the same material, when, with another stone of
suitable size, and hardness, it is fractured till a piece is
obtained sufficiently knife-like for the purpose.   Black-
boy is the colonial name of a large growing herbaceous
plant, as well as of the gutta percha-like substance
which it furnishes.   The haft, duly prepared, and
twelve inches, more or less, in length, receives a heavy
coat of the above substance, extending mid-way from
one of its extremities.   At right angles with the haft,
thus encased, is fixed the knife-like or lanciform flint,
obtained as above, and which is kept in place by the
tenacious property of the cement in which it is im-
bedded.   Then another and another is added, till half
the length of the wood is armed with these dentata.
When sufficiently socketed by additional coatings of
the gum, the whole mass, reduced to a proper bevel
and perfectly smoothed, is left to the indurating influence of the sun.   This is the finishing process.   The
percha wears a high polish.   The flint blades are of
uniform length, and they and the black-boy, which
imbeds them, are of nearly equal hardness.   For any
of the warrior's or hunter's trenchant purposes, it is
easy to infer that such an instrument would be likely
to possess a fearful efficiency.

The material and general process of axe-making are now sufficiently before the reader. He is only to suppose, the wood part being ready, that the flint axe is fitted to it as closely as possible, and that the overlying cement is, in temperature and quantity, sufficient to stick the two parts together. When this is effected, the cohesive material is applied in successive layers, till the fixation is completed. It will be sufficient to add, that the instrument in question, if intended for war, is finished by the addition of another poll, by means, and in the manner aforesaid; so as to leave it a double-edged tomahawk. If, on the other hand, it is merely designed for common use, the addition would be nothing more than what we are accustomed to call, the axe or hatchet *head.* In either case, and at any rate, the parts are as permanently and durably united as they could be by any process known to European or American artists. Waiving any reference to the known capabilities of the stone axe of the primitive Indian of this country, I shall only say, for the implement now under consideration, that it cleaves the gnarliest wood known to the Australian forests, not excepting the hard-grained mahogany.

The spear exists under three forms; as adapted to hunting, fishing, and war purposes. I am about to speak of it as an arm of war. The spear wood tree furnishes the material of the shaft. When first taken

in hand, far from being a straight, it is emphatically
"a crooked stick," and very much so, indeed. The
artist's first process is, to hold it over the fire till it is
as hot as he can handle it. His next work is the removal of obliquities. This he accomplishes with
hands and teeth; the latter being the principal appara-
tus; and the work is only finished when it is as straight
as a gun-barrel. After another heat, the whole surface is coated with black-boy, in the way of varnish.
This done, it is once more subjected to the action of
fire, which gives it extreme hardness, as well as a
high polish. When thoroughly dried in the sun, the
heavier end is tapered to a point, beginning twelve
inches from the end. This point is then properly
tempered by plunging and holding it in hot sand.
On being withdrawn, it is sufficiently heated to melt
the black-boy, and is deeply incased in that material.
In this are set three rows of the pointed flint, which
are gradually lessened—I mean the pieces—as they
approach the point of the wood; while, in the point
itself, there is infixed a piece of flint no larger than
the *point*, with less than half the *length*, of a small
penknife blade; and it is nearly as sharp, as are also
all the rest. I have said, in effect, that the head of
such a weapon, as is here described, is twelve inches
in length. Such, indeed, is its ordinary proportion,
though occasionally extended to eighteen inches. But
to return: when these flint lancets are set, the vege-

table gum is so applied as to give them all necessary
permanence, and the whole workmanship wears a
glass-like polish.

Such a spear, with a ten-foot shaft—the ordinary
length—is thrown in such a way as to produce a
screw-like motion, by means of which it opens a passage through the body of its victim, circular in form,
and in magnitude equal to the diameter formed by
the longest barbs with which the head of the instrument is armed.   Indeed, I have seen it so thrown as
to pass entirely through a human body, leaving a
perforation sufficient to admit a common-sized hand.

The hunting and fishing spears I shall not describe,
further than by saying, that, while they display equal
adaptation to their respective purposes, they involve
much less pains and labor in the making.*

But it is time for breakfast; and I must postpone to
a more favorable opportunity the further consideration
of skill in the mechanic arts among the nomades of
this island-desert.   The third day of my captivity
had elapsed before I tasted food   Then it was that I
began to look on the raw flesh with which my savage
associates regaled themselves, with feelings of lessened
aversion.   Hunger, which tames the most intractable
natures, was very sensibly doing its work upon me;
so that I was by no means sorry at the offer now made
me of a piece of kangaroo venison.   There were five

* See Appendix B.

or six pounds of it. I took it. It was partially blackened by fire and smoke; but still raw and gory. Not
yet aware of any sumptuary law of the island to the
contrary, I laid it on the fire, intending to realize the
benefit of its action in the premises. This was re-
sented. They threw it off, making signs to me that I
must eat it as it was. Compliance followed, and so
did the immediate motions of *intestine* war.—I was
sick—*dreadfully.*

An old man approached me, and muttered something. But, understanding nothing, I said nothing.
His next movement—for the reader already has before him the Esculapius of the tribe—was to gather
some herbs, warm them by the fire, and apply them
externally to the affected part. The next step in the
curative process, was this:—a piece of kangaroo skin
was burned till it was charred, and then pulverized
between two stones. Certain herbs, having been previously dried, were also rendered fine by being rubbed
between the hands. Then the two ingredients were
duly compounded, and then, aye, then, most piteous
reader, the patient was to "dare and do" the rest.
But the fact was—I may as well own it—the fact was,
that all my courage had left me in company with the
ejected kangaroo. And beside, as I was debarred the
natural right of a patient, in quizzing the practitioner,
I must own to some mortal fear of poison. The *nos-
trum* was proffered in vain. Signs, or by what the

professional man required of me, followed, which I
could not pretend to misunderstand,—signs manual,
oral, labial, lingual, and still his patient made no
swallowing preparations. To be thus trifled with,
and by an outside barbarian, exceeded the apothe-
cary's patience. He called a corps of assistants. What
could he less? Really, it seemed as if the rascals
would choke me. And so, indeed, they did till an
opening was made for the *alterative*. When this was
done, and the said alterative was past the patient's
power of rejection or recall, the strangulator very
considerately remitted his grasp. I breathed, swal-
lowed, and felt a sensation as if the sedative had descended to the very seat of the recent insurrection.

Seriously, however, the gastric disturbance was qui-
eted. To obviate its recurrence, and to save the expense of medicine and medical attendance, the crudity
of the next animal rations offered me was removed by
the action of fire. For the fricassee which ended my
long fast, I was indebted to an animal of the island
which, for the present, need not be named. The
genus is common to all countries. The particular
species, here referred to, is larger than most of my
untravelled readers have ever witnessed; unless,
perchance, some menagerie-sight-seer should form
an exception. Its length—I speak now of the individual that furnished my first breakfast—measured
little, if any, less than *thirteen feet*. This animal

is roasted first, and then eviscerated; thirdly, it is flayed; and fourthly, eaten. The penultimate act in this series—I mean the skinning—is thus performed. The neck is parted, as near the head as may be, the skin, in the mean time, remaining whole, save only the abdominal and thoracic opening, already referred to. The principal operator takes the protruded end of the headless cervex between his teeth. A boy grasps the head—the skin adhering to it as well as to the remaining carcass—and starts away in the tailward direction; and when he has measured off the thirteen feet, more or less, the eatable part of the animal is precisely in the state in which the reader may have seen a skinned eel. It only remains for the same reader to imagine that this delicious breakfast of mine is about to be made of a section of his finless, scaleless fish, with no other exceptions than that mine was originally provided with *scales*, and could run much faster on land, than his in water. I pause. The reader has now the full idea, and I am saved a more direct offence against his prejudices, which would have resulted from the needless use of a name. I said it was delicious. It was so—not because of the ravenous hunger which preceded this, my first use of it. It was a preferred article in my island diet, through the whole course of my captivity.

The only favorable time for hunting is when the weather is rainy, or windy, or both; as, then, the game is approached with comparative facility. Whereas, in a dry and still time, the noise unavoidably produced in the leaves and bushes by the numbers necessary in the native mode of hunting, gives that premature alarm to the game which baffles all stratagem. In consequence of this difficulty, we were sometimes unsuccessful in our hunting excursions, for a week to ten days together, and were obliged to subsist on the scanty supplies obtained by the women. They—the women—are always abroad on such occasions, with a bag made of kangaroo skin, by which they convey to their families whatever eatables they are so fortunate as to find. These are, now and then, an oppossum, which they kill with their sticks, and much oftener the root called *min*, which, with an exception presently to be mentioned, is nearly all the natives know of vegetable food. This root is bulbous, and of the average size of a hen's egg. When roasted, it is perfectly black, inside as well as out, and has a pungent, fiery taste, similar to that of a red pepper pod. Mashed between two stones, and kneaded with argillaceous earth, it is used for food. Its subserviency to that purpose, however, must greatly depend upon use, as I infer from the fact, that its first effect on me, was that of a violent cathartic, which continued several days. Subsequently, it became as innoxious, and probably as nutritive, to me as to any of my native acquaintances. The other indigenous vegetable, employed as food by these untamed people, is called *choocup*. The root only is edible, which is bulbous, like the min, and somewhat larger, but is met with much less frequently. To the taste, it is not unlike the potato, and is regarded as a great luxury.

When abroad for hunting purposes, the men are always provided with fire, or the means of producing it. By this means, when they have taken small game, such as the paddimelon, oppossum, or bandy goat, they roast it, in their way, and eat it on the spot; while the women, if present, sit in the background, and either eat their mins, or nothing. When these wretched serviles succeed in possessing themselves of any of the lesser animals, as is not unfrequently the case—a fact before referred to, as well as the appliances by which it is accomplished—they are expected to bring them home, untasted, to their wigwams, and then sit by, in silence, till masculine appetite is fully sated. Sometimes, indeed, the savage gourmand tosses a bone to the hungry mother, with her group of hungry children; but she may not *ask* for anything. The penalty for doing so would be—*ordinarily*; it varies with the varying humor of the fiend who inflicts it; but ordinarily, it would be—*a blow across the head with a fire-brand*. After such first offence and infliction, should she dare to say a word, he would exercise unwonted forbearance, if a stroke of his spear were not to lay her dead at his feet.

Such is man, where the humanizing influences of
Christianity, with its ever attendant civilization, is unknown. And such, too, is woman, where her lot is
unsoftened by the soothing and elevating ministers of
the Divine Mercy. Poor a Christian as I am, the most
bitter regret is awakened in my mind whenever it re-
verts, as it often does, to the dreadful condition in
which I found and left these human dwellers in the
wilderness.

As illustrative of this general subject, while at the
same time it justifies the few reflections that have been
occasioned by it, I shall close this chapter with an incident of which I was a too near witness.

I was sitting one evening before the fire of a friend
of mine. We had hunted together through the day,
and were then just returned to his lodge, weary and
hungry ; for we had taken nothing. Not so, his young
wife. She had returned before us, with an opossum,
which she had roasted, and, impelled by hunger, was
in the criminal act of eating, when we twain came in.
Doubtless, her hope was to have finished the delinquent repast, and to have obliterated every trace of it,
in anticipation of our arrival. It was too late. The
sin was a great one. Denial was out of the question.
She ate on, and said nothing. The offended sate :
rage rendered him silent. I said he was my friend ;
for to me, personally, he had ever shown more than
the average amount of savage kindness. A girl of our

tribe had inspired him with a passion very different from that which now inflamed him. He had married her; and this half-starved opossum eater, who could not have seen more than twelve or thirteen summers, was my friend *Elye-pete's* bride.

For half an hour my companion looked straight into the fire, and said not a word; for, under any great affront, the true New-Hollander stirs not nor speaks under fifteen to twenty minutes; a trait that may be more fully depicted hereafter. I watched him, as well aware that the conduct of his spouse, operating on a temper irritated by hunger and a supperless prospect, had ignited a train which must produce a fearful explosion. The flame, which threw its flickering light on the swart visage of the hunter, told but too plainly that still darker thoughts were at work within. Starting to his feet, the infuriate demon scooped his two hands full of embers and burning sand, and flung the whole into the face and bosom of the naked object of his vengeance; for I must repeat, that none of the natives wear any clothing, and that she was sitting there as nude as when she was born. The devil of his nature thus fairly roused, he sprang for his spear. It transfixed his frantic but unresisting victim. She fell dead. The wretch of a murderer muttered something about her not having *liked* him, and of his having now taken a proper revenge, both with regard to her and to his alleged rival in his young wife's affections. Whether this posthumous reflection was just, or whether it was only the natural resort of a villain, I had no means of knowing.

Save by the women of the tribe, the affair was scarcely noticed. They tore their hair, and kept up a hideous outcry for about two hours. Then they carried away the corpse, laid it on a pile of brush-wood and then burnt it to ashes. Wife-killing, among the aborigines of Australia, is frequent, and elicits neither surprise, nor any sort of animadversion.

CHAPTER X.

Warned to a general training.—Enters the ranks.—The sham-fight,
which is not all a sham.—Cadets of the chase.—Feats in target
shooting.—Puts himself upon the acquisition of both arts—the art
of hunting, and the art of war.—Acquires both, and is respected.—
Long drouth, and its effect upon the chase.—These visitations imputed to him, as a dealer in wizardism.—Tribe demands his death—
Chief's resistance—triumph—vigilance.

THE homicide was a thing of but common consequence. The day that followed it, movements were
afoot which indicated some event of real interest to the
whole community. The young men were busy with
their spears. These implements were headless, consisting of a mere shaft. Pointed, and their points
hardened, as they usually were, they were adequate to
many hunting purposes; aside from which, with occasions of divertisement, including those of the customary musters, they were seldom used. The object,
on this occasion, obviously was, to prepare, not for
killing, but for non-killing purposes; for they were
blunting and battering them against the rocks. With
these, and various kindred preparations, the day
passed away.

On the morrow, I was duly warned to take my place
in the ranks, "armed and equipped as the law directs,"
for the important purpose of doing military duty.
Repugnance to the order, though strong and sincere,
was unavailing. Commutation, by payment of a fine,
or otherwise, had not been entered in the code *mili-
taire*, at that time. As nearly as I could decipher the
law in the case, it read: Spear, or be speared; and
as the latter horn of the dilemma did not present the
more eligible point of choice, I naturally made an
election of the other.

Arrived on parade, I found myself preceded by
about forty youngsters of my own age; say, sixteen
to eighteen. They were formed in two equal divisions,
and drawn up so as to face each other at the distance
of some forty yards. Soon after I had taken the position assigned me in one of the ranks, the signal was
given, and the sham-fight began. He who could hit,
and avoid being hit, oftenest, was the "best fellow."
In both these species of exploit, the native adroitness
almost exceeds belief. Within reaching distance, the
spear is sped with a celerity and an aim which can
only be rivalled by the practised eye, and agility of
him who evades, and, by evading, baffles them. Un-
schooled in this latter, as well as in the former art,
every shaft aimed at me was all but sure to hit. And
then, as my awkwardness was as conspicuous as my
person, it excited large fun among the antagonist

party, while, at the same time it attracted a larger
proportion of their unerring javelins than would have
gone to the account of a *common* object. Well was it
for me that their points were blunted; as, otherwise,
life would have had a decided certainty of being let
out through a little less than a thousand openings. As
it was, I was so battered from head to heel that, when
morning came, I could hardly stir, tack or sheet.

This was a strictly martial exercise; a training of us
young men for war. The next day was to put us
through a course of discipline for the chase; hunting
and war being the staple employments among these
islanders — employments dearer to them than any
other, save only and always, that of having no employment at all.

Accordingly, when the sun was two hours high the
next morning—and I have elsewhere advised my
reader, that these people are never voluntarily astir
before that hour—the male juveniles appeared in busy
preparation for the fête of the day. The kangaroo
spear is always supposed to be ready polished and
pointed, either for real or mimic action. But for this
latter use, there must needs be an *object*, which for
size and motion, shall sufficiently represent the animal
itself. This is supplied by a circular piece of thin
bark, as large as the head of a flour barrel, taken from
the gum-tree of the country. Launched with a rapid,
rolling, bounding motion upon the ground, and in a

F

line parallel to that occupied by the marksmen, this measurably represents the animal in question, in that half-*leaping*, half-*flying* state in which the hunter's spear, if successful, must strike and transfix him.

The whole company of trainers are now drawn up on one straight line. Flanking them, on one hand, the left, for instance, is a small party provided with some half-dozen of the disks afore-mentioned, which it is their business to send along, at about fifty yards distance, in front of the main rank, and in a line parallel to it, as intimated above. But look! It comes! The flying target! Whizz! And half a hundred harpoons are darted at it in a jiffy. Happy is that one of the number whose aim and force, are such as to stop it in its flight. The *toga* is its owner's reward. Unless more than one spear strike it in the same *moment*, there can be no dispute as to whose the prize is, for spear and target descend together. These successful feats are by no means rare. I have seen the whizzing mark in question thrown at, ten times consecutively, and in nine instances out of that number, have seen it brought to the ground, at the distance of fifty yards.

By these two, and divers other similar methods, youthhood is trained for manhood; that is, for the honors of the hunter and the warrior. For myself, having had a forced initiation, and finding myself susceptible of improvement, I felt the kindlings of ambition to master these capital accomplishments;

and *took*, and *practised* lessons every day, accordingly;
till, in no long while, I was found a match for the
average of my companions. True, my aim never acquired all the native certainty; but this was com-
pensated by the superiority of English muscle, which
made it tell upon a more distant object. The account fairly balanced, then, and taking the spear for
the standard, I became " a man among men." The
consequence was, that, in sporting the spear, they no
longer treated me as the fool of the play; or, if they
did, they counted on prompt retribution. Another
general result was, I must hunt, when they hunted,
and fight, when they fought.

When I had been some time domesticated—how
long, I could not tell; for Sunday never comes there,
and I had not bethought me of the notched stick, as
a means of noting time—there came on a calm, dry
spell of weather, which lasted for about three weeks.
The watchful kangaroo was unapproachable. Warned
by the too audible crackling and rustling of the
leaves and brushwood, he was off with a bound beyond the reach of our missiles. Night after night we
returned to our ever-shifting encampment with the
means, not of allaying, but only of provoking hunger,
by the taste of a wallaby, a quano, a frog, or, perchance, of the *land eel*, whereof account has been
made in a preceding chapter. My full-fed reader may
feel awry, and possibly look so, at this, and similar

references in this part of my narrative. To awaken none but gustful associations in his mind, would involve the utter abandonment of my subject. If he imagine that there is no power in hunger to subdue such fastidiousness as that which now disturbs his equanimity, I have only to say; he is perfectly welcome to go to New-Holland and make the experiment. At the period, here referred to, I was beginning to think myself doomed to end my days in my island exile. At all events, I was disposed to live, as long as I *must* live *there*, by the best attainable means which I could make available for that purpose. Now, if the aforesaid reader, who, probably, thinks that instead of choosing life on the conditions now and hereafter noticed, it would have been a more decent thing in me to have starved to death; if he, I say, will bear with me for not having done so, I will not write auto-*obituarily*, but proceed, auto-*biographically*, instead.

One evening, during this long period of non-successful hunting, I was sitting by the low fire of my master's lodge, dispirited and sad. All that a mind, under such circumstances, would naturally gather around itself, was present to mine; darkening the present, and throwing still deeper darkness around the future. All at once my musings were interrupted by a general and rather tumultuous gathering of the male members of the tribe. They were without arms, and stood before the chieftain's tent. Though unable, at that time, to ascertain their object from what they *said*, I could not but make some general inferences, anything but auspicious to myself, from the tone and gesticulations of the interlocutors. To supply a full explanation at this point, where it is more natural to place it, I shall anticipate information subsequently received, and let the reader into the whole business at once. In order to this, he must excuse a little digression.

The supernaturalism of these islanders lies within a very narrow and dimly illuminated circle. With no notion of a supreme Providence, as far as I could ever ascertain, these savages, nevertheless, retain a few traces of that divine revelation which must have been deposited with the progenitors of the race, previous to the dispersion; inasmuch as these, and other unquestionable remains of it, are found among their posterity in its remotest and darkest habitations. The *immortality* of the soul is blended with its *pre-existence*, in the minds of this rude people. They believe that they existed in another and a happier state, and that the transmigration which has *degraded* them was the result of *wrong-doing* in that pristine and better condition of existence. Whether this idea of their degradation was countenanced by the original Pythagorean doctrine, with which it is now associated, and which they must have brought with them from South Eastern Asia; or whether it has originated in the occasional sight of other and happier people within the last fifty years, I leave for others to determine. Touching the soul's immortality, I can only say, judging from the fact that they always *speak* of it with reluctance, that they seldom advert to it in their *thoughts*, and never from any delight which it affords them. On the few occasions on which it was referred to, in the time of my connection with them, it was only incidental to the subjects of pre-existence, and the metempsychosis.

The notion is prevalent in all the tribes that came under my observation, of a low order of superhuman agents, chiefly, if not exclusively, of a malevolent character. These, however, though they are under a mortal dread of them, they never, as far as I know, seek to propitiate. Nor have they any magical or religious rites, or any forms of worship whatever. One thing is worthy of special notice, in this connection, and the rather, as it constitutes the point mainly aimed at in this episode, on which the explanation of the ensuing incident depends. It is this:— The tribes of this southern continent believe in witchcraft as a fixed fact. Certain arts, they suppose, enable the possessors to wield the influence of those malignant powers against whomsoever they are disposed to injure. In accordance with this superstition, they naturally resolve their adverse fortune into the interposition of some dealer with those invisible spirits. And it happens with savages who are slaves to this form of superstition, as was the case in the times of New-England witchcraft, that the conjurer, witch, or wizard, is seldom found in the person of the rich and powerful; but that *he* has the *supernatural* world under his control who has neither money nor friends in *this*. Reasoning on this approved model, the hunters of New-Holland had come to charge the bad hunting weather, from which they were suffering, to one whom the weather had thrown, helpless, on their coast, and who, beside being their captive, was suffering equally with themselves, from. the very cause for which they now intended to hold him responsible.

After charging me with the getting up of the bad hunting weather, they demanded one of two things: first, that I should be put to death; or, secondly, that I should suffer ostracism—be cast adrift into the wilderness. But the chief vetoed both proposals. They urged; but the chief stood firm, alleging that, as he had found and captured me, I was his property; and he would neither turn me away, nor suffer them to harm a hair of my head. They continued importunate, and became less deferential; till, at length, the irritated sachem snatched his weapons, and swore summary punishment, unless they instantly went about their business. They went; but it was sullen and muttering.

The more effectually to protect me against this popular attempt, the chief caused me to take the interior of the lodge again, while he laid himself down at the entrance, his spears by his side, and his battle-axe for a pillow. Like mine, his night was far from quiet. He was on the *qui vive* at every sound. Several times, starting to his feet, and poising his spear, he demanded "Who is there?" and, receiving no answer to his challenge, drove his weapon into the adjacent bush, whence the noise issued. And though returning day dispelled the more immediate apprehension, common to us both, it was several days before he allowed me to be out of his sight.

CHAPTER XI.

Temptation to attempt an escape.—Yields to the temptation, and
makes the attempt.—Strikes for the coast.—Is unprovisioned.—Miseries of hunger and thirst.—A night among native dogs.—Some account of those formidable animals.—Fruitless chase of an opossum.
—Lies down to sleep, invoking the sleep of death.—Uncaught kangaroo.—High mountain, affording a wide prospect, but no ocean in it.
—Another night, which proves terribly terraqueous.—Lightning and
the mahogany-tree.—Eighth day; discovered and taken in tow by
errant fellows of his clan.—Returns to his master.—Good-natured
reception.—Offer and refusal of human flesh.—More "land-eel."—
Private lecture from the chief.—Narrow escape of danger from that
quarter.—Further account of female vassalage.—The lagoon station,
with doings there, which suddenly change from gay to grave.

SOME days after the night scene which closes the
last chapter, but before the "bewitched weather" was
fairly over, I received my master's summons to accompany him, with the rest of our effectives, on one of
the customary hunts. To this I replied by pleading
that I was "*mendic*—sick." The consequence was, that
they went and left me—men, women and children—all
who were big enough to catch a frog, or dig a chocoup,
and some that were not; for the babies proper were
part and parcel of the expedition. In fine, I found myself left to the keeping of huts as empty as might be,

F*   Q

excepting only the little boys and girls, who were in
a state of *betweenity*, as regards the helpful and the
helpless, and consequently could have added nothing
but incumbrance to the movements of the party.

Upon finding myself thus alone, the thought of
liberty revived with fresh force. Far be it from me to
deny that it had helped to make me "*mendic.*" I will
only say that, if I had been so before the expedition
left me, I ceased to be so immediately afterward. For
a few moments I balanced chances. Some ten days
before, we had seen the sea; and though we had been
falling back into the interior in the interim, I judged
it practicable to reach the coast; in which case, it appeared equally possible to subsist on cast-ashore food,
till I could reach some settlement. The prospect was
inspiring. My courage rose. The spears were all in
the field; I took a tomahawk and started.

My course was directed by the sun. The reader
already understands that the scene of the shipwreck
and of my captivity lay on the south coast of this
vast island, otherwise called a continent. In attempting to regain that coast, then, it will be understood
that I travelled southward. Being in the southern
hemisphere, in order to get an observation of the sun,
I must look behind me; as, while I was facing south,
that luminary would cause my person, like the coming
events of the poet, to "cast its shadow before."

How I was equipped, the reader already knows;

but I have not yet informed him that, by reason of the all but utter famine then existing in our quarters, I was totally unprovisioned for my journey. Such, however, was the fact. The only eatable thing and available as such, which I met with in eight days —a trivial exception near the close of that period will be mentioned in its proper place—was now and then an innutritious root, and sometimes I travelled a day and a half, and even two, without finding one. With these general remarks, by way of anticipation, the reader will pass to the fourth night of my wilderness and lone journey.

On that night, having sunk to sleep at the foot of a large tree, I was roused, in about the middle watch, from the paradise of a hungry man's dream, by an ominous growl. Starting to my feet, I found it was the growl of the native dog, and that his family, which was in waiting, to the number of little less than a dozen, were all very impatient for supper. And they were close upon me, only, not having *reconnoitred*, they did not *rush*. On coming sufficiently to my senses, I found that, in rising, I had instinctively grasped my stick—a heavy one, which had assisted me in walking through the day, and in falling back against the trunk of the tree to prevent an attack in the rear, I found, to my unspeakable relief, that it was hollow, with an opening sufficient for my admission. I entered. These two circumstances were lucky—I ought to say *provi-*

dential—as, but for them, in all human probability, the odds against me had been fatal, and the serenade had ended much more to the satisfaction of the serenaders.

The native dog, is a term which, as applied to the animal in question, is liable to convey a wrong sense. He is not supposed to be a *native*—that is, an *original* inhabitant of the island—but to have been imported with the early colonists, from England. Like the wild, or kangaroo dog of Van Diemen's, of which this appears to be a congener, this animal appears to be the progeny of the domestic mastiff and greyhound, "littered in the bush, and allowed to run wild." His hair is long and shaggy; his head is that of the wolf, while the bushiness and length of his tail render him, in that respect, decidedly fox-like. In size, he is monstrous — exceeding the Newfoundland — which, joined with his fleetness, savage ferocity, and union of numbers, for he hunts in company, makes him the terror of the forest. Nor are the settlements unvisited by these depredators, especially in the neighboring island of Van Diemen's, where they are particularly injurious to the wool-growing interest, that great staple of both islands. "One gentleman lost, in three months, no less than 1200 lambs and sheep. Another 700—another 300."

But to return to the hollow tree. In this situation, with these enfamished monsters close upon me, gnashing their white fangs, and growling and howling, I

passed the remaining hours of that memorable night.
Ensconced, as above, I succeeded in fighting off, and
keeping at bay, my daring assailants, till the dawn
dispersed them. Never was its advent more welcome.

The day thus ushered in—the fifth of my flight—
was scarcely marked by any occurrence of sufficient
interest to the reader to warrant its record. Hunger
had ceased to torment me; but the want of sustenance
was very sensibly reducing my strength. I might
mention that, on this day, in crossing a small prairie,
an opossum started up before me, and that he befooled
me into a chase of half a mile, when I lost him in the
woods, and with him an unrequited outlay of strength,
which I could but ill afford. The only sustenance of
this day, was water, obtained by hard digging in a
dry lagoon, and which, after all, was rather a thin
mud, than proper water.

A mountain rose before me. It was nightfall. My
limbs would bear me no farther. True, the gnawings
of famine were passed; but its faintness was upon me.
It had devoured me. My whole soul was spent; and
I sank down there, at the foot of the mountain, in
utter despondence. Dark without and still darker
within, I prayed my Maker for the sleep of death—
the sleep that knows nor dream nor waking. My
desperation was complete, and I shudder as I bethink
me that, *with the means*, that dark hour had, doubtless,
wrought the end so fervently, but, alas! so madly in-

voked. Thanks to that Power who saved me, as he
did the "man of like passions," against my own
wishes.

A little refreshed by the slumbers of the night, I
addressed myself to the ascent of the mountain, with
the fond hope that it would afford me an observation
of the coast. This was the sixth morning of my
escapade. About half-way up, a large rock attracted
my attention, whose surface was moist with water,
exuding from its crevices, and held in absorption by
the moss with which it was mantled. By pressing
with my parched lips every inch of the absorbent
moss, I extracted what sufficed for their moistening.
Renewing the ascent, the remaining way was relieved
and enlivened by large numbers of the gregarious
kangaroo. So unacquainted were they with their human enemies, that they gambolled around me as if I
had been a friend. Hunger denied me the gratification of encouraging that mistake any longer than till
one of them, less timid and more curious than his
fellows, rose on his hinder feet so near as to tempt my
tomahawk. Unfortunately for me, however, the arm
that flung it was so weakened by famine, that, though
it hit and staggered him, it did not prevent his escape.

At length, exhausted, I stood on the mountain's
summit. And where was the object of this long labor?
A vast expanse lay at my feet, stretching away to an
immeasurable distance in all directions, but affording

no glimpse of the ocean.   Large lagoons were the only objects which diversified the landscape.   Some of them must have had a circumference of thirty or forty miles. These lagoons, by no means uncommon in this country, are inhabited by all the aquatics in countless numbers—the duck, the pelican, and the black swan.

Here—not in the lagoon, but on the mountain—I spent a long time in laboring to raise a fire, for the purpose of preparing food from the larva of a large insect which I found there in great numbers.   Once and again the friction process was carried to the smoking point; at which, from sheer weakness, I was finally obliged to drop it.   Of course, my food underwent no change of a culinary character; and whether finally declined or not, on that account, may safely be left to the determination of the reader.

Determining to give my subsequent course a more westerly direction, I descended the mountain; slept; arose; struggled through another day, and slept again; or rather, I disposed myself, for the purpose of doing so, and was compelled to watch with a visitant, at once very engaging and very unwelcome.   My weary head pillowed on the root of a large standing tree, I was just losing the sense of bodily and mental suffering in a first oblivious slumber, when a tempest, largely mingled with lightning, thunder, and rain,* broke

---

* "Thunder and lightning are very frequent in every part of this continent."—*Cunningham.*

upon the scene, effectually dispelling, for the rest of
the night, not only all sleep and dreams, but all dreams
of sleep. Long unaccustomed to sleep under sheets
of any kind, the reader will not wonder that I could
not sleep under a sheet of water; and, especially, with
head and ears under. My couch was thus bespread,
to the depth of six to eight inches. The consequence
was, that not only lying asleep, but lying awake, was
equally out of the question. Sitting up in bed, therefore, was the dernier resort; a posture that gave me
the full impression of the passing scene—of the water
pouring on, and rising under; of the gleaming bolt
of heaven, setting the forest in a blaze, and of the
crash which told of the nearness of its descent. The
most striking exhibition of a collision of great forces
on this occasion was that in which the electric fluid
fell upon a tree—it was a mahogany, and three feet
in diameter—rifting it from top to bottom, and utterly
demolishing its huge and gnarled structure, the splin-
tered fragments of which I found the next morning
lying in all directions around the place where I had
been sitting—a distance of forty rods. I could but
raise my heart in gratitude to that gracious Power
whose shield had covered me in that dreadful moment.

This welcome morning was the close of the eighth
day of my suffering and fruitless peregrinations. With
no reasonable hopes of reaching the ocean, but with a
much fairer prospect of feeding the native dogs, " in

lieu thereof." I now heartily wished myself reunited
with my forest-roving friends. Life, on almost any
terms, among beings of a common origin with ourselves, is found preferable, either to life in utter and
long-continued solitude, on the one hand, or to death
under the same circumstances of solitude on the other.
Destiny, with prophetic finger, seemed pointing me,
not to deliverance, but to the grave—a grave in solitude, and dug by famine! I would fain escape it on
any terms, and now fairly yearned for the sight of
even a savage fellow-man. Judge then, gentle reader,
of the emotions with which I greeted the well-known
savage yell. The morning sun was about three hours
high, and I was dragging myself slowly through the
scrub, when hailed as above, I paused to learn what
new phase of island humanity was about to cross my
path. The hunter who had surprised, had seen me.
A moment, and he was at my side. He proved to be
a member of our tribe, and I saluted him in all sin-
cerity. He was one, of a party of three, who had
separated from the main body, and not having been
at head-quarters since my desertion, was, as yet, a
stranger to that little episode in my history. How I
came to be thus abroad and alone, were questions, not
more natural for him to ask, than for me to evade.
In doing this, my inability to jabber their jargon was
not a little helpful—my ear was much better educated
than my tongue—and then, for staving off trouble

some questions, I had a tolerably fair excuse in the circumstance, that I was dying of starvation. By words, partly, but more by signs, my clansman was made acquainted with that fact, and implored for food. At this very moment, the two absent members of the little party joined us, one of whom was the welcome possessor of an opossum. A fire was kindled. The animal was half roasted, and, "courteous reader, what would you have done?"

Words and signs made me understand, what, indeed, I wished and expected, that I was to follow them. I did so, but at a very slow pace. The taste of food had suddenly changed my passive hunger into a state of tormenting activity. But the sagacity of my wardens took good care that over-eating should not kill me. I was with these stragglers seven days, making fifteen, in all, since I myself had straggled, when I once more stood before our common sachem. By this time I was nearly myself again.

His majesty very jocosely demanded of me, whether I had found it better to live in the woods alone, or with him and his; to which I made no reply. After laughing at me, and cracking several jokes at my expense, he conducted me to his wigwam, and guessing that I was hungry, gave me something to eat. It was flesh—part of the leg of an animal—*of a child!* This was the first, though I am sorry to say, not the last, instance of the kind which occurred in my intercourse

with these degraded people. Observing my hesitation, the chief made signs to me to eat it. With as
much disgust in my countenance as it . could well
express, I shook my head to say: "No. Never."
After urging me for a long time, he took it away,
and ate it with an obvious gusto, saying; " *Annon
quahki emra aubeac—this is very good.*" How this food
for the cannibal appetites of our people had been procured, together with the still more sanguinary consequences that followed, there will be occasion to notice
in the ensuing chapter. In the mean time, let not the
reader suppose that I was sent to bed without my
supper. So far was it from being so, that in conde-
scension to my undisciplined digestion, I was treated
to a large piece of my favorite *land-eel.* The entire
reptile measured fifteen feet. Save that one proscrib-
ed variety, I was now as omnivorous as any other
New-Hollander. Such is the plastic power of necessity.

When bed-time came, and I had lain down in the
chief's tent, I found that he had affected, on my return, an indifference which he by no means felt. I
have always supposed that his *acting* on that occasion, was prompted by a fear, that if he exhibited
the real state of his feelings in the presence of the
hunters, those late enemies of mine would construe it
into a license to tap some of the larger blood-vessels
of his adopted subject. However that may have been,

I was no sooner alone in his presence, than he took up a regular labor with me on the subject of my late conduct. The deeper he went into the merits of the matter, the more and more matter he found for his original displeasure. Indeed, there was a moment in which the fire of his savage nature suddenly kindled to a flame. I thought my hour had come. In another moment his fitful humor changed, and he was calm again. The crisis was over. He continued to look serious, but said no more. Doubtless he was not yet quite willing to yield the hope of making a *man* of me.

The next morning broke up the encampment. The women, who perform all the menial labor when the tribe is stationary, such as building the wigwam, and furnishing wood and water, are equally responsible for the portage of all the movables, when a new station is resolved on; which is seldom less frequent than once in two or three days. If the camp is to be pitched where there is bark for roofing the hut, the old material is left behind. This, however, is by no means common, as the tree from which it is taken is scarce, it being only found in particular locations. When, therefore, as in the present instance, the bark is to be transported, the women have to do it. Suppose, as is sometimes the case, that a mother has three children unable to travel, she is loaded thus: The bark is on her head; a child is on each shoulder; and the third, in a bag of kangaroo skin, is fastened to her back by a strap which passes round her breast. And this load she carries from fifteen to twenty miles. In the mean time, the husband and the sons, with nothing but a few weapons in hand, walk on before.

Our tents were pitched on the margin of a lagoon. For the two or three days that we remained here, we enjoyed large sport with the swans and wild ducks, with which these marshy localities abound. But an event occurred at the end of that time, which turned our spears upon objects not quite so easily terrified. That event, together with the train of circumstances following it, as well as other matters which serve to explain the causes of it, must be the subject of another chapter.

CHAPTER XII.

The nocturnal surprise.—An obstinate fight.—The author's share in it.—Is wounded, and rendered insensible.—Hospital remedy.—The enemy beaten.—Killed on both sides.—Desperate mode of fighting. —The ten prisoners.—Two of them old offenders.—Are sentenced to death.—Execution, with various savage tortures.—Defiant and unflinching conduct of sufferers.—Degradation of remaining prisoners.—Their dismissal.—Chapter concludes with the causes of the war.

WHEN it is considered, that the native tribes of this little continent are, essentially, a belligerent people, and that there is hardly ever one of them, at any one time, who have not a quarrel on their hands; and that, consequently, they never lie down to sleep without reason to expect an attack, with bloodshed and death to some of them before morning; when this, I say, is considered, it will doubtless excite the reader's admiration that they employ no night-guard, nor any other precaution whatever against a surprise. In our own present circumstances, especially, it may justly provoke astonishment that when one sleeps, all sleep; and this, too, when a neighboring people had just been goaded to retaliation by an outrage, not now to be named, but which will be related hereafter.

We were sleeping in our lagoon encampment for, I
think, the third time. The chief with his warrior-
hunters; the mothers, with their little ones, were
sleeping—the latter under the bark shelters reared by
their own hands; the former were lying around the
dull embers of the camp-fires, their long hair drenched
with the copious Australian dew. Save the stentori-
ous breathing of now and then, some over-fed gourmand, all were still as the house of death. For all
slept, and it was not far from midway between midnight and morning, when the native sleep is deepest,
and that is all but deadly. It was with all these odds
against us that we were assaulted.

What was *first*, is more than I can tell. To me, it
seemed as if it all broke upon my ear at once; the
whoop of the assailants; the alarm-cry, rapidly reiterated, as our warriors awoke; and the shrieks of the
wounded, dying, and flying women and children.
Springing to my feet, a single moment sufficed to show
me that we were surrounded by enemies, and that the
conflict on their part had already begun. The women
had snatched their children, and were rushing into
the lagoon; and I saw some of the helpless wretches
doing so with the horrid war-spear deep fixed in their
quivering flesh. My course was determined by necessity; for though, in the present case, I could pretend to no very great amount of patriotism, yet between killing and being killed—for that was the nut-

shell in which the question lay—there was no place for a moment's hesitation. Clutching a long porpoise spear—the first thing my hand fell on, and without knowing, definitely, what it was—I bounded into the area of the deadly contest. The most prominent object I could discover, by a hazy moonlight, was the figure of our chief. About thirty, light, yet lithe and sinewy, he had the courage of a lion, and was fighting like a fiend. Literally, he was sweeping everything before him.

The next object in order, was a hostile native advancing directly upon me, obviously intending to probe my pericardium without the loss of his instrument. Chary of the missive use of the spear, as the want of light rendered its recovery difficult, when spent, the parties, after the first discharge, were now mostly fighting with that instrument, hand to hand. This circumstance gives the reason why my antagonist, instead of letting fly, was intending to despatch me at spear's length, while it also shows why my longer shaft anticipated his shorter one, and why, where only one of us could live, he, rather than I, became *moribund*, as my countryman Carlyle would write it. In a word, and in better English, I hit him precisely where the son of Jesse hit, not the Hittite, but the Gittite, and with precisely the same effect: "*he fell upon his face to the earth.*"

I was now in the thick of the fight, and where my

comrades lay around me, dead and dying. Seeing a
poor fellow battling desperately with three of the
enemy, I rushed to his rescue; but before I got within
striking distance, a spear transfixed him and he fell
dead. With no *other* object in their eye at the moment, the whole trio charged me at once; but luckily
for me, not with spears. Their last passage at arms
had spoiled their last weapon of that name, and they,
like most of the other combatants, were doing battle
with the *womra*.* Spears, by this time, were nearly
all spent or broken. Mine was my only weapon
through the whole affray. When in reach of my
three enemies, having marked my man, I struck at
him; but with the true native address he sprang into
the air. The consequence was, that, instead of receiving my spear, as I meant he should, where it would
have hurt him less, and made him more quiet, the
unlucky fellow took it in the thick of his thigh, leaving a wound which, I dare say, gave him pain and
trouble afterward. It was his own fault. I meant
well. At this moment my assailants, perceiving that
some of our people were coming upon them in their
rear, rushed upon me with redoubled fury. At the

---

* All the editor knows of the womra is, that it is ordinarily employed in launching the spear at a distant object, but in what particular way does not appear. It is two feet in length, and being thin, and
made of mahogany, or other heavy wood of the island, would do much
execution as a war club, or rather as a cleaver, and such is the way the
natives use it, in default of other and better arms.

instant that my spear passed through one of their
number, and laid him in the last sleep of the hero,
another raised his womra, and dealt me a blow across
the forehead, which left me lying senseless by the side
of my slain enemy. In this condition I remained till
a number of hours after the wager of battle had been
decided—in our favor.

When consciousness returned, I found myself in the
hands of two or three women of our tribe, who were
pouring hot sand into my gashed forehead, which, as
fast as it became cool, was succeeded by more. This
is the common native treatment of all flesh wounds.
The pain in my head, generally, and in the part undergoing the actual cautery, in particular, was dreadful. When all the circumstances of my escape from
so formidable a number of the faculty are duly considered, the reader may think its claim to the hair-
breadth character superior to any other recorded in
my book. All I can say is, that I recovered ; whether
in *consequence of, or notwithstanding* the large medical
attendance, I refer to the decision of wiser heads than
mine.

But to return to matters of more public interest.
How many of our people were killed in this night-
attack, I had no exact means of knowing. On crawling abroad, however, that afternoon, I saw numbers
of our slain comrades piled on the funeral brush heap,
and turned to ashes. The reader will have occasion

to notice, that the dead are disposed of in both
ways; namely, by incineration and inhumation; to say
nothing of mastication, deglutition, digestion and as-
similation. Many of the attacking party, also, who
had been mortally wounded in the battle, were found
dead in the adjoining scrub. One body was found in
which nineteen spear holes were counted! ·

It must already have appeared that these people,
who seldom *show* mercy to an enemy, when in their
power, do their fighting in a way which proves that
they *expect* none. When an engagement becomes too
close to admit the longer use of spears, they grapple
each other by pairs. Each with one hand in the long
hair of his antagonist, with the other they mutually
ply the tomahawk or war-club.* I have seen them
thus engaged, till so worried and out of breath that
they could hardly lift the tomahawk or truncheon to
strike another blow.

As evidence of victory, our people had taken ten
prisoners. Two of these were doomed from the outset, for they were old and known aggressors. The
whole ten, however, were bound hand and foot, and
kept in durance till the next morning. This was done
with such a truly savage ingenuity, that the poor
wretches could neither lie down, nor stand, nor sit, nor
sleep.

* This is some two feet in length, and possesses nearly the hardness
and weight of iron.

When morning came, the women were found unusually active, in the wood business. This commodity,
which was collected in large quantities, was disposed
in circles around a pair of young green trees. Not in
the secret, as yet, I wondered as to what this all
tended. Nor was my admiration lessened on perceiving the youngsters, from ten to sixteen years of age,
equally active in sharpening their little spears. But
the plot was unravelled when the *sovereign of men*
arose, and, addressing the two fated captives, said, in
effect: "You have been a torment to my people long
enough. Your *run* is at an end. I mean to put you
to death this day." To this they answered with words
of taunt and scorn. They set him at defiance, and
threatened him with the vengeance of their tribe.

At the sun about three hours high, they were
brought out and prepared for execution. This was
done by first tying their hands behind them, and then
lashing them firmly each to his tree. When this had
been done, the combustibles were readjusted in such
a way as to render the fires, when kindled, sufficiently
tardy in their effect to afford the young savages the
happiness they had anticipated in sporting their spears.
Everything else being now ready, the other prisoners
were ordered out to witness the *auto da fe* of their
companions.

This done, the chief, who acted as master of ceremonies, commanded an old woman to go forward and

put fire to the two piles. When this mimic tophet
began to produce a visible effect on its two victims,
the juvenile demons received the wished-for license
to commence their work of torment. And well did
those little hands help forward the operation of vengeance. On their part, the sufferers maintained a firmness which might have done credit to the days of
martyrdom. To the last, they held the language of
insulting defiance, bidding their enemies to do their
worst. And they did it. For when the fire, aided
by the other tortures of kindred poignancy, had about
half killed its victims, the women were admitted to
their customary share in this delightful work, so emu-
lative of the employment of their sister furies of the
tartarean regions. This grateful task of theirs was
performed on this wise: First, they raked away the
fires. Then, by means of short sticks, sharpened and
kept for the purpose, they put out—aye, *dug* out—the
eyes of the tormented, and filled their empty sockets
with burning sand. And finally, the amiable creatures
broke all their toes, fingers and arms; adding a variety
of little extra touches, which were, probably, impro-
vised, and not put down in the programme. The entertainment concluded by refastening the bodies, now
nearly defunct, to the trees, rebuilding the fires in
close proximity, and turning trees, and brush, and
bodies to ashes.

The other prisoners were reserved for a destiny

which, to an islander of the male sex, is scarcely less an object of dread, and is even more ignominious. Permanent and large perforations of the cartilage of the nose were effected by means of a pointed stick, which instrument was retained *in situ* till the part was healed. Extensive scarifications, well understood as signs of deep dishonor, were made on their backs and breasts. And, to complete their degradation, the flint knife, by an exceedingly close shave of the head, deprived them of all their capillary honors. They were now unmanned; effeminated; turned into women, to all conventional intents and purposes; the last term, and that of slaves, being perfectly equivalent in the parlance of the island. In conformity with this understanding, they were now compelled to bring the wood and water, to build the wigwam, and generally, to co-operate with the women in every menial office.

But the final point to which all this humiliation tended, was to be reached by their dismissal to their own tribe, that *they* also might feel the sting of an insult intended to be as diffusive in its effect as possible. Our chief discharged them accordingly. The short and cool speech with which he did it, closed, in substance, with: "You can now go and join your tribe. Expect to share the fate of your late companions, if I ever catch you in another such scrape again. Go."

But what was the cause which instigated this sanguinary encounter, involving these revolting conse-

quences? Historic impartiality compels the answer,
painful as it is, that the cause in question was furnished by our own people. Briefly, then, it was the
following:

On what pretence of previous injury, I know not,
but, shortly before my late return, some individual or
individuals of our tribe, in strolling through the woods,
had surprised a straggling woman with her little child.
Her, they murdered on the spot. The child was
brought to our encampment, where it was also despatched, and there devoured; and the last of it was,
that same food which my cannibal master offered me,
on my return to his tent. A party of the tribe, to
which the mother and child belonged, coming soon
after to the scene of the murder, followed the track
of the perpetrators, till satisfied as to their identity
with us; when they returned, and, collecting what
force they could, came upon us, as above stated, to
execute the *lex talionis*—with what success the reader
has already seen.

CHAPTER XIII.

Author's recovery.—Social elevation.—Success in the chase, and consequent carnival.—Master and man in a kangaroo adventure.—Ditto in dogmatics; *i. e.* in a dangerous dispute with dogs.—How it ends, and the trophies borne to the encampment.—Royal entertainment.—Royal oration in honor of the adopted member of the body politic.—Large gastronomy.—Songs, the chorus, and the dance.—Author in high favor.—Matrimony as a measure of state policy.—A proposal on that subject is declined; is repeated, and redeclined.—Offer renewed under highly seductive circumstances, and still unaccepted.—Consequent ticklishness of the author's position.

SHORTLY after the tragic events related in the last chapter, we were ordered on a general hunting expedition.

It were as well, perhaps, to remark in this connection, that these general expeditions are not the more frequent modes by which game is taken. More commonly it is pursued by parties, varying in number according to circumstances; and, especially, according to the interests or caprice of the hunters themselves; these minor movements not being often interfered with by the head man of the tribe. His prerogative, though not very definite at all points, and though more or less frequently asserted, according to his dif-

ferent humors, is not expected to be exercised with relation to any, save the matters more immediately affecting the public weal.   These matters are such as the *mi-
grations* of the tribe; *peace* and *war*; *life* and *death*;
funereal and *hymeneal* matters; and, among the rest,
this matter of the *chase*, when it is wished, for any
reason, that there should be "a general turn-out."

But to return.   At the time to which the events of
this chapter stand related, I had recovered the effect
of that unlucky blow, which numbered me with the
wounded, on the battle-field, and had well nigh numbered me with the *dead*.   Being fit for duty, and having raised myself to very considerable respectability by
recent proficiency in the use of my hunting weapons,
to say nothing of exploits in the war, I was now expected to bear a hand in every enterprise.   The day
—I mean the day on which our whole force had been
rallied for the chase—was auspicious, to the extent of
our most flattering anticipations.   Eleven large kangaroo were the trophies which were borne to our quarters.   Not to have picked the bones of the whole
eleven that night, had been a sin of which these improvident gluttons are seldom guilty.   High, that
night, was the feasting, and loud the song which
celebrated the deeds of the chase.

But the chief, who appeared to watch for occasions
of getting me distinguished, and of establishing me se-
curely in the esteem of his capricious subjects, took his

o*

weapons one morning, soon after this, and ordered me to follow him. Taking my hunting gear, I followed him, accordingly. In this order we had not pursued our silent and cat-like movement long, before we came, suddenly, upon our prey; the mouse-colored marsupial, which crosses the reader's path so often in his island rambles. The flock was prodigious. The stinted trees, among which they were grazing, seemed to be alive with them. Silently, and cautiously, we crept from tree to tree, my own motions being controlled by *dumb* signs rather than *articulate.* At length the tree was indicated, behind which I was to take my final stand. On gaining this position, where the game was within an easy spear's throw, I forgot, for the moment, my subordinate relation, and that I was to wait my superior's motion; and let drive. The javelin hit, and its point passing through its victim, protruded some dozen inches on the opposite side. In the mean time, while my shaft was yet hardly launched, that of the lynx-eyed chief was on the wing, and with an aim and a force which carried an instant quietus to its object. Mine, on the other hand, though sped with equal force, had been aimed so ill, as to allow its victim to rally and join the rest of the herd in its precipitate flight. Both of us followed; nor was it long before a second spear so materially aided the effect of its predecessor, as to enable me to finish my own work by a blow of my stone axe. Proud of my new trophy, I followed the chief, while we both returned toward the point at which he had left the proof of his own superior marksmanship.

Arrived within twenty rods, we saw, standing over it, a pair of formidable competitors in the shape of two huge native dogs, who had already begun the work of appropriation; for they were swallowing it as fast as they could tear it in pieces. At a word from my superior, I threw down my burden. He threw himself into an attitude. A moment his poised spear shook in the chieftain's grasp. It was a moment and an attitude for the painter. The next moment, and like the bolt of the Grecian Jupiter—though without its thunder, and perhaps, equally defective in the dignity of its object—it flew to its mark, and the two dogs were nearly in the predicament of the two birds, so often said to have been killed by one stone. For, standing close together, as well as side by side, and exactly in a range withal, the missile passed clean through the one, and entered a matter of six or seven inches into the other. This brought on a sudden quarrel between the twain, the consequence of which was, that the off dog, who presently found himself disengaged, turned tail to and fled. The chief, withdrawing his spear from the other, gave chase to the fugitive, leaving the worse-wounded individual to keep my company, the while; and a real *tête-à-tête* we had of it. At me, he came as fierce as ten furies.

In sheer self-defence, I lifted my spear, and struck the furious brute. But its point had been blunted in the affair of the other animal, which circumstance, added to the toughness of my assailant's hide, and the interposing coat of thick hair, rendered the thrust ineffectual. The scene now became very interesting. A pair of huge jaws opened, and were in the very act of fastening on one of my *femurs*. While looking down the throat of the canine monster, it occurred, that my spear, which would enter nowhere else, might be introduced at that point to special advantage. No sooner thought than done; and my spear was in. It was his own fault, too, that in the next moment, I was compelled to lay him, keel up, by a blow of my stone hatchet. But he was by no means dead yet. One of these animals—and I have seen them three feet high, and limbed and muzzled in proportion—possesses all but a feline tenacity of life. Anxious to keep him down while he *was* down—the spear having been disenthroated during the more recent part of the scuffle—I threw my whole weight on to his carcass, and throttled him with both hands. It would have posed a looker-on for the next few minutes, to tell which of us was most to be pitied. For my part, I own to a little nervousness, and that my eye was scarcely less frequent in its glances at my unquiet protegé, than in the direction of the chief, anxious as I was to be relieved from this, too literal, *dog-watch*.

But no chief appeared, and I was prepared to adopt the former half of the couplet from the hero of Juan Fernandez :

> "I am out of humanity's reach;
> I must finish my journey alone."

The latter part of the hemistich, however, I was not yet quite willing either to sing or say. That the journey of one of us must be finished there and then, was not to be doubted ; and as the beam of the scale that balanced the question between us, still kept its doubtful level, I could see nothing but the stone hatchet that was likely to turn it in my favor. So, making one hand do double duty on the trachea of my prisoner, I succeeded, by a careful movement of the other, in grasping the *make-weight.* It fell heavy, and in the right place. The dog kicked the beam.

By the time the regal hunter returned with *his* dog, mine had surrendered his shaggy hide ; and that, gentle reader, after it had been dried and dressed, was my only bed during the residue of my sojourn among the natives. As to the preceding part of it, I had lodged nearer the ground by the difference of the dog-skin. And with regard to night-clothes, they were those worn in the day-time ; and my day-dress, with no exception worth mentioning, was exclusively constituted by a little cheap grease and paint.

Aware that most of my readers are in no mood to sympathize with habits quite so primitive as ours, I

pass over the details of disposition made of the fluid
and solid portions of *both* descriptions of our prey;
and, consequently, say nothing as to which, and how
much, were appropriated for food, either then or afterward. It is enough for the reader to know, as it is
fair to presume he does already, that stark savagism,
with no slight touch of the cannibal, eats and drinks
whatever would not offend the gusto of a famished
wolf.—Our venison, canine as well as kangarean,
though causing us a heavy load, was all safely deposited in the royal larder.

To prepare for the evening, our "first of men" ordered his wives to build a large fire in front of the
palace; and, when his liege people were in from the
chase, he made them take their seats in a circle around
the blazing pile. Me, he seated at his own side.
When the circle was completed, the presiding dignitary arose, and, pointing to me, thus announced the
object of the convocation:—"Here is the man whom
you wished, not a great while since, to put to death.
He is now almost as good a spearsman as the best of
you, who are sitting around this fire." Then, after
spinning them a yarn as long as the main-top-gallant
bow-line, he brought forward my kangaroo, and added:
"Here is a kangaroo, killed this day with his own
spear, and by his own hand. In addition to this, he
only just escaped with his life in killing a native dog.
Now, I hope you will all eat of his dog and kanga-

roo, and be as friendly to him as I have been." Upon
this, handing the head and tail of the latter—esteemed
as the choicest portions of the animal—to me, they all
fell to upon the intermediate parts without a second
invitation. That disposed of, the feast was prolonged,
first, by the remaining marsupial, and then by the tit-
bits for which we were indebted to so much hard running, and to so dangerous a scuffle, by the master and
his man.

Eating, singing, and dancing, employed the night.
The singing of these people, like that of the other
Pacific islanders, is generally, perhaps universally,
improvisatory. On this occasion, it went off, as is
usual with all savages, on the subjects of their several exploits in killing animals and men. The song,
proper, appeared to be a solo, alternated and reinforced by a general chorus. Sometimes, however, instead of the latter, after listening with deep attention
to the cantator, all would burst out into—"*Wahking !
Wahking ! Bravo ! Bravo !*" During the revel, they
painted themselves from head to foot in various gro
tesque figures, in doing which, red and white were
the only colors employed; indeed, as far as my acquaintance with the manners of the island extended,
they, with an occasional exception in favor of the
yellow, are the only colors known or used. The red,
however, it should be remarked, which is the every-
day color, and not often renewed, changes, by the ac-

tion of a hot sun and a constant accession of dirt, into a dark chocolate, but a shade short of a jet. Finally, on the subject of the carnival, when it was nearly daylight, and they could eat no more, and sing and dance no longer, every man took the way to his own wigwam.

From that date the general bearing toward me was fully changed. All were decided in the manifestations of respect and friendship, and I seemed to have been admitted to all the honors of island manhood. Of course—for that comes next—I was entitled to an island wife. And more; for, not only the nature of things, but various intimations directly and indirectly conveyed, made me sensible that it was considered a point of obligation, in these communities, that every male member should be charged with a fair proportion of individual responsibility in providing for the sex. And the rather as, beside lessening the cares of government, in the premises, by interesting as many individuals as possible in looking after those who must be dependent on somebody, it could not but be a matter of felt importance to all, and especially the ruler of such a people, to keep up such a physical force as would enable them to meet the frequently occurring exigencies of war. Ours was a strong commonwealth; but the inevitable mischances of even successful war had latterly diminished it, and the consequence was, women who had lost their husbands through those mischances, and others who had become marriageable and lacked them, from the same cause, were very unprofitably multiplied. The chief, therefore, who was bound to see them provided for, could but feel it a two-fold object to lessen his own immediate cares, and, at the same time, dispose of them in such a way as would be likely to furnish the bone and sinew indispensable to prospective security and defence.

As nearly as occasional lunar observations enabled me to approximate the point of time, I had been about nine months a sharer in the fortunes of the society, when, one day, as the chief and I were hunting together, he broached the subject of matrimony, and was answered indifferently. He continued, by referring to the number—which I knew was large—of those who had lost their husbands in battle, intimating that, if so disposed, I would be at perfect liberty to appropriate any one of them I might choose. To all of which, as I felt nothing but sincere aversion, I could manifest nothing which countenanced the royal project; and there the matter rested for the time. That time, however, was brief; for, no sooner were we arrived, and supper over in the regal household, than, first, one by one, then in pairs, and finally by whole platoons, the widows of the surrounding huts came pouring into our lodge. The chief and his *protegé* were sitting, when, in a trice, this strange assemblage disposed themselves in a curved line before the two

11

sedentary figures aforesaid. What all this imported,
was dark to me; and it is but sooth to say, that this
galaxy of woodland beauty shed no *light*, but "a pro-
fusion of soft" *darkness*, both on the subject and the
scene. Short, however, was my suspense, and few
the glances cast by the apparitions at us and at each
other, before the imperial *savage*, turning to me with
a patronizing air, substantially thus bespoke me:—
"These young women have no husbands. I have ordered them to come and stand up here. Now, if you
want one, you can pick her out." The scene was
grave throughout; an entirely business-like transaction, from beginning to end. The subjects, no less
than the agents, obviously regarded it in no other
light; and this must be my apology to the reader for
treating the matter as such, accordingly. True, there
was a cheek or two on which a searching scrutiny
might have detected a slight accession of the tinge
which constitutes the civilized blush. Together with
this, there might have been discovered the least possible leer of an eye disposed to mischief; and I once
thought that something like a half-suppressed titter
escaped from a little huzzy who was leaning on the
shoulder of her right-hand companion, and whose
face, just at that moment, was half hidden by her
hand. Thus *fairly* cornered, obliged to "face the
music," I stammered something—for, really, I have
never felt quite certain what I did say—about time

for consideration, and the fear of consequences. To
obviate all such objections, the pertinacious man
urged in reply—and, certainly, it was with an air of
great fairness on his part—that there could be no
danger in making a selection, as a return of the article and another choice would be allowable at any
time. To this, I could only say, generally, that it
was a grave subject; that it demanded time, and that
I hoped he would be so kind as not to press the matter any further, just then. To me, personally, his
general bearing *had* been kind; as much so, perhaps,
as was consistent with the decided predominance of
the animal and selfish over every other propensity of
his dark nature. | Above all, he was polite, and the
possessor of more self-control than any aboriginal co-
temporary of my acquaintance. Moved, probably, as
well by policy as kindness, he murmured a guttural
assent to my demurrer; while, with the wave of his
hand, the dark-complexioned bevy—some triple dozen,
and the number should have been given before—disappeared. The subject, however, was much upon his
mind; and it was obvious, from the frequency and
manner of his advertence to it, that he was determined
to marry me, and that it would not be exactly the
safer policy, on my part, to baulk his intention.

CHAPTER XIV.

On the coast.—Mistakes corrected, touching (1) the piscatory habits of the natives; (2) their African descent.—Their Asian origin.—Extent of exceptions to this derivation, and how accounted for.—High living.—Subject of matrimony resumed.—Surrenders to destiny, with reasons for so doing.—Marital ceremony.—General usages in regard to betrothals and marriages.—Elopements.—The *amende* honorable.—Frequency of homicides.—Fratricide and his paramour overtaken by a fearful retribution.—Acuteness of external native sense.

IT has been previously remarked, that we were seldom stationary for more than two or three days. This having been understood, I have not supposed it advisable to encumber my narrative with details relative to a subject of so frequent recurrence, unless connected with some noticeable event. As introductory to this chapter, I need only add, that, in the interim of the incidents included in it, and of those of its immediate predecessors, we had migrated from the interior to the south coast of the island.

And here, with the reader's good leave, as the present is the first occasion so fully suggestive of the subject, it may be proper to bestow a passing remark on a point regarding which the current information is more

or less at fault. Reference is here had to the general
impression made by writers on this country, that the
natives are, in a great measure, maritime in their
haunts and modes of subsistence. Indeed, one of them,
who should be paramount authority on such a subject,
though admitting that the interior of this vast island
" is very little known," says, of the known aborigines,
and without qualification, that " fishing is their main
occupation."* It would seem, indeed, that, because
the natives, when seen at all, are always on the coast,
and piscatorially employed, when employed at all, that
they have been represented as hardly living anywhere
else, and as hardly any otherwise employed. On the
contrary, in good hunting weather, the coast is seldom
visited; unless, indeed, when a wide hunting range
chances to skirt the ocean. As to any tribes, such as
the " Universal Traveller" professes to have met with,†
whose subsistence is wholly or even mainly derived
from the sea, I can only say, that, in all my time and
travels in South Australia, it was not my hap to ar-
rive at any knowledge of them. During the year a.d
a half of my connection with a community as migra-
tory in habit, perhaps, as any other, we visited the
coast but three times; at each of which times we remained, not to exceed, a period of ten to fifteen days.
And what has been asserted with regard to one tribe,

* See Morse's School Geography, p. 65.
† See a work with the above title by C. A. Goodrich, p. 437.

can be safely certified respecting many others. For during my captivity, I must have traversed, and re-traversed, in all directions, an area four hundred miles east and west by twice that distance north and south, the latter reaching directly inland. And in all that extent of actual survey, we were constantly coming in contact with tribes, or the representatives of tribes, of the same general character and habits as those of our own.

Nor would it be improper, perhaps, while so near the subject, to make another correction. And it shall be done with relation to the alleged identity of the native Australian with the native African. This identity is asserted broadly, and without a qualifying exception. " The natives are oriental negroes."* And, to preclude misapprehension, the text is pictorially il-lustrated by a bona fide negro, sure enough, and all very well done, to the ebony of the fellow's skin, and the more unmistakable frizzle of his hair.

Now, though this representation holds true enough, as limited to Sidney, on the south-eastern coast, and, perhaps, a few other points, it is very far from being applicable to that large part of the island-aborigines, who came under my observation, during my protract-ed captivity. At the points referred to, I have often seen the unequivocal traces of Negro origin; the thick lip, the flat nose, and the crisped hair, joined with the

* See McCulloch's Au. Gaz., followed by Morse's School Geography.

nearly African jet. But, for a single specimen of true
negro type, I have seen in South New-Holland, on the
coast and in the interior, hundreds, in whom the
proofs of Asiatic origin were equally indisputable.
Leaving other points of evidence to the physiologist,
I am willing to rest my conclusion on *complexion*, and
the *hair*. The former, when a faithful ablution expo-
ses its true ground-work, is nothing deeper than the
general mahogany which marks the australasiatics of
the South Sea Islands as a whole. And then, in place
of the short curled hair of the black man of Gmelin,
my Australian friends—custom forbids it to the ladies,
but the gentlemen—wear their own long locks; as
long as any of European pretensions, and not more inclined to emulate the negro frizzle.

After all, it is not improbable, that, while the proxi-
mate part of Asia, and, perhaps, even South America,
have sent the earlier and larger waves of population
to this, with most of the other, southern islands, Africa
also may have tinctured them with an early colonial
current of her own. Papua or New-Guina is clearly
an African settlement. Adventurers or castaways
from that island, or directly from the parent country,
as unquestionably landed and propagated a kindred
variety at a few points on the Australian coast.
Between these inconsiderable patches of population,
and the more widely diffused type of Australian character, there lies all, or nearly all, the difference origi-

.nally separating the brown man from the black.* The "oriental negro" population of this third continent is a fact, no otherwise than, as an immaterial exception is so in reference to the general rule to which it is related. At all events, I have stated facts. Others, if not satisfied with my inferences, must adopt others, or make their own.

This digression left us on the south coast, to which we now return. Our maritime visit was highly opportune. The shoals were thick with salmon and the porpoise, and many, of each fin, were brought up by the long-shafted fish spear, which our people could project with so sure an aim. The neighboring grove was alive with our favorite marsupial. Coyas—*frogs*, not quite so sacred, but nearly as numerous as those which plagued the Egyptians in olden time; the delicately flavored guana; the farinacious choocup, and the fiery min; all conspired, as well by their abundance as variety, to render this a time of special jubilation. As to saving any of it for a rainy day, that was out of the question. Had fish and flesh enough been piled up on that spot to rival, in magnitude, the largest pyramid of the Nile, the improvident gluttons would have picked the last bone, with any conceivable certainty staring them in the face, that half their number would starve to death before they could find another breakfast.

* See Dr. Goode.

It was on one of these days of general hilarity, that the now familiar subject of matrimony was renewed. Satisfied that it was useless to strive any longer against my destiny; uncertain, after one fruitless attempt to escape it, whether mine would not prove to be a "life membership" in this goodly society; and judging that, with another and a fairer chance of running away,* an island mate, half forced upon me, and with no "better or worse" clause in the liturgy, any how, would prove no special obstacle; I told my royal master, that I was ready to meet his wishes in the matter, and that the ensuing evening would suit my convenience as well as any time. This submission put him into great good-humor, and he declared that he would have a " *carobra*, " that is, a dance.

Accordingly, on our return to head-quarters, for we had been hunting together through the day, the auto-crat of our little empire issued his ukase for another convocation of the juvenile widowhood. If the summons was peremptory, the compliance was prompt; and the dehusbanded stood before us, as on a former

---

* "Was not that fairer chance invariably present whenever you were on the coast?" To which I reply. The farther I became acquainted with the coast; the number of broad rivers, with their broader embouchures; the numerous bays, with their far-reaching indentations; the more hopeless was the prospect of ever reaching an English settlement in any other character than that of a sailor. In a word. I was satisfied that my escape must depend on the coincidence of our tribe's return to the coast, with the landing of some vessel. But in order to this, I must needs bide my time.

H

occasion. Why the spinsters were not included, must be told at another time. Suffice it, for the present, to say, that they were a species of property not at the disposal of the executive, and that the operation of immemorial custom makes its acquisition a matter of much longer time than was consistent with the present emergency. I said, they stood before us; and it were superfluous to add, that the ceremonies of the toilette had been the occasion of no vexatious delay, or that whatever of diversity existed in the darkly fair assemblage, on the score of native loveliness, was present without *disguise*. The object who fixed my attention, was a weedless widow of about seventeen.[*] "Popping the question," that awkward consequence which waits on civilized courtship, was no affair of mine. To choose, was my right. To intimate my choice, not to the chosen subject, but to the sovereign, was my duty. The right was exercised in *one* moment. The duty was the work of the *next*. What remained was exclusively between the royal pontiff and the bride elect, and was despatched in the brief terms of the following question and answer.

Question.—"Yenec annan yoructongur coopul?—Do you want to live with this man?"

Answer.—"Quop, ki emeran beac.—Yes, if he wishes to take me."

---

[*] Her name, *Ekyepeet*, is the native word for the guana, a large land lizard, much used for food.

Upon this, she was *ordered* to sit down in *our* wigwam. As for the rest, they were informed that they
could now retire; and they did so, neither they, nor
detenu, nor, indeed, any individual of the sex, appearing
or reappearing to grace any part of the subsequent ceremony; unless making and maintaining the fire, and
hovering and looking on at a distance, might be
thought to constitute exceptions. As my master did
not choose to allow us a separate establishment, *Mrs.*
J. became a permanent inmate of the royal lodge;
and the only respect paid her on this her bridal night
was permission to look from the interior of her new
abode on the out-door show, got up in honor—not of
her, but of her husband—and to witness, in common
with the other menials, the havoc wrought by the
chivalry of the tribe on the viands of the evening.

The sons of the chief were ordered to procure a
couple of poles, some dozen feet in length. These
were stripped of their bark, painted with various colors, hung with a diversity of gaudy flowers and feathers, and then fixed perpendicularly in the ground.
While this was going on, the ladies were gathering
fuel. This they piled in the form of a half-circle, and
in such a way as to leave the ornamented poles as
nearly in the centre as might be; the same circumference being equal to a line of four or more rods. This
completed, they set it on fire, and had no more to do
than to bring and heap on fuel enough, from time to

time, to keep the whole line in undiminished glow, till their gallant husbands had exhausted their faculties of enjoyment. As this was a royal feast, sumptuary custom demanded of the guests, that they should array themselves for it with due particularity. This was done in the following manner: The whole exterior of each individual was treated to a coat of fresh paint, diversified, on this occasion, with white and yellow, in addition to the every-day red. Every breast bore the figure of a large white cross; while those of the kangaroo, the wallaby, red and white, the white cockatoo, and the emu,* all were crowded on to the same moving canvas.

When the men, all decorated as above, were assembled and seated at the fire, the boys, acting as servitors on the occasion, brought forward the fish, flesh and vegetables, gathered during the day. At this point, the chief man of the nation, who was something of a wag, and whose self-esteem, *a la phrenologie*, must have been very large indeed, arose once more to act the orator. On me, though now a measurable proficient in their elegant vernacular, its more exquisite touches were nearly lost. My fellow-auditors, however, obviously understood the address to be, if not witty, at least facetious; for they encored it most vociferously. When the speech was done, and in salt phrase, it was a " yarn as long as a jib-don-all," there came off the reg-

* Some account of this winged animal may be found in Chap. XVI.

ular eating match. A general dance around the two
poles succeeded. And to this, succeeded singing, in
which all were performers. This held till midnight,
when they all returned to the unfinished feast, at which
they continued their devoirs till every gastric capacity
was tasked to its uttermost distension. As to the distantly attendant ladies, their participation of the entertainment, beside the gratification of looking on,
consisted, as on less extra occasions, of the final odds
and ends; preceded, now and then, by—what the reader has already found admissible under the eating
laws of our society—the *bone fide* bonus of a bone.

Unless the native swain should be willing to take
his chance among the widowed fair, as I did, he bar-
gains for his wife, soon after she is born. In this
species of traffic, the mother has no voice, and is not
consulted. If the father and the applicant agree, the
child is the property of the latter, and he returns, accordingly, to claim it, as soon as it is old enough to
follow him; which is at about the completion of its
third year; and she continues to attend him in all his
fortunes, till old enough to become his wife. Instances occurred in our own tribe, and under my own immediate notice, of female infants disposed of, in this
way, to individuals of another tribe, whose hunting
ground was four or five hundred miles distant. For,
however roving in their habits, each tribe has, what they
claim, and other tribes admit to be, their own domain.

When the father of a family dies, his oldest son is considered the owner of all his wives, whether more or less. And on *his* demise, without a son, he is succeeded by his next oldest brother; and so on, through the family.

If a woman lose her husband, unless some kinsman claim her, she is the protegée of the chief, who has authority, as we have already seen, to dispose of her to whom he pleases.

As in more refined communities, elopements are by no means rare occurrences. Mutual fancy influencing, one man takes the wife of another, and escapes to a distant tribe, where he keeps her for a longer or shorter time. The longer, may sometimes be for life; but, if so, it is without my knowledge. I speak of things merely as I saw them. Ordinarily, then, the time in question terminates in seven or eight months, when the faithless wife is redelivered to her husband, between whom and the abductor there is a settlement on this wise. The wife-stealer stands before the wronged party, at the distance of some thirty yards, and the latter throws *nine* spears, only. If one of any less number hit him, he must own himself satisfied, and the other is discharged. If none of the whole number take effect, however, the injured party is at his option to consider himself made good, in the matter of his wounded honor, or to demand further satisfaction. In this latter case, two men approach the seducer and hold him, while the cuckold drives a spear through one of his femural appendages. This is the end of the law in the case; after which the delinquent is at liberty to go where he pleases, and the dishon-ored husband is perfectly satisfied. While all this is going on, the other wives of the latter party, in some cases as many as seven or eight, fall upon their frail sister, and, before leaving, half kill her with their heavy sticks. And if the husband should not think proper to finish the business by taking the rest of her life, at that time, she must attend him wherever he goes, nor ever venture out of his sight again, while she lives. Repetition of the offence and the being subsequently taken, is certain death; and this holds, as well with regard to the seducer, as the seduced.

Homicides are so common, that there is hardly one in a hundred, who has arrived at the age of sixteen, whose hands have not been imbued in the blood of some human being, otherwise than under the pretext of war. The following instance is given, as having fallen out under my own observation, partly because it is illustrative of the preceding remark, and partly, as throwing light on some of the other habits of a fierce and sanguinary people.

Two brothers were fishing on the coast; one a bachelor, and the other a benedict. The bachelor had taken a fancy to the young wife of his brother; and, having exhausted the arts which usually induce an

elopement, without success, took the opportunity,
while his brother was spearing fish from a rock, to
push him into the surf, where he was drowned. The
object of his passion, now a widow, accepted the protection of the fratricide, and both decamped to a distant tribe in the eastern part of the island. The case
being more atrocious than common murder, the men
of our tribe were moved by a common and a fixed purpose of punishing the criminal upon the earliest opportunity. After an absence of seven months, he had
the temerity to return. He was first seen and recognized, by some of our people, on a rock, some way out
in the surf, where he also was fishing with his spear,
as the brother had been whose life he sacrificed to his
lawless passion. In this insulated situation, he suddenly found his retreat intercepted by a dozen clansmen, who had sworn vengeance, and were armed to
execute it. Spear after spear was launched, which
his extreme adroitness of evasion rendered harmless.
The consequence of such a waste of projectiles was,
that the assailing party found it expedient to call a
pause. Unwilling to risk a close engagement with
one of the best spearsmen of the tribe, and a man of
formidable prowess, they despatched a boy to the encampment for a fresh supply of spears. Chancing to
be at one of the wigwams when the messenger came
in, I snatched a handful of the flint-headed shafts, and
started for the scene of action. Arrived, there stood

the avengers of blood, resolute and determined, and there, too, on his rock, stood the manslayer, the fratricide, like a lion at bay, fierce, and hurling defiance at his assailants. But his bravado availed him nothing. He was a doomed man. As in the case of the first shedder of a brother's blood, there was a clamor for vengeance, which nothing but the blood of the murderer. could appease. When our men were once more fully armed, we drew up in single file, and then, instead of the succession of single discharges, which his dodging art had enabled him to elude, a large dozen of the barbed missiles were on the wing at once, and under nearly as many wounds the wretch descended after his victim to a watery grave.

His less guilty paramour became the next object of the vindictive passion, now fairly roused. It was reasonably presumed that she had accompanied his return, and either was, or recently had been, in the vicinity. Accordingly, after a long search, one of our party fell upon her trail. This was fate. The native senses of sight and smell possess an exquisiteness, which enable their possessor to follow the traces of an object, which, to a civilized man, would be totally undistinguishable. Thus furnished, the aboriginal Australian, when sufficiently stimulated by cupidity or revenge, pursues his victim for a hundred miles, and nothing but a fall of rain can baffle his unerring pursuit. He has no difficulty in distinguishing the foot-

print of a boy from that of a girl; a man's from a
woman's; or that of a boy, girl, man, or woman, of
his own tribe, from one of either, or all the four, belonging to any other. To return. The pursuing
party, after about three miles, found the wretched
fugitive in the hollow of a large peppermint-tree. A
jerk dislodged, and a stroke of the tomahawk, followed by another of the spear, laid her lifeless. The
women were then ordered to raise and kindle the
funeral pile, and the incineration of the remains of one,
"more sinned against, than sinning," concluded the
tragedy.

"Horror covers all the heath:
Clouds of carnage blot the sun:
Sisters! weave the web of death.
Sisters! cease, the work is done!

CHAPTER XV.

Three murders and two murderers.—The latter are surprised.—Both
fly ; are pursued ; one taken.—His confession and execution.—More
extensive retaliation resolved on.—Spies.—Short preparation.—
Further traits of native character.—All on the war path.—A forced
march.—A division of forces.—The midnight reconnoissance.—The
ambush.—The surprise.—The onslaught.—Heroic, but ineffectual
resistance.—Touching incident.—Revolting allusion.—Brief homiletic
" on the state of nature."

IN a few days subsequent to the events last recorded,
I was one of a party of seven, who were abroad in
the bush, in quest of game; when suddenly a sound,
as of human voices, struck our ear. Listening, we
ascertained the quarter from whence it issued, and advanced, as cautiously as possible, till, at a distance of
forty rods, we discovered a couple of men on their
knees, apparently engaged as if in cutting up some
animal, taken in the chase. The discovery was mutual. They started, and fled. We called, in order to
stop them, but it only added wings to their flight.
We gave chase, and kept them in sight for half an
hour, in which time, such was their fleetness, that
they held us at about the original distance. It
chanced, however, that in leaping a narrow stream,

in which there were some six feet of water, that one
of them was stopped on the further shore, by the dis-
location of an ankle. We leaped after and made him
a prisoner. The other escaped us. On overhauling
our prize, whom should I find, but the veritable gentleman with whom I had had that memorable passage
at arms in the affair of the lagoon, and whose womra
all but dealt me the true *coup de grace.* A moment
of exultation, on finding him in my power, was exchanged for a feeling of commiseration toward the
wretched savage, long before death relieved him of
his miseries. But this is anticipation. The reader
will soon perceive the ground on which it arises.
With our prisoner in custody, we returned to the spot
where he and his comrade were first discovered. There,
to our great consternation, lay the dead body of a
clansman of ours, pierced by many a spear. And
there, too, half cut into pieces, lay the remains of his
two little children, girls, eighteen months, and three
years old.

For further explanation, which is more properly
supplied at this point, I must avail myself of the matter of the prisoner's subsequent confession, as well as
of information derived from the surviving wife and
mother of the murdered man and children. While
travelling through the woods, with his wife and children, the man had been taken sick. After lying some
time on the spot where we found him, his wife had been

sent away to gather some herbs for medicine, the two
children, in the mean time, remaining with their father.
Shortly after this separation, the prisoner and his
companion, belonging to a hostile tribe, discovered
the pitiable group, sarcastically remarking, as they
advanced upon it with lifted spears : " You and your
children are the first game we have met to-day. We
are hungry." The poor fellow sprang to his feet
and fought desperately, as knowing that it was for his
life, as well as that of his children. The event is
with the reader. He was slain. The two children,
beside their butchery, were in course of preparation
for a purpose but too common in this land of cannibals. The prisoner, not in the way of compunction,
but as matter of boast, declared that, when interrupted,
he and his more fortunate comrade, having done the
killing, were about to satisfy their hunger with their
infant victims.

 While we were yet standing over the scene of this
revolting transaction, the mother returned. Her maternal transports may be imagined, not described.
Whether grief or revenge was the master passion, it
were hardly safe to say, for both were so outrageous,
that, after having torn out her own hair, she flew upon
the prisoner and, unrestrained, had soon made the
number of his pieces equal to those of her children.
But this would have been a mercy which was not to
soften the doom to which he was reserved. Details,

under the head now referred to, are not intended, save in an instance or two, by which the occasion stands distinguished from the subject of a previous description; and for all of which I expect the reader of cultivated sensibility, if his good sense has been equally cultivated, will accord me his ready pardon.

After *Anthropophagus* had been marched, or rather, dragged, for he could not walk, to the encampment, he was tied to a tree, with a piece of wood, some seventy pounds in weight, made fast to either hand; in which situation, with a number of our people to watch him, he was kept till morning. The preparations were as usual, save that, being unable to walk, the culprit was carried to the place of execution. As matter of compensation to the widowed and childless mother, she was admitted to the grateful office of putting fire to the pile; and, after a few minutes of incipient burning, the fire was drawn from around the victim, and he was conveyed to another, which the bereaved and distressed lady had prepared in the interim. In this, for her special comfort, four men held his two feet till they were nearly consumed. While this protracted operation was going on, the still disconsolate mourner exhibited various violent antics, together with certain vociferations, which made it obvious that, if she was influenced by the feelings of a human mother, on the one hand, she was still more strongly actuated by the malignity of a *she* infernal, on the other. But being

pledged to avoid unnecessary repetition in the notice
of this class of cases, we say nothing of the furthei
gratification of the chief mourner by means of the
burning sand, with which she plied the object of her
yet hotter wrath, nor of the number of bones she
broke, and with what an eager gusto. Life by this
time was but faintly lingering. Sensation must have
been utterly extinct. It only remained to remand
the subject to his tree, where, in a few moments, the
renovated flames turned him to ashes.

This was retaliation. But it was only the prelude.
Born, and trained, and steeped in murder and cannibalism, themselves, they were now to find and punish
that depraved community which had furnished a single
pair of murderers and man-eaters. Such was the will
of our potent sachem. As yet, however, all was dark
to me; for when the crafty potentate was hatching
any plot of more than common treachery and mischief against a belligerent neighbor, his wont was to
exclude me from his counsels. In this instance, how
ever, I was not left to vague inference, from the omi
nous movements afoot, that some great event was pend
ing. There was *one* who, with a curiosity characteristic
of the sex of every clime, had applied her ear to the
key-hole of the dark conclave, and consequently, as a
true wife should, let her husband into the secret of
the whole business, several days before it would have
transpired by the more ordinary process. Spies were

out in different directions, to ascertain the whereabouts of the enemy. After an absence of five days, some of them came in with the information, that a small party had been discovered, who were stopping at the foot of a mountain called *Buckinbuck.* This was so joyfully exciting a piece of intelligence, that it lost us—the chief and me—the uneaten half of our dinner.

The necessary number of his warriors not being present, our puissant leader snatched a handful of spears, and bade me follow him. I snatched a couple, and followed. And he strode away, and was followed, till we found ourselves on the summit of a mountain —*Corinuck*—distant, by approximation, a matter of ten to twelve miles. Here we kindled a large fire, which was the conventional point and signal of a general rally. But as time must be allowed for its effect on a widely scattered band of hunters, after waiting by it for a while, we went away, killed some small game, and roasted and ate. Near sunset our people began to make their appearance: presently, they came pouring in from all directions; so that, by the time the sun was fairly down, we numbered upward of a hundred. Having effected so large a rendezvous, our chieftain led us on the homeward path about four miles, where we slept. In the morning, resuming our way, we had the good fortune of taking a dozen fine kangaroo, averaging, I suppose, a hundred and fifty pounds each. A quickly kindled fire gave the flesh the requisite blackening, and, in less than an hour, not a vestige of it was left. From this, with previous intimations, the reader is already aware of the "large alimentiveness" of these associates of mine. For his more accurate information on this head, I add, that, after one of their long fasts, I have seen one of them devour ten to twelve pounds of flesh, and to follow it with water in fair proportion. Of course, like a true savage, he would then court inaction, and a long siesta; against which, in time of peace, there is no law. But that spirit was now awake, and its restless fires burning fiercely in every bosom, which, in the savage, sways all the other appetites of his nature; a spirit which had now transformed his habitual indolence into the stronger and more habitual activity of revenge and the thirst for blood.

On returning to our huts, we were greeted by the sight of nearly all our warriors, many of whom had been coming in, in the interim of our absence. Our whole number of effective men, as I may not have remarked before, was said—how correctly, I had no exact means of knowing—to be about seven hundred. But, with the loose discipline to which they were subject, more or less of them were always absent on any given emergency.* Decampment, so to speak, was

* What, after all, was the number of fighting-men accompanying this expedition, the editor has no definite means of determining. It

but the work of a moment, and warriors, women, and children, were all on the long war-path. During the first three days, we were only allowed time sufficient for sleep; and we tasted, absolutely, nothing, save now and then a mouthful of water, which was generally half mud, and sometimes brackish at that. Standing around the mud-hole, or rather scrambling to obtain a handful of its contents, nothing is more common than for native men to growl and snarl at each other, like the same number of native dogs over the carcass of a dead kangaroo.

When the three days' stage of our march was measured, the tents were pitched, the fires were kindled, and a short hunt supplied a very scanty meal. The next morning, leaving a hundred men to garrison the encampment, we resumed the path which some heroic muse has celebrated as

" Leading to glory or the grave."

During this day, as we were nearing the enemy, every tread was cautious, and every eye was frequent and searching in its glances to detect an ambuscade. At dark, not daring to light a fire, we laid ourselves down and slept upon our arms till midnight. According to the information of the spies, who accompanied us as guides in this expedition, we were now so near the quarters of the enemy, that we could reach them at

appears to have been less than the whole number; and it might have been so by the difference of a hundred, more or less.

that chosen hour when they would be found in their
deepest sleep—a sleep which proved to many of them,
as it was intended to be, the sleep of death.

Resuming our arms and our march at midnight,
two or three hours brought us in sight of hostile fires.
Here we paused. Agreeably to the order of attack,
we were divided into two parties. One was to surprise and attack, while the other, at a distance of forty
rods, was to surround the encampment, for the purpose of intercepting and cutting off the fugitives. I
was detailed on this latter service.

The charging party had advanced to within some
fifteen to twenty rods of our unsuspecting victims,
when one, more watchful than his fellows, caught the
sound of approaching footsteps, and yelled the alarm.
Before it was fairly uttered, a volley of missiles laid
him dead. The projectors followed the projectiles,
and with nearly equal swiftness. The strife which
ensued was hand to hand; but it was unequal. Many
were struck before they could get to their feet. The
outcry of terror and death was horrible. Women,
with their children, were flying and falling in all directions, while the mere handful of surviving men,
with a valor unsurpassed by the palmiest exploits of
ancient or modern chivalry, stood and fought like
tigers. By the clear light of the moon, which rendered most of the scene distinctly and fearfully visible, I beheld a poor woman, with a child under each

arm, flying from the stormed encampment, hard by
the point at which I was posted. The sight roused
my pity. Unfaithful to my painful trust, I determined to permit her escape, and pretended to be looking another way. Ill-fated mother and children!
The sight had attracted an eye that knew not to pity,
and the barbed weapon which pierced the maternal
bosom, reached it by passing through one of the children; and, the next moment, I saw the tomahawk
despatch the little survivor.

The time of this massacre did not occupy more than
half an hour; and small, indeed, must have been the
number who escaped to tell its ensanguined tale.
When the work of destruction was ascertained to be
complete, and before daylight broke upon the scene,
we left it; but not before some of the victors had
availed themselves of the opportunity of allaying their
cannibal hunger.

Let those, who are impatient of the influences and
restraints of Christianity and its institutions, and who
pine for the larger liberty of the "state of nature,"
have the full consent of their neighbors to emigrate to
Australia, or any other spot equally favored by the
absence of those influences. Once there, they could
hardly fail to feel the full force of the contrast between the presence and absence of those disrelished
influences, in their effects on human interests.

CHAPTER XVI.

Return to camp.—Superfamished.—Resort to the chase.—Quest of a private adventure.—Finds it in a Miss Emu.—How she is *struck*, and how she *strikes*.—Adventurer finds himself in a twofold misadventure.—Is extricated.—Hostile encroachments.—Opposing forces meet.—Parley between chiefs.—The enemy's champion, and his challenge.—A pitched battle.—Rout and loss of the enemy.—Brief cessation of hostilities.—Capture and execution of a spy.—Descent to the coast.—The stranded whale, and a " whaling" feast.—Harassed by the enemy.—" Heir apparent" and his attendant slain.— A princely funeral.

OUR backward tramp held us from a little before daylight, which closed the bloody drama of the night before, till the ensuing nightfall. Arrived at home, we yielded at once to such sleep and dreams as are common to weary and famished wolves and warriors. With quite as much sympathy with the former, as the latter class of heroes, we awoke. Revenge had been sated, and we must needs lose no time now in satisfying hunger. A couple of miles brought us upon a fine herd of our staple game. Instead of scattering, however, as usual, which would have equalized the chances of a shot, they darted off in single file. The consequence was that my spear was unthrown. Not so with all; a few were so well aimed as to produce immediate death; more were carried away by the wounded; which latter circumstance induced the customary pursuit. Aware that a whole army was to be provisioned, and that, while all were nearly hungry enough to swallow one another, I could count on the exercise of no great degree of hospitality, I determined to part company with my comrades, and strike off in pursuit of an adventure of my own.

Having picked up a pair of opossums, I was casting around for something a little more worthy of a hunter's ambition, when, suddenly, a long-measured tread, with a continuous crashing and crackling accompaniment, broke on my auditory sense. Listening, the tramp and the crash grew nearer. A moment, and a full-grown emu crossed my path at a few yards. The reader, it is presumed, will excuse a short episode enlightening him at a few points—should he chance to need it—on the subject of the natural history of this *rare avis*.

Briefly then: the emu is the ostrich of Australia. Like its African congener, it runs rather than flies; or, more accurately, it does both at once. Though the size and construction of its wings unfit it for independent flight, they add so much to its pedal propulsion as to give it a velocity to which no mere mammal, biped, or quadruped, can make any just pretension. True, she is run down by the native dog; but it is owing to her want of wind, and to the curves

and doublings of her course; in avoiding which, as
well as in his greater power of endurance, her pursuer
finds the whole of his advantage.   Her ordinary
stature is that of an ordinary man.   When erecting
herself to her greatest height, she stands full eight
feet, perpendicular.   Great timidity and vigilance,
with clairvoyant eyes, peering from the pinnacle of
such a walking observatory, render her an object of
very difficult and unfrequent acquisition.   To make
the reader sensible that this is a perfectly logical conclusion—this of the difficulty and infrequency of emu-
catching—he is to remember, first and last, that her
arrowy swiftness is worthy of that divine eulogy bestowed on her Arabian cousin thirty-five hundred
years ago—

> " What time she lifteth herself on high,
>   She scorneth the horse and his rider."

Before re-conducting the reader to the subject of the
narrative, I shall merely remark, that the force, as
well as the magnitude, of this mammoth bird may
be judged of from the fact, that her kick is sufficient
to break an arm, or even the leg of a man.   But more
of her capabilities anon.

We tie the broken ends of my story together, gentle reader, at that critical moment in which the rapid
fugitive was shooting across my way.   Very well; it
was in that moment that a well-aimed shaft entered
just below her short wing, and away she went, lance

and all. It was in the next breath, when I was on
the point of giving chase, that a large native dog offered
me a mark for another spear.* It took him in the
shoulder, and sent him limping on a different tack.
Having made acquaintance with this description of
gentry some time before, as the reader remembers, I
thought, instead of holding him by the button, I
would insinuate myself a little farther into the good
graces of *Miss Emu.* The visible traces of her flight
precluded all difficulty in the pursuit, which had been
continued but a short distance, when I discovered her
in the act of endeavoring to disengage herself from
the incumbrance of my spear. This offered me the
opportunity of following it with another. The effect
of this was that, rearing for another half-running and
half-flying effort, she bore herself a matter of a hundred yards, and fell. Supposing her tame enough,
by this time, I very innocently took her by her ante-
rior extremities, when, suddenly, drawing them up,
she let fly, with a force which laid me up at the distance of a rod, or thereabouts, a little *more* senseless
than I had been the moment before. In a word, as
nearly as I could ever know, I knew just nothing at
all for the next quarter of an hour. My totally dissi-
pated wits, however, slowly returned, and with such
an *accession,* as made me a little cautious of taking a

* The emu was his game, and he was in hot pursuit of her when
the adventurous spear encountered him.

bird of that particular feather by the *hind* leg, till
pretty sure that she was past kicking. It was in that
safe state that I found her, but with the earth so torn
and rent, as satisfied me, that *mine* was, by no means,
the final kick. To restrain the reader from treating
this little affair, between the *kicker* and *kickee*, with
undue levity, he should know that, up to the time of
its occurrence, I was innocent of any experience in the
class of cases to which it belonged; and, then, he
might do well to remember, that some of the more
valuable portions of his own wit—if he have any—
were probably impressed by means not totally dis-
similar to that which gave me mine.

Hunger and thirst being equally extreme, for I had
hardly tasted either drink or food since "the last
war," my hunting knife effected a speedy opening of
resources for allaying both; and the reader needs no
very broad intimation that the opportunity was duly
honored. But fresh troubles awaited me; for, though
my fair captive was lighter by the weight of her blood
and other appurtenances, my full strength was inadequate to raise her to my shoulder, and bear her to our
quarters; and I make this remark, partly, that the
reader may have a more just conception of her true
magnitude. In effecting a return to camp, however,
it is but sooth to own, that my incompetency was not
less mental than physical. Plainly, and honestly, I was
bewildered. In such cases, fire is the native expedi-

I   13

ent. I struck it, and raised both *it*, and my *voice* to as high a pitch as possible. In about two hours, I heard a distant answer, and answered it. Shout responded to shout, till, shortly, I was joined by several of my late companions. In answer to their repeated questions, I could only say—mortifying as it was— " *Nothing* is the matter; only I have lost my reckoning." It was clear that my island education was sadly defective, for a real islander is never at a loss for his direction. However mazy, he can find and keep it, by light or in darkness, indifferently. When occasion requires, he drops an article—a spear, or an axe, for instance—pursues his journey for any number of hundred miles, and in every conceivable direction through the pathless wilderness, till, wonderfully enough, re-.urning to the spot, he picks it up: if in the day-time, well; if in the darkest night—never mind; he has got it. The child of instinct, instinct is his guide, and it never guides him amiss.

We were once more in our quarters. The plucked emu, along with various contributions from the other followers of the chase, had undergone due dissection; the parts had received the customary blackening, and eager appetite was causing their rapid disappearance, when a scout brought in the intelligence that an enemy had invaded our hunting ground, and that, from all appearance, they had come to offer us battle.*

* The memoranda are silent as to the identity of the invading party,

Instantly, the reeking meat fell untasted, and the luxury of the feast gave place to preparations for the greater luxury of war. Nor was the time allowed for preparation long. For, while the warriors were giving their weapons a brief inspection, female hands were putting the other movables into portable con dition; so that when the former were armed, the lat ter were loaded for the march.

In a few minutes from the sound of the tocsin, we were waiting for the word which was to set our whole train in motion. It came, and all were on our way to find, and chastise the foe. Nor did he compel us to a protracted search. In less than four miles their shouts of defiance broke upon us, and were echoed with due emphasis. We found them posted in a wood. An American and a western man would have called it an *opening*. The trees were large, but sparse, and without the impediment of an undergrowth. The consequence was, that it presented a fair field, and brought the two parties into mutual view, at a desirable distance previously to the onset. The reader will not fail to perceive that this is the only case, recorded in connection with my island residence, of anything like a pitched battle. Skirmishings; night attacks; and other speci-

es, also, touching the cause for which they had sought the pending contest. If they were the main body to which the party belonged, that had been so severely handled in the recent night attack, they must not only have received the most prompt notice of it, but made a very forced march, in order to be in readiness for the ensuing encounter.

mens of desultory fighting were by no means wanting; but this is the first and only instance, which fell out in that connection, of the meeting of large forces, deliberately, in the day-time, and with what we are accustomed to consider,

> "The pomp and circumstance of glorious war."

When within some hundred yards of each other, the two armies halted, and formed in order of battle. Then the two chieftains strode out on to the middle ground, till they had reached a distance suitable for the purpose, when they fell into a long parley. Whether it contemplated a pacification, I had no means of knowing; but from the result, as well as from a general knowledge of savage character, I presumed it was meant for nothing more than a part of the aforesaid "pomp and circumstance." This ceremony was followed by another of a less questionable character. When the chiefs had terminated their interview, an armed man advanced a few paces toward us from the opposing ranks, who performed a number of antics, and displayed a deal of grimace and gesticulation of a violent character. Then, squaring himself, in true martial style, he poised and shot his war spear directly into our lines. This was the unmistakable " throwing down of the gauntlet," and, perhaps, included the ceremony of devoting us to the infernal gods. At all events, it was followed by immediate action.

For about the space of three hours, the death-dealing missiles were showered as thick as hail. Within such a time, projectiles would not only begin to fail, but the combatants, waxing impetuous, would be fain to mix themselves in strife of a more personal and deadly kind. It was so in this case. The original distance had been gradually lessened, so that, as spears and patience failed, they were ready to grapple each other in *pairs*. From this period, the style of the contest was merged in the duello, in which each seized the other by the hair, and, with his war-hatchet, either cleft his cranium, or plied it for that purpose, till he had hardly strength for another blow. For a long time the scale of battle hung on an even beam. Every man fought as if he were conscious that the issue depended on his single arm. At length, however, the enemy gave way. The rest of the action was a rout, on their part, attended with a slaughter unprecedented by the whole of the regular engagement. For half an hour we hung upon their flying squadrons, when, too much spent for a longer pursuit, our leader called a halt; and each party, satisfied in its own way, retraced the path by which it had sought the war.

The changes which occur in savage society, while in a state of repose, are few and unconnected, for the most part, with incidents of any interest to the readers of narrative. Such a society, itself, looks on those incidents with a stolid indifference. Instinct, the necessi ties of nature, and brute force, give law to all their actions. Love, whether conjugal, filial, parental, or social, as well as hatred, aversion, and desire, with every other passion, are unquelled by the influence of any moral sense, or sentiment, whatever. The *animal* is fully formed. The *man*, contemplated as a moral intelligence, acquainted with, and feeling his obligations, to his Creator and fellow-men, is yet to be *born*. He knows nothing of *God ;* nothing of his own *soul.* Nothing turns his thoughts *within ;* nothing lifts them *above*, or sends them on to the *future.* Uncheered, unsoftened by the sympathies and charities of home and kindred ; bookless, sabbathless, friendless, hopeless, Godless ;

> " He eats, and drinks, and sleeps, and then
> He eats, and drinks, and sleeps again."

But however waveless and tideless, like the sea of Sodom, may be the savage mind, when no longer lashed by its only great passion, *revenge ;* the reader can but have seen, that, when excited by that passion, it exhibits a patience, a firmness, and a force, which would have given it distinction in a nation of heroes.

Our inglorious rest was of but brief duration. One day while a small party of us were engaged in the ordinary avocations of the chase, we started up, not another *feathered*, but an *unfeathered* biped. He fled, showing himself an enemy. We followed, and, after a hot chase of four miles, overtook, and captured him.

Proving himself a spy from our late enemy, we marched him into camp. He was bound, and kept in the usual durance till the following day. Then, as his life was forfeit, as well by the rules of savage, as of civilized war, the customary preparations were made for the customary execution.

When led out to meet his fate, he displayed the same haughty indifference to death, the same proud scorn of his enemies, which characterize the native hero. He threatened us with the vengeance of his tribe. Our chief, little thinking that it would fall so soon, and upon himself, merely replied, that he ought to have stayed at home. I have implied that the circumstances of this infliction were such as ordinarily enter into cases of the kind. They were so, save that the bearing of the prisoner was marked by a bolder defiance, and more bitter taunts. The bitterest, and that which stung the native pride most sensibly, was that which told the chief, that he and his men were "no better than so many women." The consequence of this was, that he and they essayed their very utmost to convince him, that he had underrated their merits, and that, by consequence, his comparison was not more unmannerly than it was unjust.

The law thus duly satisfied, and the fire that had satisfied it hardly extinguished, we took our traps, and once more wended our way to the coast. The reader will be aided, to some extent, in his imagination of distances, by being informed that our seaward journey in this instance, occupied us during the whole of fourteen consecutive days; in which time we travelled, by approximation, three hundred or more miles. The famine, caused by bad hunting weather, which had precipitated this long journey, wrought incredible suffering among our people, till our arrival on the coast. Nor did we meet with anything much more auspicious, even then. With a heavy surf breaking upon the rocks—our old fishing stations—nothing could be effected in that line; and fifteen hundred people, already famished, were left for three days to the scanty gleanage of a few shell-fish.

On the fourth day, however, my companions experienced the truth of our civilized adage touching "an ill wind;" for they found that—all but the blubber—it had blown ashore what was once a whale. The unctuous exterior long since gone home to Nantucket or New-Bedford, the balance had been left for our special benefit. Sea-salt, thrown over it by the surf, and crystallized by the sun, had invested it with a coating of snow-like whiteness; while, within, owing to the time that life had been absent, and of its exposure to a high temperature, it was absolutely and deeply green. Thus it struck the optics; but the olfactories—Attar of Roses! Eau-de-Cologne, and all ye odorous powers! Need the reader be explicitly informed, that this was a god-send to my hungry

clanspeople? Indeed, with their habits, it would
have furnished a welcome change of diet at *any* time.
How much more, then, when a long famine had rendered them absolutely ravenous? A fire was kindled. Every knife was in requisition. Flesh supplied
the *inner* man and woman, and oil, the *outer*. In short,
all were soon as happy as full feeding, with plenty of
grease and paint, could make them. In vain was I
invited to eat, grease, and be happy, also. In vain,
too, did my newly-anointed spouse press me to the
banquet, and offer her personal aid in applying the
odorous unguent. I turned away. The unbreathable
perfume filled a wide circumference. I took my
spears and struck for the woods. Here, passing two,
and sometimes, three days without tasting food, I
remained, till the long carnival was over. On falling
back into the interior, though compelled to join my
tribe, yet, as the atmosphere of the feast still surrounded the persons of my fellow-travellers, by reason of
the reeking unction afore-mentioned, it was long before I could abide any but the most distant of admissible civilities.

A sharp look-out was now felt to be indispensable.
From various indications, it was ascertained that our
movements were under the espionage of our watchful
adversary, whose scouts would be likely to cut off any
who straggled far from our quarters. Nor was it long
before they found their opportunity. Our chief had

I*

a son, some seventeen years of age. He was a man;
for manhood and womanhood come early in these savage constitutions. Venturing into the scrub, one day,
with an attendant, they were both waylaid and slain.
On a slight inspection it was obvious that the two
deaths had been caused by those who knew the person
of the *hair-apparent*, and who intended something more
than a common retaliation. His remains, beside being transfixed by a stake to the ground, exhibited no
less than fifteen spear holes, with other mutilations
and indignities, too revolting, as well as "too numerous to mention."

As nearly as appearances could be trusted, this ne-
farious transaction must have occurred about three
days before a party of us made the above discovery.
On depositing the mutilated remains of the high-born
youth, with those of his attendant, before the chieftain's lodge, his imperial majesty tore his hair, gestic-
ulated and vociferated dreadfully, and swore the death
of every man, woman, and child, belonging to the
offending tribe—as soon as he could catch them.

A common death occasions little or no ceremony.
We were now, however, to celebrate the obsequies
of a prince. For this purpose, the men were ordered
to dig a grave. To save labor, it was to be made
large enough for the two-fold interment which the
occasion demanded. When eighteen inches deep,
however, it was divided so as to form two compart-

ments, with a bar of unbroken earth between them ; after which, they were respectively sunk some two feet deeper. In accomplishing this, it was observable that all the roots which came in their way—and they were not a few—instead of being cut, were uniformly broken by hand. When, at length, the excavation was completed, the naked bodies were deposited, and well *trodden down*. Then the *princely* remains were covered with bark, from a neighboring mahogany, which was also trodden down ; after which, there was another and a *transverse* layer of the bark. The earth, thrown from the pit, was not to be used for filling it. The women were sent to procure, and bring the requisite quantity, from a distance. When, by this means, the excavation had been filled to a little less than even with the surface, the chief broke a spear, and laid it over the remains of his son. Then the womra belonging to the deceased was split, and the two parts fixed, perpendicularly, at the two extremities of the grave. The next thing in order, which, like the placing of the broken, and riven war-weapons, was the work of the principal mourner, was the removal of a circle of bark from every tree within thirty yards of the place of sepulture, in all directions. The concluding rite was performed by means of a quantity of bones, of different animals, about a foot in length. These were obtained from the women. For what purposes they are in the habit of preserving them, unless for those akin to this, I am unable to say. These, the paternal monarch fixed in the earth within three inches of each other, till his son's compartment of the grave was completely impaled.

Inhumation, as the reader has probably inferred, is not the common practice. Indeed, the present, is the only instance of it within my recollection. Without professing certainty, I presume that the opposite practice rests solely on the ground of convenience; and that inhumation is held to be more honorable, for the reason that it is more expensive, if for no other. One more remark shall end this digression. The silence of survivors, in relation to the dead, is more remarkable here, than among any other people within my knowledge, whether savage or civilized. To utter a name of the dead, is sure to give offence. Indeed, there is no custom more sacred than that which utterly forbids it.

We now return to the grave, for a very different purpose from that of listening to some monitory thought—some hortatory or benedictory effusion. The regal priest had satisfied his affection, such as it was, and his piety, if he had any. It only remained to satisfy his *vengeance*. He had already sworn it once; and here, at the grave of his child, he *re*-swore it. The next chapter will inform thee, oh, reader! whether he needed absolution or not from his reiterated vow.

CHAPTER XVII

Retaliatory war.—Deaths on both sides.—The surprise.—The flight.—
The pursuit.—The rescue.—Rescuers rescued.—Two prisoners.—One
escapes death by dying.—The other dies by being put to death.—
Final visit to the coast.—Fishing; in which the fisher, by being
fished, has a narrow escape of becoming food for fishes.—Finally,
the adventurer gives his mahogany-colored friends and relations the
slip, by escaping on shipboard; and how.

RETURNING from the only grave which I had seen
opened and closed, with due ceremony, out of the pale
of Christendom, we followed our chief's example, by
sharpening our tools for making *another* grave. We
had made a common one for a couple of *friends*. We
were now to prepare another for more than twice as
many hundred of our *enemies*. Our good spears were
once more rebarbed. Our wigwams were broken up;
and we were again upon the war-path. Stopping only
to sleep, and only a night in a place, we found ourselves, after a long and wearying march, on the hunting ground of our enemies. There was an oath, or
rather a couple of oaths, between us. They had sworn
our deaths; we had sworn theirs.

Our warriors were divided into four parties, with

orders to patrol the hostile territory, and spare neither age, sex or condition. And literally—too literally—were those atrocious orders obeyed, during the six weeks of interskirmish which ensued. How many our arms destroyed in that time, we had no means of knowing, with any great definiteness. But, upon a comparison of accounts, our chieftain comforted himself by believing that the number of *men* was little, if any, less than two hundred, beside large lots of women and children. True, we paid for this princely satisfaction by some large losses of our own. We had gone into the enemy's ground with seven hundred warriors—a little over one hundred of whom were missing when we left it—as, at that time, we could hardly muster six hundred. This septimation of our men was accompanied by a proportionate riddance of such encumbrances of the expedition as wore the shape of women and little ones. For such as they—a hundred, more or less—are hardly included in the loss-account; especially, when, as in the present case, we had the proud satisfaction of having been the killers of two hundred male enemies, full grown, with only a little more than half as many of our male effectives killed.

But, as I was very near being included in this latter list, I must close the history of this "last war," in which I served my—*country,* I can hardly say—so I will say, my *countrymen*—by a short yarn on the sub-

ject. It was the closing scene of the drama, and my
last passage at arms. Tired of killing men, and out-
rageously hungry, at the same time, I thought, one
day, I would try to put the life out of something that
was not human, and which I could appropriate for
food, without violating what my comrades in man-
slaughter ridiculed as a foolish prejudice of education.
Bent on this little piece of self-gratification, I had
strolled away into the scrub, about a couple of miles
from the place of our intended encampment for the
night. Having killed an opossum, I was sitting by my
fire in the act of barbacuing it for breakfast, dinner
and supper, when it occurred to me that I was on an
enemy's ground, and that it might be well to reconnoitre. Rising to suit the action to the thought, the
sight of three naked native figures, convinced me that
the thought was by no means premature. Their ad-
vance was rapid. At a glance, I knew them for enemies; and that, being so, it would not be their fault
if they did not eat my opossum, and me to boot. It
happened, just then, that neither of the two alterna-
tives was precisely eligible. To lose life or dinner,
and especially the latter, already half devoured by anticipation, was not to be thought of. Snatching it
with one hand, and my spears with the other, I fled
for life, and for my—*opossum*. It was well for both
that I had a pretty good start of my pursuers. Looking over my shoulder, after running about a quarter

of a mile, I thought the rascals were gaining upon me
a little. That put me to the tip-top of my speed, and
though no time was wasted on another observation,
I have always flattered myself since, that I held them
at that distance till the race was up. My bearing was
as direct as possible, for a point at which I expected
to find a number of our clansmen. On entering a
thicket, I thought, for a moment, of attempting to
give my enemies the dodge. Recollecting, however,
that the hounds who were on my track could both
scent and *see* it, I dismissed all idea of the *ruse*, and
was tearing through the thick scrub like a young
whirlwind, when, all at once, I heard a tremendous
yell. A clansman of mine had seen the chase, had
concealed himself in the chapparal, and when I had
passed him, and my pursuers were passing, rose and
yelled, and threw. One of the three was stopped.
The thunder did not kill him, but the lightning did.

In the mean time, another of our men, who was at a
distance, hearing the war-shout, answered it, and
presently joined his comrade in chase of the two survivors. In the same time, too, having become satisfied that both shouts proved the interference, not of
enemies, but friends, I had put about, in order to help
my helpers. As soon as the two fugitives found that
the number of their pursuers was only equal to their
own, they halted, determined to try the chances of a
fight. When I came in sight, spears had been thrown,

and, hand in hair, the belligerents were plying the
deadly battle-axe. On gaining the proper distance,
I hurled my womra. It hit, broke and fell; and with
it fell the head that broke it. Dashing on, I found
my other clansman engaged with a powerful fellow,
decidedly his superior, and literally covered, and
nearly suffocated, with his own blood. A spear transfixed the herculean foe. His grasp relaxed. The consequence was, that the weaker party, who had been
held up for some time by the strong arm of his enemy,
dropped at his feet. The savage Sampson, on receiving my spear, eyed me for a moment, and exclaimed:
" *Yennuck jonnuck !—You are the devil !*" and fell.

Both the vanquished were marched toward our
camp; though their situation made it necessary that
we should frequently stop, in order to afford them
rest. During the night, however, one life escaped by
way of the outlet opened by the spear of the previous
day. The survivor was led out to an open space,
and set up for a mark, at the distance of thirty yards.
He was allowed his perfect liberty ; and so well did
he use it, as to elude every spear, as long as spears
came singly. Long did our most expert marksmen
continue to throw their pointed shafts, while the fellow's adroitness of evasion enabled him to hold them
perfectly at bay. In all probability, the whole day
might have been spent with the same result. At
length, however, maddened with mortification, they

14

all let fly at once. He *fell*, and still he *stood*. The explanation is, that his nearly dead weight was arrested, midway in its fall, by the number of spears which the poor fellow had received. A fire, kindled for the purpose, received his remains, and converted them to ashes.

The pastime of war was now over. Our chief delivered it as his opinion, that our enemies would hardly trouble us again, and that it was now about time for us to return. After a hungry march of ten days, we encamped once more on our own hunting-ground, where it was thought safe to remain the unusual time of seven days. Here, the success of the chase, like that of the recent war, equalled our reasonable wishes. The day was spent in the field, and the night in feasting, alternated with the chant of their various feats in battle.

Our next adjournment was to the sea-coast. The order, like each of its predecessors to the same effect, re-enkindled my languishing hopes that Providence would open some way for my escape from an irksome bondage. After five or six encampments, the blue expanse of the Pacific once more opened before us. The tents were set up—of course, by the women. The fishing-gear was got in readiness; and soon a long extent of the beach was lined by several hundred hungry men, whose fish-spears were to feed themselves, and more than twice as many hungry women and children.

Perched on a rock, I had not waited long before a

large school of porpoises came floating in the clear
water, till, at length, they were at the foot of the
rock, and in easy reach of my spear.   My aim was true.
A large porpoise was fast at one end of the spear, and
I, as a fish-spearer's duty is in such a case, was fast
at the other.   And now the question was: which
shall be pulled out, or which in?   The struggle was
desperate, but it was short.   The rock was slippery;
I lost my foothold; and, with a souse, I was among
the fish.   If the top of the rock was so slippery that
I could not help getting *in*, the side was more than
enough so to keep me from getting *out*.   What made
it worse for me, was, as the reader has had occasion
of noticing before, that I could not swim, and the
water was so deep, that no way remained of reaching
land, but by diving for it.   In brief, then, as the case
stood, the prospect was, that, instead of a supper on
fish, the fish would make a supper on me.   And so
they would, but that the whole scene had fallen out
under the eye of a native friend, who, at the moment
in which the porpoise got the better of me, was standing on another rock, some forty rods distant.   The
sight of my plunge brought him to my relief.   By
reaching me the end of his spear, he succeeded in
towing me round the rock; when, after drinking more
"salt-water grog" than either health or comfort exactly demanded, half pulled and half crawling, I once
more regained my proper position in society.

We were on the coast a fortnight. During this time, I saw three ships—the first I had seen since the wreck of the Pyramus—standing to the west; but none of them near enough to afford me the needed assistance. At the end of that time, all, but myself, were willing to take the bush again. At the end of the first day, after our re-migration into the country, we found ourselves on the margin of a large lagoon, where we stopped for a few days. On the second of these days, one of our men, on coming in from hunting, proceeded to the wigwam of the chief with the information that he had seen a "*kibra*"—*ship*—standing off shore. The chief asked him where she was. He replied that, when he saw her, she was coming into the bay. This was in the evening. The chief dismissed the conversation by saying, that he would go and see her the next day. All this, being in an adjoining lodge, I distinctly overheard. In a few minutes, I was gratified by hearing myself called, and asked, whether I would not like to go and see a *kibra*, which was lying in the bay. Fearing some sinister intention on the part of the questioner, I replied, evasively, that I did not care much about it—that I was quite contented where I was.

The next morning my master told me to get ready, and go with him. This I did with a feeling and purpose, which it was well for me that he was far enough from suspecting. Six of us—five beside myself—

were the chief's attendants on this occasion : a number which, whether intended, among other purposes,
to guard against my possible escape, or not, was certainly calculated to lessen the chances in favor of
such an occurrence. That such a motive operated the
arrangement in question, is the more probable from
the consideration, that my attendance would naturally
be thought important, as the capital to be made out
of the people of the *kibra* would be readily associated,
in the ruling mind, with the facilities for that purpose
to be derived from my qualification to act as a common interpreter ; while, at the same time, it is hardly
imaginable that my juxtaposition with white men,
should not suggest the possibility of an abduction.

Near nightfall, our party encamped on the beach
of the bay. Its native name is *Elyepete.* As the
reader finds this name appropriated to *persons*, and,
among others, to my native spouse, it may not be in-
apposite to remark, as I have partly done before, that
it stands for *guana*, a land animal of the lizard kind,
eighteen inches to two feet in length, and highly esteemed among the islanders as an article of food.
While on the subject of *names*, it may be proper to
add, that they are borrowed from bays, rivers, trees,
mountains, day and night, sun, moon, and stars, wind
and rain, thunder and lightning, birds, beasts, fishes,
and, in a word, from all sensible objects.

The sun rose on the last day of my captivity. It

showed us the ship, lying about three miles from
shore. After waiting anxiously for some time, we saw
her lower and man a boat, which pulled away for an
island situated in the centre of the bay; from which
it was obvious they were wooding and watering the
ship. I told the chief, that he had better light a fire,
and raise a large smoke, which the people of the *kibra*
would understand as a signal that we wanted them to
send a boat ashore. He did so. We also suspended
two or three kangaroo skins on as many spears, which
we waved for the same purpose. After signalling, by
these means, for about an hour, we saw the starboard
quarter boat lowered from the brig, and pulled directly
toward us. When within hailing distance, they hove
to, and demanded what we wanted. I answered, that
I had been cast away on the coast in the Carib, and
wanted them to come ashore. They next demanded,
if there would not be danger from the natives, and
were assured that there would not; for, indeed, I had
taken the precaution to induce them to put their
spears away in the bush, telling them that, unless
they did so, the white men would not come ashore.
Upon this they pulled up near the shore, where they
lay a long time, chaffering about the safety of proceeding further, and sometimes inclining to put about,
and return to the ship. At length, however, my mingled entreaties and assurances prevailed. They leaped
ashore, and pulled the boat out of the surf.

The natives pressed around the craft, hugely surprised and delighted with the harpoons, lances, and other matters connected with the whaling business, which were lying in the bottom of the boat. The chief asked me if the white men would not give him . one. I told him, that the white men, in the ship, were wanting some meat, and that, if he would go and kill them a kangaroo, they would give him one. What most captivated his fancy was a hatchet. He appeared to want that, above all things. Of course, he was told, that, if he brought the kangaroo, they would make him a present of the hatchet, in the bargain. Pledging himself for the venison, and that he would be back with it "short metre," he disappeared among the scrub; and with him—to insure the greater despatch, and which even exceeded my hopes—*three* of the royal guard.

As soon as they were out of the way, I told the mate, that if he would be so kind as to take me to the ship, this was the time to do it. Still inclined to talk, rather than act, he asked me how long I·had been with the natives. I told him I had lost all dates, and could not tell. But when he had named the passing month and day, I replied, that I had been there seventeen months, and twenty-eight days. Then, falling back upon the main subject, he confessed his fears that, if he undertook to get me away, the remaining natives would attack us. Begging him to hold on a bit, I said to one of the natives: " Where is there some water? Go and get some." He took a calabash and started. The other was told to go and fetch some wood, to make a fire. He also cut stick, and was gone. " *This*," I said to the mate, " is our only moment." The boat was launched. We were in it, in a trice, and pulling away from shore, with might and main. The chap who was to accommodate us with the wood, not being fairly out of sight, chanced to look over his shoulder at the very nick of time in which we

" Shov'd our light shallop from the shore."

When he saw the movement, and that I was included in it, he yelled, and bounded for his spears. His tom-fool of a comrade heard him, and, yelling an answer, dropped his calabash, and ran with the speed of a frightened kangaroo. Their arrowy course along the beach was marked by jets of sand, rising, in manner and extent, like the puffs from a pair of runaway locomotives.*

By the time the two worthies had recovered their spears, and gained the place of our disembarkation, we were sixty rods from shore. At that distance, feeling ourselves beyond the reach of harm, we hove to, that we might observe their manœuvres. First,

* In running on the beach, a native employs his feet in such a manner as to flirt the sand over his head, as high as twenty or thirty feet. Such is the fact. The explanation would accompany it, could it be as briefly given.

they essayed to coax me to return, and wait till the chief should come back from hunting. Then, finding that I was not soft-soapable, they exhausted the whole vocabulary of native abuse, not omitting to notify me as to what I might expect, should I ever set foot on their shores again. At the mate's request, all this, or the substance of it, was done into English for his special enlightenment; upon which he thought it time to stand away for the brig. She was the Camilla, Capt. Thompson, belonging to Hobart-Town.

When we came alongside, the captain and crew were looking down with a fixed stare on the nude specimen of island zoology. The captain demanded of the mate, what he had on board; and was answered, that it was a man who had been cast away on the coast, seventeen or eighteen months before.* He next inquired, if I was an Indian, or what country I was from; and was informed, that I called myself an Englishman. Upon this the captain swore that I was no Englishman; adding, that if I only had curly hair, he should think I came straight from the coast of Africa. By this time, I had ascended the ship's side, and stood upon the deck. What ensued in that immediate connection, together with a final shore-scene, must be reserved for the next chapter.

* The original papers, which would naturally be expected to shed some light on the fate of the other survivors of the Carib, leave it entirely in the dark. Indeed, the editor cannot find that they contain any reference to that subject whatever.

K

CHAPTER XVIII.

Curiosity and surprise on shipboard.—Kind reception.—Metamorphosis.—Final shore-scene.—*Exeunt omnes.*—Whaling cruise off the coast.—King George's Sound.—Ships for Canton.—Renewed kindness of Capt. T.—Arrival at Canton.—Protracted opportunity for observation.—Notes on the Chinese.—Anecdote illustrative of character.—Return voyage.—Succession of disasters.—Arrival in Swan River.

THE last chapter, having shown that I had *cut* my Australian acquaintance, and how I did it, left me standing on the deck of the whale-ship Camilla, Capt. Thompson, of Hobart-Town. This, then, is the true point of resumption; and here it was that the good-natured captain catechized me, as to who I was, and where I had been, and how long, and how I came there. When he had *put me through* on all these points, to his heart's content, and when all his doubts were obviated, he called the cook, and ordered him to give me the benefit of plenty of soap and warm water. The wash-deck-tub, with all the other abluent appliances, were, accordingly, put into speedy requisition. And when the process, aided by the friendly office of the cook, was completed, it was found that the *wash* and the *washed* had made a very perceptible exchange of com-

plexions. The former had turned decidedly dark
the latter, with a fair allowance for the roasting, which
had been doing it browner and browner for the last
eighteen months, appeared as if it might be distantly
related to some dark-skinned English family. The
captain then called me down into the cabin, and presented me with a good suit of clothes, and soon saw
that I knew how to put them on; though, the fact
was, that, from long disuse, I felt, for some time,
awkward and uncomfortable enough in my new rig.

In about two hours after I reached the brig, there
was a new movement on the beach. By the occasional
use of the captain's glass, I saw that the chief and
his party had returned with the kangaroo. Presently,
the signal fire blazed again, and the signal skins were
waving in the air. When he had signalled us, in
vain, for about an hour, they fought among themselves
for about half that time; and then disappeared in the
woods, and we saw them no more.

We lay here five days longer, taking in wood and
water from the island. And such was the kindness
of the skipper's treatment, that I was not allowed to
do any work, either in the time mentioned, nor for
more than a week afterward.

April 2, 1839. We weighed anchor on this day,
and dropped it again in King George's on the 27th of
the following June; having cruised along the coast,
and taken five sperm whales, in the interim.

In a few days after we anchored in the Sound, a brig came in which was short of hands. She was the John Hendee, Capt. Lean, bound to Canton. I shipped. Before sailing, however, my noble-hearted benefactor, Capt. T., came on board, bringing with him a farther supply of clothing, which he also gave me. He expressed regret that he had no place for me in his ship, and when he was going over the brig's side, he called, and shook me by the hand, in which he left two sovereigns.

July 14. We got under weigh, steering N. W. for the coast of China. As nothing of note occurred on the passage, I have noted nothing.

September 30. Our ship hove to before Canton, the great commercial emporium of the Celestial Empire. As Capt. Lean, beside being captain, was owner of the merchantman, and trading on his own account, he chose to lie here four months, in order to suit himself with a cargo. This length of time, during nearly every day of which we were on shore, and in more or less intercourse with the natives, gave me an opportunity of noticing various things touching the manners, customs, and other peculiarities of this very peculiar people. And I shall set down the result of my observations as independently as if, instead of belonging to the forecastle of a trader, I had been a member of a *corps scientifique*, and carried the queen's commission in my portfolio. In doing this, I shall but repeat, to some of my readers, the substance of what they knew before; while, to others of them, this part of my journal will not prove to be entirely destitute of interest.

The native complexion of the Chinese is a yellowish brown, with scarcely ever the slightest tinge of red. So that, with nothing but the knowledge of this fact to depend on, it were fair to presume that, as a celestial maiden is incapable of a blush, she is allowed to *conjugate*, without learning to lisp the pretty falsehood;—"I blush; thou blushest," et cet. The cranium of a Chinaman is nearly square; his cheek-bones are prominent; his face flat; his eyes are black and small; his chin is rather prominent, and his hair black, and scanty.

Between the natives of this country and those of Tartary there is no very wide difference. Generally, the former are taller, and more slender; while the latter, being thicker set, and more robust, are capable of more hardship, while, at the same time, they possess superior activity. The people of China are mild, inoffensive, contented, cheerful, and courteous. Altogether, they are prepossessing, above any people I have ever met with, whose grade of civilization is the same, or not superior. They seldom use abusive language. If, at any time, they are betrayed into a quarrel, it scarcely ever ends in anything worse than pulling hair, and tearing clothes. Their timidity is extreme,

Personal courage, and presence of mind in the hour
of danger, do not seem to have been provided for in
the native constitution. I have seen this verified,
when some of our men, on shore, in consequence of
drink, have become a little bellicose. The following
is an instance.

Jack had liquored, at a native dram-shop, a little
freely; and, of course, was a *little* inclined to quarrel
with *somebody*. This bred an altercation. The altercation excited extra curiosity. The curiosity attracted spectators. The number of spectators—more than
thirty—made Jack think that it was just the time for
a glorious row. The consequence was, that, drawing
his knife, the madcap made a charge at one of the
celestials; when the whole thirty—shop-keeper and
all—bolted, as for life, leaving my shipmate in full
charge. Nor did any one return to eject or molest
the *barbarian,** till he had capsized everything he
could lay hands on, and, beside helping the rest, had
helped himself to the liquor, till we were obliged to
carry him down to the boat, where we hired a couple
of Tartars to take him off to the ship.

Dress is regulated by law, according to the rank
and situation in life of the wearer. Yellow is sacred
to the imperial household. Red, on days of ceremony,
is the costume of the mandarins: on all other occa-

---

* The reader is, probably, aware, that, in China, *barbarian* and
foreigner are convertible terms.

sions they are restricted to black, blue, or violet. The common people are confined to black, or blue cotton. White is for mourning; but even that must be assumed only upon the death of a father or mother. He who assumes it upon one of those occasions, however, must wear nothing else for three years; after which, he is not allowed to change his black cotton for blue, nor *vice versa*—he can only appear in one color. The general style of a *man's* cap resembles that of the other sex in this country. As worn by the higher classes, it is jewelled, and otherwise highly ornamented.

As all are aware, who have had the benefit of any information on the subject, the common diet is decidedly very poor. The animal part of it involves details which, beside being so well known, are so distasteful to readers of any delicacy, that I shall pass it *sub silentio.* After all, the common Chinaman is little else than animalized rice. It is his breakfast, dinner, and supper, three hundred and sixty-five days in a year, and his hut contains little, in the way of furniture, save the pot that cooks it, together with a frying-pan, two or three coarse jars, and a few basins. Some of them have fire-places; but stoves are far more common. Chairs and tables are hardly so much as known even in name. The iron-pot is the great family centre at meal-times, around which, squatted on their feet, each, having filled his basin, holds it near his mouth, into which, with the two "chop-sticks" in his dexter hand, he flirts the food as fast as he can swallow it; and he swallows it incredibly fast.

Public or social diversions are very limited. Card and dice-playing constitute nearly the sole exceptions. I might instance cock-fighting; but it does not appear to be in great favor, and, I suspect, is Anglican, and consequently recent in its origin.* The other games referred to, are of almost universal prevalence. Nearly every man, and every boy who is old enough, carry in their pockets the well-worn cards and dice. Companies of players may, generally, be seen at any out-of-the-way place, in the open air,—nor is it uncommon for some of these groups to remain thus engaged for days together.

Jan. 5, 1840. We made sail for Swan River, on the south-western coast of New-Holland. Our cargo consisted of silks and tea. Fifteen days out, we encountered a heavy gale, which carried away our fore-top-mast and sprung the fore-mast. At the moment of the former disaster, two men were furling the jib, and when the mast went, it carried the jib-boom, and the two poor fellows with it. Alas! We saw them

---

* For this conjecture, as well as for all other than matters of naked fact, the editor only is responsible. He thinks it less probable *since*, than *before* he penned it. By the way, the author, excepting his facts, proper, appears to have made himself indebted for several of his observations on this general subject, to a well-known publication, embodying, among other kindred matters, various notices of Chinese character, &c.

directly under the ship's bows; but she was tearing through the water like a race-horse, and no human power could save them. The gale lasted forty-eight hours. We repaired the ship, but sighed to think of our shipmates—a loss which we could not repair.

As the ship was found to have sprung a leak, incessant labor at the pumps rendered the remaining part of our passage anything but comfortable. With no other accident, however, we arrived off Swan River. Here we encountered another gale, in which we lost both fore and main-masts, and were left as a floating wreck. What rendered our situation peculiarly distressing, was the want of a spar, to get up a jurymast. Providentially, however, favorable weather followed the gale, which was but a short one, and, after drifting about at the mercy of the elements for ten days, we were picked up by the Wallaby, Capt. ——, and towed into the river.

x* 15

CHAPTER XIX.

· ·¬e months in an American whaler.—Again at King George's Sound.
—Three months as an *attaché* of a surveying party in the back-
woods.—Despatched for supplies.—Lost, famished, tricked by natives.—Regains the settlement.—Delivers despatches, and declines
the service.—Ships in a whaler.—How the whalers whaled the
whales, and the whales whaled the whalers.—Returns to the Sound.
—Four months in harvest.—On a lee-shore.—Wrecked.—Desperate
struggle *for*, and narrow escape *with*, life.—Portuguese sailors.—
Once more in the Sound.—Articles for another whaling cruise.

As our cruise was up, we took our wages, and, as
soon as we could spend them, which, of course, was
no very long while—for Jack never wants for the sort
of friends who are peculiarly helpful in relieving him
of a little troublesome cash—I went and shipped in
an American whaler, the Palladium, Capt. ——. In
five months we returned to the Sound, with only two
hundred and fifty barrels of oil; one hundred and
fifty of right whale, and one hundred of sperm.
Thinking this rather too slow a business, and not having engaged for more than the cruise, I left.

Here, meeting with, what appeared to be, a fair
opening for another land-cruise, I entered it, by joining a surveying party, under orders from deputy-gov-

ernor Franklin. When we had been three months
out, our provisions were so far spent that it became
advisable to send down to the settlement for a fresh
supply. Another man and myself were detailed on
this service. Our outfit consisted of our blankets,
tomahawks, and two horses, with the quantity of provisions supposed to be ample for the time that our
journey to the settlement was expected to require.
Our pocket compasses—and they were parts of the
general equipment—enabled us to keep our course,
without difficulty, till, unfobbing one of the instru-
ments, we found the needle nodding to every point in
the horizon. And, to increase our consternation, we,
presently, discovered that the other was dancing to
the same tune. Just before rendering a verdict of
witchcraft, in the premises, we bethought us of the
possible neighborhood of iron ore; when, on examination, we found ourselves out-flanked to an unknown
extent, by a tract strongly impregnated with that min-
eral. This whole country, *as* a whole, is highly ferru-
ginous. The reader will, presently, perceive, that
the iron region, here immediately referred to, must
have been very large ; and such, if not more extensive, it will be found, whenever those interior depths
shall be explored, with which my late captivity made
me acquainted.

In hope of out-travelling the difficulty, we kept on,
as nearly in the direction of the settlement as we

could, under the circumstances, till the fifth day;
when our stock of provisions failed, and we began to
suffer for food. At this juncture, we fell in with a
party of natives, who appeared to be friendly. Hoping
that the language, acquired at so much expense,
would prove available, I addressed them in it, telling
them, that we wanted to go to the settlement. It was
Greek to the lubbers, and they stared, vacantly, and
shook their heads. On translating our question into
the language of signs, we were made to understand,
through the same medium, that the answer to it could
only be purchased at the expense of our blankets and
tomahawks. Reluctant as we were to make the sacrifice, the object appeared to demand, and we made it.
Upon this, our mercenaries accompanied us for a short
distance, till we found ourselves in a thicket of spear-
wood, so tangled that it was with extreme difficulty
we could proceed with our horses. Of course, we
proceeded slowly. Our guides, as guides *should* do,
walked ahead of us. But, presently, they were out
of sight. We hailed, but got no answer. The greasy,
and rascally copper-skins were gone, blankets, and
hatchets, and all !

The day was now spent. Benighted, as well as be-
thicketed and betricked, we laid ourselves down, un-
covered and fireless, for the night. The next morning,
with such appliances as we could yet command for
the purpose, we killed one of the horses; and, after

some time and difficulty in raising a fire, we satisfied
our hunger, roasted as much more of the flesh as we
could conveniently carry, and resumed progress. The
sun was still our only guide; for our compasses remained as useless as ever. While our "*fresh*" lasted,
our only suffering was for water; a state of things
which, neither in that respect, nor any other, met with
any alleviation during the next three days.

At the expiration of that time, we entered a tract
of sandy land, and found, to our great joy, that our
compass needles traversed. Still, as the line of coast,
occupied by the settlement, was quite limited, it was
impossible for us to tell which, of a given number of
directions, would intersect it. Adjusting this point,
however, as satisfactorily as possible, we proceeded
three or four hours, when we found ourselves intercepted by a lagoon, some ten miles in circumference.
At least, we hoped that the place, for the delay it was
to occasion us, would afford us water. But the month
was December, which, though early summer in the
southern temperate zone, had left us to the necessity
of digging for water, or doing without it. The former being the more eligible horn of an unpleasant
dilemma, we sharpened our sticks, and at it we went.
A depth of two feet, brought us what we were fain to
take for water; though *mud* is the word that would
have better suited the purpose of exact description.

On we went. Night came again. We slept, or

rather essayed to do so; but in vain, for we were fire-less, and the copious Australian dew made our teeth chatter the livelong night. And morning came, and with it our horse-beef breakfast. The beef was well enough; but—accidents will happen—it had become putrid, and bred—"what?" Fie! reader; fie! you know *what*, as well as anybody.

This day brought us the welcome sight of the ocean. At first we thought it was "*Oyster harbor*," which is situated ten miles east of King George's Sound; instead of which, after a little observation, we found, to our great chagrin, that it was Wilson's inlet. I had visited it before, and knew it to be thirty miles east of the Sound, and that we had to make a circuit of forty miles to avoid the inlet.

Leaving our surviving horse, now completely worn out with hardship, we shaped our course eastward, and, before the ensuing night, brought to, at the house of a settler, on the east side of the inlet, whose name was Craig. The hospitality so very promptly and kindly rendered us by this gentleman and his family, was not more grateful than it was necessary; for this was the fifteenth day since we had left our party at Cugenap.* Mr. C. insisted that we were unfit to proceed to the settlement; that we must stop with him

* The notes make no other mention of this place. It appears to have been the head-quarters of the party; but how situated, with regard to direction, or distance, from the Sound, we are left to infer from circumstances. The presumption is not improbable, that the

a number of days, after which, as he was going to that place with a wagon, he would carry us. Acting on this kind invitation, we arrived at the settlement, in company with Mr. C., twenty days after commencing our journey.

On presenting our returns to the commissary, Mr. Neal, that gentleman said, that we could have the supplies as soon as we pleased. To which I replied, that I was not able, and did not wish to return; suggesting, at the same time, that he had better send as soon as possible, as the party were much in need of provisions. To effect this, he was obliged to call on Mr. Warburton, the military commandant, who despatched the supplies by a party of soldiers.

In two weeks, when we were tolerably recruited, I asked the late companion of my land fortunes, who also, I had forgotten to say, was a brother salt, whether we should return to the surveying party, or go back on shipboard? To which he replied, that he chose rather to find himself on a lee-shore in a gale; and that, between being eaten by the sharks, or the native dogs of New-Holland, he had a decided preference for the former. And we shaped our course, accordingly; applying for, and receiving our wages of Mr. Phelps, and then shipping in the Garlin, Capt. Day, the only

name in question designates the site of a projected settlement on some river emptying into the ocean on the west coast, and probably much nearer the ocean in that, than in a southern direction.

craft then in the Sound, that was short of hands. She
was a whaler.

We were scarcely outside of Bald-Head, when we
fell in with a large school of sperm whale. Hauling
up close on the wind, till we were abreast of them,
the captain ordered the mate to back the main-yards,
and clear away the boats. The boats were lowered,
and pulled away; but just before we reached them,
they went down. We hove to, and waited. I was in
the mate's boat, and they came up close to us. The
mate told the boat-steerer to stand up and fasten to one
of them. This was no sooner done than the wounded
monster began to flurry at such a rate as to frighten
the rest, and scatter them in all directions. This
hugest of animals, as most readers are aware, moves
in its native element by the perpendicular action of a
horizontal tail, five feet long, by twenty-five in width,
more or less. Consequently, when a boat falls in with
such a motion, it is carried up or down, according as
that motion is ascending or descending, at the time.
To return to the hurry scurry, caused by the fright,
aforesaid; it chanced that one of the headlong cetacea,
found our boat a little in his tail's way; when, what
does he, but, very unceremoniously, put us out of
it. "In which direction? Upward or downward?"
Upward, reader of mine. The caudal force, at the
moment of contact, was acting in that direction; and
when that force was spent, and we, with the frag-

ments of our boat, had attained the culminating point,
my judgment was, that we were sprawling one dozen
feet in air. For my part, as compared with a sub-
marine journey, I was pleased with this short aerial excursion. For first; sent off in this direction, we were
almost sure of coming back again. Whereas, started
in the other, we, and especially I—*non natant*, as the
reader remembers me—could have counted on that
event with far less confidence. And then—but why
need my choice be justified by referring to the copious draughts of salt-water grog that had already fallen
to my share,—and to the natural aversion growing out
of a surfeit?

On descending to the water, nothing more was
necessary than for each of us to avail himself of as
large a piece of the wreck as he could, and 'bide his
time for being picked up. This we naturally expected from one of the boats, and pretty soon. But they
left us to spout, while they were paying *pointed* attention to other spouters. After having been an hour in
the water, we were picked up by the ship.

On gaining the ship, we immediately took a boat
from the *bearers*, and pulled off to help those who did
not help us. We found them, fast to two whales.
Just before reaching them, however, we heard a *blow*
to leeward, and before grampus went down, we had
fastened to him. He *sounded;* but before our line
was out, a *drag* had been bent on to the end of it. He

rose a mile to windward, and we pulled after, seized
the drag, got it into the boat, and pulled in our line.
Before we could reach him, however, he sounded
again; but not so deep as before. On his next appearance, and before he had time to go down again,
a lance reached his seat of life. He spouted blood.
By the time he *flurried* we were five miles from the
ship, and so far windward, that we were obliged to
tow him two hours, before the ship could pick him
up. When "cut in," which was not till the next
day, he filled ninety-two barrels; while each of the
other two made but thirty.

The next day, while "trying out," we saw signs
of more sperm, at a distance of three miles. We
lowered our boats, and took four of them. In short,
in this off-shore cruise of four months, we filled five
hundred and fifty barrels of sperm oil.

May, 1842, we returned to the Sound, where, as I
only engaged for the cruise, I received my share of
the oil, and disposed of it to good advantage. Thirty-
three miles from the Sound, is Two Peoples Bay.
Hearing that a ship was there, short of hands, I went
to the place. It is much frequented by whale ships.
After considerable hesitation, I went on board the
Harvest, Capt. Pendleton, of New-London, for the
season. In four months we had only taken four hundred and fifty barrels of right whale; and that, reader,
means nothing better than so much common *train* oil.

Nothing else—and that was a small exception—happened, till

Aug. 28th, when it came on to blow a gale. We were anchored in the bay, and were about trying out the blubber of a right whale, taken the day before. The swells rolled in from the sea at such a rate that we were obliged to let the try-works rest. Riding at anchor, we were very comfortable through the day, and felt safe. Toward sun-down, however, the gale increased, and still we felt secure. But, at about nine in the evening, our starboard chain parted, and before the other cable brought the ship's head to the wind, it parted also. Most of our sails were unbent, at this crisis, and had it even been otherwise, it would have been impossible to beat out of the bay in the teeth of such a wind. It was now plain, that the ship must go ashore. While drifting to our fate, we passed within a biscuit's throw of one of two other ships, in the bay at the same time, both of which rode out the gale in perfect safety. The one that we came so very near carrying with us, was a namesake—the bark Harvest, of Fair Haven; the other was the Peruvian, of the neighboring sea-port of New-London, Conn.

In nearly half an hour after parting our cables, we struck the beach. The sea was tremendous. The ship's bottom was out of her, and everything swept from her decks in an instant. The only chance of saving the crew, was by getting a line on shore. The

mate first, and I next, volunteered for that dangerous
service; presently, the requisite number, four, was
ready. As soon as it lulled a little, we lowered the
quarter-boat; but before her stern could be got to the
surf, a heavy roller struck her, capsized her, and in
that situation, threw us, boat and all, high on the
beach. But it was not high enough to prevent our
being carried nearly back to the wreck by the refluent
sea. The next surge, however, threw us so far out of
water, that, clutching some portions of the ship's
wreck, lying still farther out of it, we made good our
landing.

As soon as we had fairly regained our senses, we
looked for, and found our boat, which was lying a
few rods from us, bottom side up. She was immediately righted, and the ship was hailed, to pull her off.
But the wild uproar of the elements drowned our
voices. Then we *signalled* by pulling the line which
was attached to the ship; immediately upon which,
we were gratified by finding the boat in motion. She
went to the wreck; we pulled her to the shore;
again she was pulled to the ship, and yet again we
pulled her back to shore. By these means, though
she capsized in the time, and met with various mischances, we made her bring away the people of the
ship, till an accidental collision knocked in her bow,
rendering her useless. On pulling her to the beach,
we looked around in despair, as to any means of re-

lieving the rest of our companions, till joyfully surprised by finding our stern-boat lying at some distance
on the beach. And on overhauling her, our joy was
greatly increased when we found her whole. Soon
our lines were bent, and she was plying between the
ship and shore, which she continued to do, till, at
length, we sent her off for the captain and second
mate, the only persons remaining on the wreck. On
coming to, for the purpose of taking them in, she had
the misfortune to have a hole knocked in one of her
sides. After pulling her once more to the beach, and
seeing her situation, we were again at our wits' end.
After casting about some time for the means of repair, I told the mate that my oil-cloth jacket would
stop the hole, if we only had the means of nailing it.
Providentially, the means were in his pocket. The
breach was stopped; the boat was launched; but we
found no answering pull, and we were left to the
painful conclusion, that our poor captain and mate
had nobly labored to save the lives of others, till too
much spent to lend a hand in saving their own. To
leave them to their fate, was impossible. Three of us
threw ourselves into the boat, and put off; but when
we were alongside the ship, we got under her counter,
capsized, and were so nearly drowned when thrown
upon the beach, that it cost our comrades some little
time and labor to restore us. To be brief with what
remains, the boat. which was better manned for the

next effort, returned with the two officers; so that, between one and two in the morning, we were all on the beach, and, thank God! all alive.

A little circumstance, illustrative of a national peculiarity, may be worth mentioning. Belonging to the ship's crew were a couple of Portuguese, unable to speak a word of English. They had been shipped at Fayal, one of the western islands. As soon as the ship struck the beach, and was fairly on her beam-ends, the two poor fellows clasped the fife-rail, hard by the main-mast, and began praying right lustily for help, to *Saint Antonio!*

That morning the gale abated. We got what we could from the ship; stripped the rigging from the mast; and everything was sold at auction to the English settlers, who came down from King George's. Proceeding to that place, I entered the whale ship Elizabeth, Capt. Eastham, of New-Bedford.

CHAPTER XX.

Cape Rich, on the east coast, for supplies.—Sails for Australian gulf.—
Success there.—The Fegee islands.—Off and on at Rotuma.—Trade
with the natives.—Their friendliness, with other characteristics.—
Ashore on liberty.—Absconds.—Is concealed.—Betrayed.—Discovered.—Reclaimed.—Moral.—Four months in Otaheite.—Otaheite
and the Otaheitans.

SEPTEMBER 8, 1842. As the captain wished a supply
of vegetables, things not to be obtained at this place,
our anchors were shipped, our canvass was given to
the breeze, and we stood away for the eastern coast
of the island. Entering Cape Rich, we took in our
supplies, and then made sail for our fishing ground in
the Australian gulf. In the fear that a repetition of
details on the subject of this cruise would give my
narrative an overcharge of the *fishy* odor, I shall only
say, generally, that our success was equal to our
reasonable wishes.

Taking in sail, and heaving to, every night, for our
greater security, while navigating these reefy seas, we
sailed for the eastern islands, with the purpose, for the
present, of trading with the natives, as well as of obtaining supplies of water and fresh provisions; the

Elizabeth, like many other whale ships, having brought out goods for the former of these purposes. It was decided to take Otaheite and the Sandwich Islands, with a few intermediate places, in our way, and then to complete our cargo on the north-west coast of America.

We sailed by the Fegee islands; the Fegeans, having the reputation of being both inhospitable and treacherous, and most villanous cannibals, withal, we did not care to make their acquaintance.*

The wind being favorable, we made the little island of Rotuma. This island is situated in the twelfth degree of south latitude. Being very fertile, it is also very populous. All the productions of the most favored of the South Sea islands abound here. The day following our arrival, the natives, who seem to be a harmless people, came off in their canoes, in swarms, bringing every variety of fancy and useful article, which their little country afforded. Among the former, were sea-shells, spears, war-clubs, and, perhaps I should include, very fine mats, together with cocoa wood, for canes. The latter, included hogs, oranges, limes, lemons, pine-apples, mangroves, yams, with sweet potatoes, and pumpkins. Of money, they knew not the use. Two or three *hands* of tobacco would purchase four or five dollars worth of shells, and a

---

* According to recent intelligence, the king of these islands has embraced the gospel. Dec. 1850.

In about two hours, my guide returned, in company
with another native. He called, but received no answer. After waiting, and reconnoitring, however, till
satisfied that I was not ambushed, I made my appearance, and was introduced to the chief. Upon this, I
was reconducted to the beach, where, on coming to a
house, my two conductors led me in.

The first object which engaged my attention, was a
large basket, made of cocoa leaves and the bark of the
banana. It was full of provisions, and suspended over-
head, in the middle of the house. By means of a
pully, over which the suspending rope passed, it was
raised or lowered, as occasion required. Besides
baked swine's flesh, it contained baked yams, bananas,
and a root called *ofela*, resembling our potato. The
baking process is very neatly done, in the following
manner. Whatever is to be cooked in that way, is
first deposited in a cocoa leaf basket. The basket is
then deposited in a hole, dug in the ground, for the
purpose, and covered over with banana leaves. On
these, they place hot stones, prepared for the purpose,
and then cover the whole with earth, in which state it
is left till the confined heat has done its work. Thus
prepared, the edibles, either hot or cold, are laid on
wooden plates of their own manufacture, and these, on
a clean mat, spread out in the middle of the floor,
around which the guests gather, and every man helps
himself. Being invited, I took my seat in such a fes-

tive circle, and, bating the absence of salt, or other seasoning, made a very comfortable repast.

Dinner over, my new friends informed me, that I could not safely remain where I was, the ship being in plain sight, as also the boats in plying between the former and the shore. Accordingly, I was conducted to another house, in a more retired part of the town. Here there was a large pile of mats, and I was told that, if covered up in them, none would be able to find me. After some hesitation, I consented, and was so closely packed away, as to bring on a speedy and most beautiful perspiration. But, without exaggeration, the heat, together with the want of respirable air, was intolerable, and I bolted, though strongly urged by my benevolent wardens to remain passive. I had been seated a few moments when a posse of natives came up, and halted outside of the house. On looking through a low crevice, I saw, among several pairs of *naked* legs, one that was, unmistakably, *trousered.* Looking again, and listening withal, I heard one of the natives say—" *There !*" and saw him point to the door. The trousers entered, and—just as I feared—the skipper was in them, and he was armed with a musket. To his question, whether I did not want to return on shipboard, I answered, "No ;" and added, that I did not intend to do it. He rejoined, that he had none too many hands, and that I would have to go. My final answer was, point blank, " I

will do no such thing." On his part, the negotiation
ended with—"There can be no use in your cutting up
any capers. All the law there is in the island, is in
my own hands." As he said this, the "*law*" to which
he referred as being in his "own hands," was very
closely applied to my case, indeed; a case which I was
not exactly willing to have *opened* just then. To
quash so dangerous a proceeding—but I must drop
the legal allusions to tell how it *was* done—I dashed
aside the muzzle of the musket, and grappled the
skipper. Well was it for him, and perhaps for both
of us, that his native assistants were on hand in goodly
numbers. They seized me, carried me down to the
boat, and threw me in; the captain ordering the men
to lie off at some distance till he should be ready to
go off to the ship. Then, discharging the musket, he
gave it to the natives, telling them that it would pay
them for their trouble. In fact, they deserved good
pay, and there is little doubt that the rogues expected
it from the very first. Enticing a sailor to leave ship;
concealing him; then giving information, and aiding
in the capture and recovery of the runaway, is, probably, one of the oldest, and most profitable games
known to these shrewd people; and the remark is
more or less applicable to all the inhabitants of these
bland and happy islands. I was duped, hoaxed, hum-
bugged, in their most fashionable style. "I will stow
you away!" Umph! But a truce to all non-compla-

cent recollections. The skipper soon returned, and was taken into the boat, when we all returned on board the ship; the boat was hoisted up, the yards were braced forward, and that very night we stood out to sea.

As I was clearly in the wrong, in the whole of this island affair, it is but too obvious that the recital can procure me no sympathy from the intelligent and upright reader. It is matter of just regret to the writer, that the *moral* of this adventure, as well as that of several others, related, and to be related, is not less exceptionable. He offers, however, this compensating observation—or rather, that Providence offers it, who rules over the affairs of men—that whenever he is found astray from the path of rectitude, he is not only not a gainer by it, but a loser and sufferer. And so, on the whole, it ever must be, till moral order is reversed, and the fruit of the forbidden tree is *life*, instead of *death*.

Passing the Marquesas Islands, then under the protection of the French government, we rode into the most beautiful harbor of that most beautiful island of all islands, Otaheite, the gem of the South Pacific. The harbor, excepting a passage barely wide enough for a single ship, is completely shut in from the ocean by a bold coral reef. Once in, vessels are safe, and can ride at anchor, or, such is the boldness of the shore, haul up, and make fast to the cocoa-nut, or other

trees. Thus commodious for shipping, affording excellent water, and abounding in all the vegetable lux-
uries of a tropical climate, it is highly desirable, and
much frequented for refitting and recruiting purposes,
by all who use these seas. Its surpassing fruitfulness
denominates it The garden of the South Sea Islands ;
and well does it deserve that enviable distinction.
Field, or garden culture, is very little practised, and
what there is, is almost exclusively in the hands of
foreign residents. When, therefore, I say that there
is scarcely a rod of this island not yielding fruit, the
reader will understand me as referring mainly to the
indigenous productions of the country, as the bread-
fruit, banana, cocoa, with many others. I have seen
the ground so nearly covered with these and the other
varieties of fruit, and that too on the very margin of
the harbor, and in other situations where it was most
exposed, that it was all but literally impossible to
avoid treading on it. We lay here four months.

The custom of *making friends*, among the Otaheitans, is perhaps the best illustration with which the
reader can be furnished, of the amiable simplicity of
character by which they are distinguished.

When a ship comes into harbor, and before she is
fairly anchored, the native canoes are dancing around
her on every wave. Suppose yourself among the
new-comers, and that the eager islanders are permitted
to come aboard. You are accosted with : " You my

frenny *me*, me my frenny *you*." This, you perceive,
is a proposition that, if you will be a friend to him,
he will be a friend to you. If you assent to this offer,
you find yourself immediately presented with a basket
of fruit, by way of ratifying the engagement. From
that moment till you leave the island, he espouses your
interests with all the cordiality of a true attachment.
Every morning, about eight o'clock, you are sure to
see him alongside, with, most generally, a basket of
fruit, and a bottle of lime juice; and he expects you
to visit his house, and to share every accommodation
it can afford. In a word, he supplies you with everything you want. Of course, he expects, before you
leave, that you will remunerate him. If you are an
officer, he will probably think you ought to give him
a ruffled shirt, or a coat; or, perhaps, both. But, if
you belong to the forecastle, he appreciates the bestow-
ment of a cotton shirt, or a pair of duck trousers, and
he leaves you satisfied, and even thankful.

Like many of the Pacific and Indian islands, Otaheite has received the gospel. Indeed, she was among
the first who were visited by its benign influence. It
is deeply to be deplored that, from the greater activity
of secular enterprise, the *vices* of Christendom usually
out-travel its *virtues*, and are the first to strike root
and bear fruit in heathen countries. At best, if the
latter are ever beforehand, the former are sure to follow in their train. So that, while some are regenerate

by the one, others degenerate under the easily propagated influence of the other.   But the greatest obstacle to the elevation of these races, is their constitutional indolence.   Their physical wants being but few,
and simple ; the climate superseding the necessity of
clothing, and all they need for food springing sponta-
neously from the soil, it seems unreasonable to expect
that they should ever rise above the very lowest grade
of civilization, or that they should cultivate any of
the virtues, except such as are consistent with the
most fixed habits of disinclination to active and long-
sustained effort.   At all events, if any nation within
the tropics shall ever rise to a higher destiny, it will
be an occurrence unknown, as yet, to the history of
our race.   Reasoning from analogous cases, the presumption is, that, in the lapse of time, these island
communities will be amalgamated with offshoots of the
hardier and more enterprising nations of the Cauca-
sian type.   If such be the inevitable tendency of
events, under the operation of the fixed laws of Heaven, Christianity will *save* these imbecile people, not
by preserving, but by *destroying* their nationality.

L*

CHAPTER XXI.

Otaheite, and the Otaheitans, continued; wherein is contained an account of the author's twofold captivity, by the captivating islanders;
as, first, how he ran away, because he was captivated; and, secondly,
how he was captivated because he had run away—the latter branch
of the subject being unfolded to the reader in various captivating
details, which end the chapter.

NOTWITHSTANDING the recent maladventure among
the Rotumese, all the incentives of it were still existing, and in active operation. To which was added, in
the way of natural consequence, the desire of resto-
ring myself to my own, rather large, sense of self-
complacency, and, at the same time, to vindicate myself from the dishonor I was under, in the estimation
of others, from that ill-managed enterprise. And
then—it may as well be honestly confessed, for the
reader will more than half suspect me of it, at any
rate—that I was not totally insensible to the attrac-
tions of this island-paradise. In a word, I was faily
captivated. The upshot was, that, from the moment
this scene of enchantment first broke upon my sight, I
was decided to add another to the number of its free
and happy inhabitants, at the earliest opportunity.
This, however, did not occur till two days before

the ship was to leave port. On the occasion, here referred to, being ashore on liberty, with a couple of my shipmates, we agreed on a stroll up into the country, to a place which I must phonographize, as *Townore*. In many other cases, indeed, as well as in this, I am left to the necessity of writing foreign names, phonetically—*i. e.* according to the real "*Anglo Sacsun*" of things. Should the reader ever visit the place, he will find it at the distance of one and a half miles from Barkadas,* the town before which the good ship Elizabeth was now lying at anchor.

Here, deeming that the proper moment for effecting my cherished purpose had arrived, I invented a pretext for leaving my comrades for a few moments, which I had no sooner effected, than I struck for the back part of the island. When the reader perceives, as he soon will, that this was the day of the Otaheitan Sabbath, he is to conclude neither favorably nor unfavorably in regard to our seafaring morality. The fact is, that the reckoning of time in the island, places their Sunday a day too soon, according to ours. And it comes from this: that, instead of reaching the place by way of Cape Horn, as our ship did, the missionaries, whose computation of time was naturally adopted by their converts, came to the island by way of Cape Good Hope.† Pursuing my upland path

* "Papèta."—McCulloch.

† "In consequence of the early missionaries having reached this

three or four miles, it led me to a native place of worship. As it had the appearance of containing an assembly, I went to the door. It was sermon time. Satisfied, by listening a moment, that the discourse, which was in the vernacular of the audience, could minister nothing of special utility to me, I silently withdrew. As I was doing this, however, an undevout outsider accosted me in broken English, asking where I was going. My reply, which was evasive, contained something about returning to my ship; and it hardly need be said that my disappearance was in that direction. But then, as soon as the church was fairly lost sight of, I left the road, and resumed the ascent of the shaded slope leading to the top of the island.

In explanation of the sudden change of scene, about to be introduced, the reader will naturally infer that my comrades, on missing me, returned to the beach, and, the skipper being there, reported my disappear-

place by way of the Cape of Good Hope, they were a day before us in their time. We were, therefore, yesterday—Saturday, by our reckoning, and Sunday by theirs—presented with a most striking proof of the alteration in their habits since the time of Wallace and Cook. Not a canoe was seen afloat; but the people cleanly dressed, and the women with bonnets, after the European fashion, were observed returning from divine service, with their psalm books under their arms, and proceeding quietly to their homes, after stopping on their way to gaze at the English man-of-war, which they had so long expected. But this morning brought to our view quite a different scene. All was bustle. The ship was surrounded with canoes, filled with fruit, &c., and the men were not a little astonished and hurt, when repulsed in the attempt to come on board, in the droves that offered.—*MS. Journal of a Voyage of Discovery.*"

ance.　He will naturally infer, also, that that gentleman, with his knowledge of something a little like
errantry in the habits of the absentee, had enlisted the
male natives in my recapture, by the offer of a sufficiently stimulating reward.　These preliminaries are
due, no less to my amiable island friends, as excusa-
tory of the part they are about to act, than to myself,
for not acting my own part any better, after having
been on the stage before in the same character.　The
fact is, reader, though I was very slow in coming to
the knowledge of it, that successful desertion, from
any branch of sea service, among these islands, is
next to impossible.　The skippers' longer purse always
enables him to render it an object with the native population to make common cause against all interlopers.

Having left the native church, in the way already
noted, I was climbing the acclivity of the mountain
landscape, full of the bright dreams which the prospect of life in this enchanted island was so well calculated to inspire, when, all at once—it was sudden as
the bolt of fate—I first measured my full length on
the ground, and was then dragged down hill, till I
landed in the road.　Without knowing *how*, any more
than *why*, I found myself in the hands of four sturdy
Otaheitans.　Nearly as soon as the road arrested the
down-hill tumble, I was once more on my feet, and
one of my fine fellows was on his beam-ends.　The
rest would have followed in quick succession, but for

the conclusion they appeared to have come to, that *driving*, rather than *leading*, would be the safer *modus operandum*. One of them went ahead; the rest brought up the rear. Before being able to settle upon any plan of freeing myself from my escort, we were nearing a large house. The van leader entered, the main procession, in the mean time, continuing to descend the road till, on entering a bridge which led over a brook, I saw a heavy stick beneath me on the ground, and near the side of the stream. Leaping from the bridge and taking it in my hand, I told my pursuers, with a significant flourish of the crab-stick to enforce it, to keep at a due distance, or——. At this moment he who had entered the house, reappeared, advancing upon me with a quick step, bringing with him a carpenter's adze, together with some ten fathoms of rope.

When within ten yards, he ordered me to stop; notwithstanding which, I continued my retreat, still keeping my face to the foe, all of whom, save the one with the adze, were armed with bludgeons. Satisfied, by my bearing, that capitulation was out of the question, they now charged, and the adze missed my head by about two inches. Plainly enough, the affair was to end in no child's play. My shellala anticipated the next stroke from my most dangerous assailant, and his calabash rattled like a miss's bag of biscuit. He reeled and fell. This took them all aback, and they were only prepared to renew the onset when reinforced by a couple of men from a neighboring house. Not counting the wounded, there were now five of them, and all armed; and so thick were the cudgels that hung over my head, that, finding I could not raise mine, to hit another cranium, I made it tell upon a pair of shins. The consequence was a sudden bow, which reached the ground. But my part in the game of sticks was now up. The undisabled four were all upon me at once. Indeed, from the moment my stick became useless, the contest was as good as ended; for, though a rather hard fist fell fast and heavy, clubs were harder, and fell faster. But even the power of pommelling them was soon taken away, by these loving friends of mine; for as my arm was raised to repay the heavy debt I owed them, it was suddenly arrested. They had come upon me from behind, and, in a trice, my arms were pinioned. True, the struggle was desperate; but even the tiger gnashes and writhes in vain, when once fairly entangled with the boa-constrictor. More luckless than the hero of "*Sampson Agonistes,*" I could not say:

"My *heel* is fettered, but my *fist* is free;"

for, however free the former, the latter was powerless, alike, for good or evil.

To heighten the interest of the scene, the hero of the long rope, who had been left astern on his beam-

ends, now righted ship, and came up, muttering and
staggering, and rubbing the sore place on his head.
But he had not forgotten the rope. This enabled my
captors, by belaying my two hands behind me with
one end, to tow me wherever they pleased with the
other. When they had walked me on our back track,
a short distance, a sense of the indignity of my position rose to such a pitch, that I could not resist the
temptation to try the effect of my right boot on the
stern-post of him who was leading me by one end of
the towline, while I was ignominiously following at
the other. The distance that parted us varied from
eighteen to twenty-four feet, as the rope was slack or
otherwise.—A sea-boot, by the way, and that, reader,
was the style of boot in question, is not exactly an
imponderable, nor, consequently, an altogether *bootless*
affair.—Its sudden and rather forcible application, aided the effect of a natural surprise, so that the fellow
went ahead in the world, at least six feet, before he
knew it, and then he wondered some time, as to what
it was that sent him. It became probable, however,
that by some means the boot got into his philosophy of
the case; for he took smart care to keep it at such a
safe distance, that I could hardly "bid him the time
of day," till we brought to, at the house which had
kindly furnished the rope.

Into this, I was pushed and pulled, and when in,
was made fast to the central post, by which the roof

was sustained. After keeping me here an hour, they *cast me loose*, ordering me to walk across the road to a small house standing hard by the sea-shore. As soon as I was unfastened, they began to knock and kick me about, in a manner so unprisoner-like, that I was compelled to use the whole pair of sea-boots to convince them that, if they *would* play at that sort of game they could not have it all to themselves, any how. This demonstration induced a change of purpose, in favor of remanding me to the centre-post of my recent quarters. This they did in such a way as left me no power of moving, either hand or foot, and with such a force of ligature as stopped the circulation in all my limbs, especially in my arms, causing a sensation as if a hundred pounds' weight were suspended by each of my fingers. It was in vain that I implored them to ease away upon the rope. The cente-post could have been as easily propitiated. At this crisis, a native entered who belonged to the queen's army, then lying at the back side of the island. To him, I offered a quarter of a dollar if he would slack the rope, which, after talking to the rest a while in their common language, he did, to my unspeakable relief. Soon after this, the rope was once more *unbent* from the post, and I was dragged with great violence, toward the place of my former destination. Seeing a party of white men coming up the road, at a distance, my loving attendants, fearing a rescue, were in the act of throwing me over the fence,

17

in order to the greater security of the interest they had
in me. This attempt, however, was prevented by the
coming up of the party. My first impression of them
was, that they were man-of-war's men; but a nearer observation showed them to be gun-room stewards, captain's clerk, purser, and others of that sort of gentry,
from whom a common sailor can expect but precious
little sympathy.

Telling them who I was, and the name of my ship,
I asked them to help me out of a bad scrape. They
wished to know if I desired them to accompany me to
my ship. Of course, I answered affirmatively. And
then it was that I once more reckoned without my
host; for, feeling certain that I was on the point of
parting with my dear native friends, it appeared no
more than fair, that they should be settled with for all
the trouble they had given themselves on my account;
and so, without any more words on the subject, I
"pitched into them, right and left." Upon this, what
did those half-salt chaps do, seeing that I was not quite
ready to accept of their protection, but take themselves off, leaving me to finish my adventure in my
own way. The lubbers! I was now in a worse box
than ever; for, as soon as the fear of a rescue was
over—I was too busy at the moment to notice it myself—they began to pull away upon the rope. The
reader, probably enough, thinks that it would have
been wise to postpone this thrashing operation till I

had been fairly loose. But who can think of so many
things at once? This time the towline pulled in the
backward direction of the calaboose. Thither, when,
they had dragged me, and in a style which was plainly meant to offset against the thrashing account, they
tied me, for the third time, to the perpendicular fixture, afore-described, where I was kept for the rest of
the day. At night, I was permitted to lie down, my
hands being fastened to the post. Then, fixing a large
bamboo stick in the ground, they placed a cocoa-nut
shell filled with oil, having a wick in it, by way of lamp,
on the top of it. It only remained that they should
divide the night into watches; and, to render them
effective, they were armed with a couple of muskets
obtained, in the way of trade, with foreign ships.

In the morning a native came in, who had the use
of a little English. I told him that I wanted to see
the American consul. After communicating with the
rest, one of them said he would go and see that officer,
and left for that purpose; though he did not return
till nearly noon. In all this time, there was not offered me a mouthful of food. The messenger reported
the consul as saying, that he knew nothing about me:
that they must bring me down to town, when he would
be able to tell what ship I belonged to. Whereupon,
without loss of time, the towline was stretched in the
townward direction. In about two miles, we were
met by a gentleman on horseback, who proved to be

that gentleman himself. As he was about to pass, I ventured to say, that I wished to speak with him; upon which he stopped. I then said: "I belong to the ship Elizabeth, of New Bedford. I came ashore yesterday on liberty, and in two hours was taken up by the natives, on suspicion of having run away from my ship." The worthy gentleman replied, that he was going round to the backside of the island, and could not spend time to talk with me then. But, after speaking a few words with my attendants in their language, he added: " I have told them to take you back to the place from which they brought you, and to fetch you to my house to-morrow. I am in a hurry, and have not time to see about it to-day." So saying, he gave his horse the spur, and left me to my native friends, and my native reflections.

With some exceptions, a common sailor may as well " whistle to a milestone," as talk to a consul. He *never* has time to attend to *him*. But let a captain go ashore with a barrel of beef or pork, or even a good smoked ham or two, and that agent is always at leisure, and is all attention to the slightest wish of his nautical friend. All this comes of money, or the want of it.

My attendants immediately countermarched me, till the consul was out of sight, when they suddenly put about, and with a rap of one of their sticks, and other signs, manual and oral, made me understand that this

was the way to my ship. On arriving at the beach
—and there were more than fifty aborigines about me
by that time—they brought me to the house where
Capt. Eastham was stopping. Sending them on with
me to the boat, the captain followed, and, with me
and my original captors, went off to the ship. Ten
dollars, paid these precious fellows, left them, I dare
say, very well satisfied; though, considering numbers,
time, and divers little items of tribulation in the
premises, as the reader has seen, I must say, as an
impartial umpire, that it was none too much.

The skipper returned on shore. The ship, with
orders to stand off and on for three days, got under
weigh, and I was left in irons for that length of time,
that I might mature my captivating fancies on the
captivating charms of a charming life among the
captivating inhabitants of the charming little island
of Otaheite.

CHAPTER XXII.

Touches at the Sandwich Islands.—Their volcanic origin.—Soil and climate.—Spontaneous productions.—General state of cultivation. —Hawaii and its fire-crowned mountain.—Oahu with its capital and royal city.—The islands indebted, for their rescue from savagism, to the gospel.—Their progress in civilization and the arts.— Cruise on the N.W. coast.—Success there.—The two unfortunate ships.—Return to the Sandwich group.—Cruise off New Zealand.— Doubling the Horn.—Touches at Tristran da Cunha for water.— Notice of the place.—Quarrel between the captain and mate.— Sails for Brazil.—Stops at Trinidade.—Eaters the harbor of Bahia. —Sale of cargo.—Tranships to a Brazilian man-of-war.—Regulations of Brazilian and Argentine naval service.—Incidents of a six months' service.

IT was on the third day of my painful separation from this gem of an island—and I was prepared to testify that its inhabitants had very " *taking* ways ;" that they had very forcibly *impressed* me in their favor, and that I was so *loaded* by the obligations they had laid me under, and bore so many *marks* of their *overpowering* regard, that I was unfit for duty, and could hardly rest day or night—it was on that day, that our good ship, standing in shore, sent off the captain's gig, which brought that important functionary to his more immediate post of duty on our quarterdeck. This, as will naturally be concluded, was an

event not altogether unwelcome to me, as it closed
the period of that disability under which I had been
laboring from the operation of causes now sufficiently
familiar to the reader. *En route* for the north-west
coast of America,

May 1, 1843, we arrived at the Sandwich Islands,
where we lay fourteen days. This length of time,
with another, much more considerable, on our return,
afforded opportunity for a few observations, which
will be thrown together in this place.

These islands are ten in number; and, like the Marquesas, are supposed to be of volcanic origin.* They
lie within the tropic of Cancer, about one third of the
distance from the western shore of America to the
eastern coast of China. Thus situated, in reference to
the equator; the larger, rising into lofty mountains,
and all surrounded by the ocean; they enjoy a climate as salubrious and agreeable as their soil is fertile. The bread-fruit, the cocoa-nut, the orange, and
other fruits, together with the taro, and many other
edible roots, are produced in great abundance, and
some of them entirely without cultivation. As distinguished from other kindred branches of rural industry, agriculture is hardly known among these
rich and beautiful islands.† And so abundant are
the spontaneous productions of the soil, that it can
hardly ever be expected to yield a native population

* See Appendix C. † See Appendix D.

distinguished for enterprise, in that, or, indeed, in any direction. Hawaii is the largest of the group, and is crowned with a mountain—Mouna Roa—which rises 16,000 feet above the level of the ocean; while Kirauea invests it with a grandeur more than equal to its queenly dignity. Oahu, however, is the island, and Honolulu—otherwise, Honoruru—the city, of the royal residence. This island, while the whole group is supposed to have a population of 140,000, contains, by approximation, 20,000, and the capital 7,000. Oahu is the most romantic, and is thought to be the most fertile of any of the group. It is 46 miles in length, and about 23 miles broad. Its appearance, from the sea, is remarkably picturesque. A chain of lofty mountains rises near the centre of the eastern part of the island, and extends nearly twenty miles.* It has a good harbor; is already inhabited by many foreigners, chiefly Americans and English, who have established themselves here for purposes of trade; while, at the same time, the place is the resort of the numerous whale ships in this part of the Pacific.

To estimate the value of the changes in the social and moral condition of these islanders, consequent on Christian influence, one should be definitely advised as to their previous actual state. He should have seen them, as Cook saw them, living in voluptuous idleness; in promiscuous debauchery; in the prac-

* Sailors' Magazine.

tices of cannibalism and infanticide; ignorant of God as the beasts that perish. And then, before denouncing as insignificant the changes in question, he should have counted their cost—the severe, patient, long-continued labor, by which the habits of such a people must have been eradicated, and a taste for industry, and the arts and usages of civilized life implanted in their stead. Then let him look into the native schools; introduce him to the domestic circle, and especially at the moment when the Hawaian Gazette arrives, moist from the press; let him mark the quietness of one of their rural Sabbaths; follow the cleanly groups of glad-hearted parents and children to the secluded church; listen to their hymns; see them bowed in prayer, or, with eyes beaming intelligence, catching the accents of the word of life. Let him, I say, do all this, and then, if he have the heart to do it, pronounce the Christianity and civilization of these islands a failure. For more ample information on these subjects, however, the reader must look beyond the limits of these pages.

Having now recruited ship, we made sail for the N.W. coast, where, in four months, we only took six hundred barrels of right whale, while other ships, on the same ground, and in the same time, took three thousand, and over. While here, we spoke a ship from Newport, which had lost her captain and a boat's

M

crew; and a French ship, which had lost three boats' crews.

But the season was up, and being warned away from these high latitudes by the premonitory blasts of an arctic winter, we headed once more for the Sandwich group; where, after remaining a month, we recrossed the equator, cruised on the coast of New Zealand four months, and then sailed round the Horn.

Being short of water, we hove to, off one of the "Nightingale Isles," named—probably by its Portuguese discoverers—*Tristran da Canha.** The agricultural enterprise and thrift of the little English settlement on this island, enable them to supply the ships which stop, as many do, for the purpose, with most of the vegetables, including a superior quality of potatoes, as well as various other things, which are needed. But, as already intimated, our leading object was water.

The landing-place, which was naturally poor, is rendered much worse by an almost constantly heavy surf. We had landed seven pipes, and filled them with water of a most delicious quality, which gushes from the rocks hard by the landing, when, the wind springing up, in the mean time, the captain, who was on shore, sent the boat off to the ship, with orders to keep a sharp lookout for his signal, which was to denote the earliest opportunity of getting off the water;

* For a highly interesting note on this island, see Appendix E.

upon which the boat was to returr, and bring it and him aboard ship. Now, while the land is fruitful, as we have seen, the adjacent waters are prolific of the most delightful fish. It fell out, in consequence, that the mate, thinking more of a nice *chowder* than of the skipper's signal, took a boat's crew rnd put off for the *wherewithal.* As for the signal afor said, it had been flying so long before he saw it and got to shore, that the skipper was brimful of wrath. The way he swore and called names was awful. At length the subaltern so far forgot his propriety, that, withott the shadow of a license from his superior, he swore and called names by way of retaliation, and ended with a wish— the exact words in which such things are done are considered out of place in a book; but the substance of the wish was, that skipper and ship wert both in a very uncomfortable place. Now, the reader must be sensible, that, in all well-regulated ships, from a whaler to a man-of-war, the right of personal invective, as between a superior and his subordinates, is a regular monopoly in the hands of the former. Such an outrage on his dearest rights deserved the most summary punishment on the spot, and would have met it, had not the perpetrator eluded a heavy blow, aimed at his unmannerly caput, by the outraged and outrageous skipper. The breach was now past healing. Indeed, the fact was, that things had been coming to this complexion for some time, and if forecastle

gossip told true, the two had not pulled well together
from the very time of leaving New-Bedford. The
mate—this appellation being always used, by way of
eminence, for the *first*-mate—the mate was sent off to
the ship, as a prisoner, in custody of the third-mate,
with orders to the second-mate, then on board the
ship, to take the command till the captain's arrival.

After we got on board, however, the deposed officer
called all hands aft, on to the quarter-deck; stated his
grievance, and told them, that they were not *men*, if
they would do another *handsturn* of work, before they
saw him put to his duty. But, poor fellow! it was
all day with him; for, except in his own boat's crew,
he was not exactly popular among the men. Had
the second-mate been in his place, I believe there was
not a man on board that would not have stood by him
to the last shot in the locker. As it was, though none
of the men were precisely indifferent, none felt quite
willing to hazard a mutiny in his favor; a result
which the captain shortly provoked by carrying his
resentment beyond all just limits.

When the excited skipper came aboard, and found
the *ci-devant* still walking the quarter-deck, he ordered
him to walk forward, and never show himself there
again, as long as he remained in the ship. This was,
probably, right enough, and at any rate, it was looked for, as a thing of course, and the degraded officer
went forward into the waist, and seated himself on the

top of the bulwarks. This latter act having been noticed by the excited skipper, he came forward, first venting the most violent abuse, and finally striking the object of his passion in such a way, as all but sent him overboard. The ex-mate's boat-steerer, who was not far off, and saw the outrage, dashed between the parties, and grappled the captain. This, with the interference of the second-mate, was the signal of a scene of disorder which must soon have ended in an open mutiny, had not the skipper seen that he was getting on to a lee-shore, and showed himself willing to get off without as great a loss of authority, as he had already suffered in point of dignity.

To conciliate us all, we were called to the quarter-deck, soon after this *emeute*, and asked, whether we wished to cruise off shore till we had got 400 barrels more of right whale, or whether we had better proceed to the coast of Brazil, and see if we could find a market for what we already had. We declared unanimously for the Brazils. So leaving Tristran, water-pipes and all, we stood away that very night, crowding all sail for the coast. The want of water induced us to stop at the island of *Trinidade*—not the West Indian *Trinidad*—but lying off the coast of Brazil. Our search for water was fruitless; for, save a stinted growth of wood, the island is bare of everything. With a few boat-loads of the latter, we returned to the ship, and continued our course till we gained the an-

cient harbor of San Salvador, now Bahia, in about the
twelfth degree of south latitude. Here we quenched
our thirst, and sold our cargo. And here, too, a fair
opportunity offering, I quitted the Elizabeth, and
identified my fortunes, for six months, with a Brazilian
man-of-war—the Cassadore.

Before noticing the few events—and they are but a
few—connected with this short period of my history,
it seems proper, with the reader's good leave, to refer,
briefly, to Brazilian matters generally, and to the state
of the naval war-service, in particular.

It will, of course, be recollected, that all the American colonies of Spain and Portugal, taking advantage
of the domestic troubles of the parent States near the
commencement of the present century, revolted, and
succeeded in effecting their independence. These
countries are now divided into a great number of
separate, and ill-governed republics, with the exception of Brazil, which is a monarchy, whose chief wears
the title of Emperor. It must be equally known, that
these states, nearly ever since they became independent, on one pretext and another, have been engaged
in mutual wars. This is, especially, true of the Empire of Brazil, on the one hand, and her jealous and
powerful neighbor, the Argentine Republic on the
other. At the period now referred to, hostilities were
in a state of great activity, and carried on with a ran-
cor totally unworthy of civilized and Christian nations.

Of this, however, the reader will find more in another
place.

The regulations of their naval service differ from
those of the British and American, chiefly in the
greater frequency and severity of punishment. For
instance—and I name it, because it belongs to a class
of cases incomparably larger than any other—a man
is aloft furling or unfurling sail, or exercising the top-
gallant mast or yard, and does something wrong: he
is called down; takes a hundred lashes, while the
other men remain aloft, and is then sent back to finish
his work. The hundred, however, is the *minimum*
for that class of offences. I have seen a case of that
kind—followed by three hundred, and confinement
in double irons. But as there is likely to be occasion
for renewing this subject, in connection with some
future service in the Buenos Ayrean navy, I drop it
for the present, to remark, in a word, on the kindred
subject of rations.

Of meat, the per diem allowance is half a pound.
Of bread, a half pound goes to each meal; to which,
with the meat, there is added, in the morning, a half-
pint of coffee. Dinner, beside the allowance of bread
and meat, is attended with a poor soup, made of the
water in which the meat has been boiled. And, to
finish the daily fare, the second and third meals are
accompanied by a *stew*, of a black kind of bean, made
palatable by a seasoning of sweet oil. And then there

is the grog; a glass at 11 A. M; another at 12 M., and
the third at sundown. The application of these
stimuli to the *stomach*, is just as unfailing as that of the
bamboo to the back, in default of the veriest punctilio
in handling the ropes and canvass of the ship—I say
bamboo, in this place, having omitted it in its more
fitting connection—for, instead of honorably flogging
a fellow with the cat, as if he were a *man*, they outrage
his self-respect, by caning him, as if he were a *dog*.

These general remarks, applying, as they do, to the
Brazilian and Buenos Ayrean naval service, indifferently, will have their use when the subject of this narrative is found acting, as, after a little interlude, he will
be, in connection with the naval operations of the
belligerent republicans. In the mean time, the matters
relating to his present position will be despatched in
the two ensuing paragraphs, with which it is intended
to close this chapter.

After lying five weeks at the island of Fernando,
on the northern coast of the empire, for the purpose
of protecting the interests of our commerce in those
parts, we returned to Pernambuco. On our arrival,
we received orders to proceed immediately to Bahia;
and, accordingly, got under weigh for that place the
same night. On making that point, the Deucalion, the
commodore's ship, made a signal for our commander
to come on board.

Belonging to the captain's gig, I was a witness of

what passed between the two officers. It appears that the commodore had received certain complaints against the captain. At all events, there was hard talk between the two, which ended in an order to our captain to return to his ship, and confine himself to his cabin, till superseded in his command, when he was to be sent to Rio Janeiro, to be tried by a court-martial. In three or four days the *supercedaneum* took command of us; and we of the forecastle pretty much agreed that he was an improvement. However, before that question was fully settled, the term of my enlistment—six months—was ended, and so also is this chapter.

M*   18

CHAPTER XXIII.

Sins against his English conscience, by joining the crew of a slave ship.—Reach the coast.—The slave factor.—The live cargo.—The home passage.—Chased by a British man-of-war.—Narrow escape of being boarded by one of his boats.—Make the coast of Brazil.—Another escape, though not without a scratch for it, which proves a little sanguinary.—Land the cargo.—Leaves the slaver, with fair promises never to give his countrymen another chance of hanging him to the yard-arm for a pirate.

As these sketches have been drawn up with the determination of making them true to the shadows as well as the lights of my humble life, the reader is now to be made acquainted with what he will, probably, regard, as, indeed, I do, as the darkest portion of my history. I speak of my connection with the slave trade.

A shipmate of mine in the Cassadore, went ashore with me at the Rio, who was a Portuguese, from one of the western islands. To keep his company was the more of an object, as his native language, while I was with him in this part of the world, was likely to be of special service to me, and might prove a matter of high importance ; especially as he had the command of my vernacular as well as his own. Our first object was the merchant service. But, failing in that, and falling in with the captain of a slave-trader, in an evil hour we both shipped with him for a piratical cruise to the coast of Africa. She was owned and fitted out in Bahia, by a Frenchman, who ought to have been hung, by the name of Gauterpe. The *name* may possibly be *wrong.* The *hanging*, to a certainty, would have been *right.* Our wages were $25 per month, with a bonus of 400 millreas, *provided* we returned without being taken by an English or American man-of-war.

We sailed with a crew of thirty-five men, and five guns, beside four twelve-pound carronades, and a long thirty-two pounder in midships. Our passage out was quick, and, however perilous, brought us into no actual contact with anti-piratical guns and cutlasses.

To obviate the consequences of more than the least possible delay, there were standing arrangements with agents on the coast to have everything in readiness. As soon as we arrived in the bay, therefore, without letting go an anchor, we backed our main-top-sail, and raised our signal ; when we soon saw a canoe coming off, pulled by four negroes, with a large mulatto, seated in the stern. This was the *slave-factor.* The rum, beads, and tobacco, had enabled him to buy up the requisite quota, and nothing remained but to send them off as fast as a fleet of canoes and paddles could do it. Short was the conference between the yellow scamp and the whitish one. " *Quick*"—was the word with

which they parted. " *Quick!—Quick!*"—went boom-
ing after the yellow rascal, as his black minions pulled
him away for the beach: and "Quick!—Quick!"—
were echoed back to the *whitish* villain from his half-
bleached brother. And the freighting operation was
done accordingly. For scarcely had the conscienceless
mulatto gained the shore, when a large flotilla of
canoes was thrown into a state of high activity, and
began to come off with the coffled victims of the ac-
cursed traffic, about as fast as our weasel-faced French
skipper could tumble them into the hold. Our ship
would contain five hundred, and I believe we left the
coast with our full complement. While this dark
transaction was going forward—and blackballing would
not have improved the beautiful jet of its complexion—
we were standing off and on, with a sharp lookout
for the cruisers. Scarcely had the two hundred and
fiftieth pair of the chained wretches been tumbled down
the hatchway, and the hatches were not yet fairly
closed, when a favorable wind was fast bearing us
away from the negro's home.

As my duties confined me exclusively to the working
of the ship, while she was taking in her human cargo,
I was by no means sorry that, save occasionally and
at a distance, I did not even witness the *handling* of it
by others. This reflection is certainly a very inadequate protection to an enlightened conscience; but
poor as it is, it is better than nothing. But what I

wished to say is this: the circumstance of my position, during the shipment of the slaves, puts it out of my power to inform the reader, positively, as to their age and sex. My impression is, however—and, by means not now remembered, it has come to be a fixed one—that the people we brought away were all young men and boys. Most of the latter must have been taken from their mothers, and some of them were young enough to *need* them. Of the former, all were old enough to have contracted marriage, while not a few must have been *fathers* as well as *husbands*. But to return to matters that are less out of my line.

At half-past one the next morning, mine being the morning watch, I saw, by the clear moonlight, a sail on our weather bow, which I took to be an English man-of-war brig. Whoever he was it was as clear as moonlight could make it, that he felt an interest in us, for he was crowding all sail in chase. "Sail ho!". from the masthead, was followed by the skipper's quick—"Where away?" and this was answered by—"A point and a half on the weather-bow." With true Gallic agility he sprang to the masthead, when no sooner did he bring his glass to bear than, with the usual—*Sacre Dieu!* he pronounced: "Dat ish von shairk." It was in vain that we piled on the canvass. The breeze freshened; and it was in his favor, till we double-reefed our top-sails. For the next forty-eight hours, he had as much as he could do to keep in sight

of us. Then the wind died away, and he was overhauling us again, till we raised our sweeps—eight of
them; four on a side—which carried us at the rate of
three or four knots an hour; while the chase, being
nearly becalmed, must have seen that, as things were
going, we were likely to get away from him.

At this juncture, he lowered a couple of his boats,
and *bent* them on to the brig, for the purpose of towing her up to us. Still we had the satisfaction of seeing that our sweeps were slowly increasing the distance
between us. Then it was, that one of the boats, with
a lieutenant, put off with the obvious intention of
boarding us. Aware that if John Bull catched me
on board a slaver, it would be mighty apt to go hard
with me, I could only resolve, first, to fight hard, and
so, if possible, keep off his grappling irons; or, secondly, worst coming to worst, to use my little stock
of Portuguese in such a way as, if possible, to prevent
a recognition by my brother Britishers, altogether.
Still, it was easy to see, that if my brave countrymen
were once aboard of us, the chances would be sadly
against me, and occasional glimpses of futurity, made
me think I saw a figure dancing at the yard-arm, bearing an uncomfortable resemblance to *William Jackman*.

Our guns were double-shotted with grape and ball,
and we pulled away at the sweeps; but the hostile
boat was now in hailing distance. With a pistol in
each hand, the skipper paced the quarter-deck, with

a quick step, and throwing quick glances, the while,
at the approaching enemy, as if to measure the lessening distance between them and us.   On the eve of
what appeared likely to prove a deadly conflict, he
ejaculated his orders, relating, alternately, to the working of the ship, and to the working of guns and cutlasses.   By the former, we were to keep clear of the
man-of-war, and by the latter, he hoped to beat off
the determined fellows who proposed to board us from
the boat.   Now came words of encouragement and
promise; and anon a dark avalanche of mingled
threats and curses.   The upshot of it all was, that, if
necessary, we must all fight like the ——, till we were
all dead, at any rate; and how much longer, he did
not say.   And, for the special encouragement, as I
thought, of the Portuguese, who are unconscionable
cowards; he swore that he would blow out the brains
of the first man who faltered in his duty.

As soon as *le capitaine* thought the boat was near
enough, he hailed the officer to say, that he did not
wish to hurt him, but that, if he came any nearer, he
would fire into him; adding, that he had better return
before getting himself into trouble.   The boat said
nothing, but pulled ahead.   The warning was quickly
repeated, but with the same effect.   The Frenchman
snatched and discharged a musket, which broke the
Englishman's arm; and still, without a word, he pulled
right on.   In this crisis, not willing, as yet, to call

the men from the sweeps, and thus endanger a nearer
acquaintance with the brig, the man at the wheel and
the first and second mates were called to the small
arms, which were lying ready-loaded on the deck,
when they, with the captain, levelled and fired, with
such effect, that two of the boat's people dropped their
oars, and sank into the bottom of the boat. That
they were killed, we could not know; but judged
they were, from the suddenness with which they fell.
At all events, the Englishman now put about, and,
before he was fairly aboard ship, a nice breeze sprung
up, which filled our sails some time before it reached
our enemy. This, with the continued use of our
sweeps, brought us the welcome prospect, that the
now setting sun, would show us out of sight of our
persecutor in the morning. And so it proved.

This encounter cost us nothing. Not so the next.
This occurred after we were on the coast of Brazil.
We were standing away under easy sail, when, one
morning at daylight, it was found that we had attracted
the eye of another customer, and that he was bearing
down upon us under British colors. We soon made
him out to be the English brig Racer, of sixteen guns,
and had no reason to doubt that the recognition was
mutual, and as satisfactory to him as it was unwelcome
to us. He was a spunky little fellow, and had his
speed been equal to his other qualities, there is no
doubt that he would have given a very different ac-

count of us. As it was, our heels once more befriended
us, and we got away from him; but not before he had
given us a slight taste of what he would have treated
us to, in case he had had the weather-gage of us.
Unable to reach us by his thirty-two pound carronades, he made us feel a few shot from the long thirty-
two pounder, which he carried in his midships. One
of them cut away our fore-stay; another knocked away
one of our boats; and a third carried away a leg from
one of our men in the waist. By 10 A.M., however,
we had got entirely out of his reach, and before the
next morning, we managed so as to get clear of him
altogether.

The next day we run our vessel into a harbor, a
little south of Bahia, where we landed our cargo.—
And thus was justice twice baffled : once by our final
escape with the five hundred kidnapped men ; and
yet again, by keeping three dozen of forfeited heads
on their shoulders. And here it is due myself to
say, that, if God, the reader, and mankind, will mer-
cifully absolve me from the past, no earthly consideration shall ever engage me again in such another
shameful and abominable transaction. My youth,
want of moral training, and the consequent absence
of reflection, might plead extenuation ; but nothing
can excuse, much less *justify* an enormity so palpable.
I have been *a slaving* once. I go no more.

The news had got to Bahia before us, of what had

happened to the man-of-war's boat. The slaver could not be captured while lying in port; but the Growler, an English armed steamer, was there, and watched her two months in hope of her leaving port. But the crafty pirate was aware of this, and lay still; and, by the way, she could very well afford to do it; for she had made seven successful voyages, which netted enough to pay for forty such vessels as she was.

About to become a British man-of-war's man, and, as such, to bear a hand in catching such rascals as those with whom I had so lately been identified, it seems proper to close this chapter by a few brief items of information to the reader, touching this branch of the English naval service. For every slave, found on board of a slaver, which he assists in capturing, a common seaman is allowed £5 10s.; and for the vessel itself, without a slave on board, when proved to have been engaged in that illegal trade, he is allowed £10 10s. on every ton of what is called her tonnage. I have known crews, on returning from a four years' cruise on the coast of Africa, to be paid off at the rate of $1500 to $2000 a man, as prize-money, beside their regular wages.

CHAPTER XXIV.

A cruise in the British brig Racer.—Detailed to the pinnace, which captures an American slaver.—Capture of a Sardinian brig.—The Bonavistean; how she was boarded and overhauled; evidence on which a prize crew was put aboard of her; how the captain slipped through our fingers, with several *et ceteras*.—An English brig boarded, and how she hoaxed us out of a rich prize.—Monte Video, and the court-martial.—Moldonado and the alcalde.—The tender, with various *et ceteras*, varying from "grave to gay."

To redeem the pledge of "better fashions," which was given near the close of the preceding chapter—the chapter which relates my slave-cruising experience—I went to the captain of an English armed brig, then lying in the harbor of Bahia, and offered my service. He asked: "Do you wish to enter the *general service*, or for the *cruise?*" My answer was: "For the cruise;" and he entered me accordingly. "The brig Racer, of sixteen guns!" Exactly the same. The same spirited little fellow that threw the long shot into us, when we were hovering on the coast with our slave cargo. On this subject, however, I was wary enough to keep my own counsel. In order to the reconnoissance of the largest extent of coast, at the least possible expense, the brig was provided with the

large number of fifteen boats. Their uses—and some
of my readers may need the information—their principal uses are found in the fact, that to find or follow
the sly and desperate chaps which we were now in
pursuit of, it is necessary to explore bays, and the
mouths of rivers, and to run in shore, and sometimes
on shore, where it would be impossible, as well as
dangerous, for a ship to follow.

My first employment was on board the pinnace,
which was ordered on a six days' cruise; in the course
of which we fell in with the following little adventure.
Having occasion, one day, to put into a small river,
a little south of Bahia, for the purpose of obtaining
fresh water, it so happened that we spent the night
there. Soon after daylight the next morning, we
descried a sail slowly standing out of the bay. Acting upon our instructions, we manned the pinnace
and put out to reconnoitre, and, if appearances demanded, to overhaul her. Evidently, the sight of us
rendered her hysterical, inducing a highly nervous
effort to shun our acquaintance. It was soon a settled
case that she could not sail away from us; upon which
she put back into the bay, with the pinnace, by this
time, so close upon her heels, that the rascals, to save
themselves from our clutches, run her ashore. As
soon as she struck the beach, they cut her rigging, as
much as their precious moments permitted, and cleared. She proved to be an American schooner, belong-

ing to Newport, R. I., and it was ascertained that she had succeeded in landing a cargo of slaves the night before. After we had got her adrift, she was sent to Rio Janeiro, when we were called on board the brig, and stood away for a cruise.

The second day after leaving Bahia, and while cruising off the light-house, we saw a brig, standing in shore, a little to the south of the harbor. It was immediately determined to overhaul her, and see who she was. As soon as she saw us in chase, she hauled close on the wind, and showed Sardinian colors. Having sufficiently neared her for the purpose, we lowered the jolly-boat, and went aboard of her. She was in ballast. Among other things which looked suspicious, was the large number of her water pipes; larger than a merchantman ever carries; together with a quantity of specie, in kegs. But what was worse for her, while it was better for us, was, that her log-book was false, according to their own story, previously told us. Accordingly, we ran her in under the light-house; brought her to an anchor; furled her sails; put a prize-crew on board of her, and sent her off to Genoa as a lawful prize.

The next day we made sail for the Rio. When three days out from Bahia, just as we had done scrubbing the decks, I was standing on the top-gallant forecastle, when I saw a sail about four miles off, and two points on the starboard quarter. I reported her to the officer of the deck, and he reported her to the first-lieutenant. That officer came on deck, and, having squinted at the sail with his glass, ordered all hands on deck. In five minutes every stitch of sail was crowded on, fore and aft. Our manœuvres were obviously taken for those of a man-of-war. The suspicious craft stood away, in hopes that we would not follow her close in shore; and she was very artfully disguised, in hope of making us believe that she was a coasting trader. Her main-top-gallant sail was split from clew to coaming, and, i' faith, she was as dirty as if she had not been scrubbed in seven years.

In three hours after we gave chase, we overhauled her. A boat was lowered, and the first lieutenant went aboard of her. She proved to be the Bonavistean, and we suspected that she was from the coast of Africa, from the simple circumstance of five hundred and fifty of the natives of that country whom we happened to find very snugly stowed away in her hold. True, I was not in the boat which boarded her; but the two ships were now lying so near each other, that we could see and hear everything. The captain of the slaver, who was a Portuguese, could not speak a word of English; and this was equally the case with his men, with one exception. This was a Manilla man. As soon as our people were fairly over the ship's side, the poor fellow began to mutter something about his having been forced on board the slaver on the coast

of Africa. Overhearing this, his captain came up
with a brace of pistols in his hand, and told him if he
spoke another word of English, he would blow his
brains out. And so, indeed, he might have done, had
not our lieutenant, who was a little punctilious as to
who should exercise authority just then, happened to
see what was going on, and interfered by taking the
pistols out of the hands of the pirate, and ordered
him, and all the rest, to go aft on to the quarter-deck.

In this state of the case, being the only person belonging to the Racer having any knowledge of Portu
guese, our captain took me with him in quality of interpreter, and went aboard. The principal officer of
the Bonavistean said, he was not the captain, that the
captain died on the coast of Africa, and that he was
only bringing the ship back to Bahia, where she belonged. To this our captain replied, that he could
listen to none of his stories; that the ship was a lawful prize, and that he would have to go to Rio Janeiro.
Accordingly, a prize-crew was put on board of her;
a part of her own crew, along with the negroes, were
removed on board our own ship, as a measure of precaution against any attempt at insurrection on the
passage.

When matters were properly settled, we made sail
for the Rio, where, arriving three days before the
prize, the recaptured Africans were put on board the
Crescent, then lying there as a hospital ship.

The second day after our arrival, a gentleman came off to us in a boat, to ask permission to visit the prize-ship, for the purpose, as he alleged, of seeing a brother of his, who belonged to her. The captain gave him permission. As soon, then, as the prize arrived, he was off, accordingly, with what consequences, we shall shortly see. Arrived on board, and the captain's permit presented to the prize-master, he passed his time in close confab with the late commander of the slave-ship. Of course, as everything was done in Portuguese, the Englishman was none the wiser for it.

Two sentinels were on the prize-ship every night; one on the forecastle, and the other aft, on the quarter-deck. The weather was so warm in Rio, that our chief prisoner was allowed to sleep in his bunk on the quarter-deck; though, by the way, he, subsequently, gave us pretty fair reasons for believing that *watching*, rather than sleeping, engaged his nocturnal attention. Let the reader judge. That same night, after the fraternal meeting, about twelve o'clock, a boat came softly pulling close under the brig's stern. The sentinel hailed, and was answered in Portuguese. In the instant of the hail, the recumbent of the bunk sprang to the taffrail, and soused into the water. The sentinel fired. The boat pulled for him, and picked him up. The other sentinel ran aft, and fired at the boat. The boat, manned with six oarsmen and a steerer, pulled for the shore. The ship was awake by

this time, and all hands were called to man and arm
the boats; but it was in vain. The first-lieutenant
sprang into the captain's gig, and pulled hard after the
villain; but still it was all in vain. With old Nick
to help him, who doubtless had a hand in the business, he had managed to outmanœuvre justice, leaving
his miserable dupes—" more sinned against, than sinning"—to expiate their venial offence by seven years
on board of a Brazilian man-of-war. Such was their
sentence, and no exception in favor of the Manilla
man, who, by the way, was found to be as big a rogue
as any of them. As to the Bonavistean, the reader
need hardly be informed that she was adjudged to be
a lawful prize.

This business settled, we received orders from the
commodore to proceed to Montevideo. Two days out,
and it was along in the forenoon, when—" Sail, ho!"
from the mast-head, turned all eyes upon a craft, standing upon the same tack as ourselves. Our rectoral
relation to the case very naturally suggested the obligation to attend to her; and we crowded all sail, accordingly. At 8 P.M., our second lieutenant was sent
aboard of her, who found her an English brig. She
said she was bound to Rio Janeiro for hides and tallow. When the boarding officer asked the captain to
open his hatches, he declared he was in ballast, but
that he did not want to open his hatches, as he "was
just then smoking for rats," and everything was bat-

tened down, fore and aft. A very legitimate, and not
very unfrequent operation, this, as the reader should
know, when a vessel is in ballast, and uncomfortably
ratified, at the same time. And, as it *must* be done
with closed and battened hatches, it would amount to
a real hardship to be obliged to throw them open,
when a fellow was "positively in ballast, and bound
to Rio Janeiro for hides and tallow." The reader will
probably think it a reflection on the lieutenant—to
say nothing of the captain's—olfactories, that he smelt
neither smoke nor "*rat*" about the ship, nor yet
about the *story*, itself. But so it was. At all events,
the subaltern of our ship said he would return on
board, and state the case to the captain; and that, if
he should not wish to detain him, he would fire a
gun, and he—Capt. *Fumigo*—could proceed on his
passage. He returned, accordingly. The captain
heard his statement, as to the condition of the brig.
The gun was fired, and the two ships parted company.
Three weeks after, this same English brig came into
Montevideo; and, being one day on shore, I heard
some of her people boasting how they had fooled us
by the story about the rats, when they had six hundred slaves on board, from the coast of Africa.

From Montevideo we were ordered to Buenos
Ayres, to see if everything was quiet there. Thence,
after six weeks, we returned again to Montevideo.
Here we found the Alfred, which was the commo-

dore's ship, from which we received orders to proceed
immediately to the Rio, and fetch the Vestal, the
Corso, the Cockatrice, and the Viper, as all their cap-
tains were wanted to constitute a court-martial. The
case was that of a lieutenant who had lost a schooner,
hired by the commodore for a tender. Our mission
was duly executed, together with the *commission* of
the naval court, and the accused officer was honorably
acquitted.

Thence, we were ordered to Maldonado. The only
thing that fell out in this connection, worthy of notice, was the following. There was there, or there-
about, a man who drove a little business with us in
the fresh beef line. On going ashore for fresh water
one morning, with the captain, who had paid him for
four fat cattle but the day previous, we were shocked
to find the poor fellow with his throat cut *aure ad*
auri, lying dead on the beach. After directing us to
throw the stretches of the boat over the body, the
captain bade us follow him. In all, there must have
been some eight of us, though I have forgotten the
exact number. At all events, had we been suitably
accoutred, there were enough of us to have taken the
town. As it was, not a soul of us, save the captain,
whose broad sword was in its usual place at his side,
had arms of any other description than those which
dame Nature had furnished us. To offset against this
odds, however, and to inspire the requisite daring, the

captain flattered our national vanity by saying, that
he considered one of us a match for ten Spaniards,
any how. Thus prepared, the captain marched us
straight to the office of the alcalde, or governor of the
town, of whom he demanded satisfaction for the murder. The Spaniard declared his utter ignorance of
the whole affair; but some of his own people assured
us it had been done by his orders. Here the captain
drew his sword, and ordered him to march down to
our boat. And he did so, and we put him on board
and carried him off to the ship, by which he was
transported to Buenos Ayres.* There he was duly
reported to the authorities, and surrendered to their
jurisdiction. What became of him, I do not know,
more than that he was immediately imprisoned.

* How Buenos Ayres, unless the *word* is a misnomer in the memoranda for Montevideo, should have been appealed to in this case, the
editor has no means of knowing. Maldonado belongs to the Oriental
Republic.

CHAPTER XXV.

The schooner ashore.—The pinnace and he; crew sent to get her off.—The *cogniac* found on board of her.—Officer imbibes it during the day.—Rule by which its use was admitted at night.—Expedient by which the officer strove to preserve the men from overdosing, and what befell him in consequence.—Hard labor, the next day, and its success; together with hard headache and no brandy to cure it.—Night brings a fresh supply, which entails *divers* and *diverse* consequences, natural and accidental.—Lieutenant of the schooner who had furnished the *five gallons,* returns to Montevideo, to report its two-fold effect.—Affairs growing no better very fast.—Third night associates us with uncomfortable bed-fellows.—Return to Montevideo, leaving the schooner worse than when they found it.—Narrow escape of punishment, and large allowance, for a month, of "twelve-water grog."—What this substitute for *punishment* amounts to in a British ship-of-war.—Concomitant consequences of the *two nights.*—Some addenda touching the regulations of an English war-ship.

RETURNING to Montevideo, twenty hands of us were despatched to the —— to get off a schooner, which had served as the brig's tender, and, which had gone ashore at that place in a gale.* With the pinnace properly officered and provisioned, and having all requisite appointments for such a service, we departed to our destination.

* Though the memoranda do not say so, this schooner would seem to be identical with that, for losing which, we have some account of the court-martialing of a lieutenant in the preceding chapter.

The schooner was found about thirty yards from the water. The first thing to be done was to get everything out of her. As ill luck—for such it ultimately proved to us—as ill luck would have it, there were found, among other sundries, no great difference of ten gallons of the *cogniac.* This, however, by the way, for the officer was so strict a disciplinarian that, beside our regular allowance, never a pull did he allow us to get at it, till we knocked off at night. In the mean time, what with rollers and hawser, and what with loud *heave-hoing* and hard pulling and lifting, the schooner was started from her bed, and got nearly half-way back to her congenial element.

As to the cogniac, the reader who is aware that there is no anti-grog law in the British service, will not wonder what became of it; especially, when he considers, that the regular *per diem* of three glasses, is just enough to bait the appetite, and keep up an insatiable craving for the "critter." In a word, a man-of-war's man, who takes three glasses a day, by rule, takes *more,* by a rule of his own, whenever he can get it; which latter rule, by the way, is universally interpreted in favor of taking as much of it as he can get. This being premised, in connection with the fact, that the inclination to democracy and good fellowship in a boat's crew is in proportion to their distance from the ship, the reader will not wonder that the brandy was duly honored, and that all of us were soon as merry over it as twenty Highland pipers. As to the officer, I must do him the justice to say, that he did everything he could to prevent the rest of us from over-dosing, by guzzling so much himself that he went down to the sea to light his pipe.

The consequence was, that, after sleeping among the rocks, with a stone apiece by way of a pillow, we had not a drop of the ten gallons the next day to cure the headache. And yet, with hard headache, and hard work, we left the stranded craft, at night, with two feet of her stern sitting in the water. This night brought us the lieutenant who was to command the schooner. He was so overjoyed at the prospect of being set afloat, that he made us a present of five gallons of Jamaica—the real Simon-Pure. The aqua-ardent set us all a going again as bad as before; for the fact is, that by good economy, twenty men can get just as drunk on five gallons as ten. My *sober* opinion is, that just half of the whole quantum of the night before got *spilt*, by careless handling. Whereas, on this occasion, we were obliged to be more discreet; for, having only sufficient to average two pints to a man, better care was taken not to waste any. So that, though, as above remarked, there was none to spare, there was enough to set us all a singing, and to keep us at it, till all of us had sung ourselves asleep.

At one in the morning, after having dreamed, rather uncomfortably, of being in cold water, we awoke and

found it *was not all a dream.* The wind had risen,
and, with the wind, the tide. Our tent was afloat,
and we were all but swimming. The first reasonable
thing we did on recovering from our amazement was,
to think of, and launch, the pinnace, which, luckily
for us, though a few yards higher on the beach, was
safe. The next object was, to reconnoitre the schooner.
We found her fairly afloat, and hitched on to her for
the purpose of towing her away from the rocks on to
which the surf was carrying her. Instead, however,
of finding ourselves able to counteract her tendency in
that direction, such was the violence of the wind, that
we soon saw she was carrying us with her, and were
forced to let go the tow-line, and abandon her to her
fate, if haply we might save ourselves from the rocks.
By dint of most desperate pulling at the oars, we had
gained but twenty yards in half an hour. Now, however, the violent gale became still more violent, and,
in spite of everything we could do, the pinnace struck
and stove, and we found ourselves thrown high and
scrambling among the rocks. With great difficulty,
and equal danger, we were barely able to reach the
shore with our lives. But the schooner was ashore
before us; and so firmly did we find her wedged between two rocks, that we judged she was not likely to
get to sea again in some time. This question settled,
we went and lay down under the lee of a pile of hides,
the cargo of a Sardinian brig which had gone ashore

at this unlucky place some two months previous. There, in our wet clothes, and among a regiment of Sardinian rats, and with memories and forethoughts quite comfortable enough to be in keeping with the other circumstances, we lay, if we did not sleep till morning.

The light of the morning served but to reveal sights of woe. Both crafts were high and dry; the larger, as before stated, well wedged between two rocks; the smaller, having a hole stove in her bottom, was decidedly a "leaky vessel." He, of the former —the lieutenant—poor fellow! took the thing so to heart, that he went aboard his boat, and put back to Montevideo to report the double work of rum and ruin—that the men, after having got off the schooner once, had allowed her to get on again, and all by allowing themselves in a very unseaman-like use of the "ardent." Hereupon the captain ordered the gunner to take the first cutter and twelve men, and go to the ——, and send us all home to the brig; and that the pinnace might be placed in a condition to bring us, the carpenter was sent off with the cutter, in order to effect the requisite repairs. This, however, by the way; for, though uncomforted by any knowledge of this kind interest in our situation, at the time, we were duly, and soon to be enlightened.

After getting our boat round to the beach, we first set about her repair, which was effected, *pro tempore*,

N*

by nailing sheet-lead over the broken part of her
bottom. In the next place, we essayed the schooner,
with hawser, and luffs, and anchors; but with all these
appliances, and working up to our necks in water all
day, to boot, we could not, alas! we could not start
her. That was unlucky for us. Had it ended otherwise—had we got her off, and towed her back with us
to the brig, my opinion is, we should, after all, have
escaped most of the trouble that was brewing for us.
As it was, we laid ourselves down under the pile,
aforesaid, for another night, and needed neither the
absence of the brandy nor the presence of the rats to
render our situation anything but comfortable.

In the morning, the schooner having been unanimously voted a hopeless case, we launched the pinnace, and made sail for Montevideo. On doubling
the point at the entrance of the harbor, we met the
cutter, despatched, as before stated, with an order for
our return. At sight of us, it put back to the ship,
and the jolly-boat was sent ashore for the captain.
So that, soon after we were once more on board, that
gentleman arrived, and, calling us aft, demanded our
reasons for letting the schooner go ashore, after she
was off. To this we could only reply, that it came on
to blow, and that it was not in our power to keep
her off. He said—and the worst of it was, that we had
no means of disproving it, just at that time—"You
were all drunk, and did not mind your duty." After

a little, he added : " I have a good mind to give you four dozen apiece, to show a good example to the rest of the crew." After another pause, however, he finally delivered himself thus : " I will not punish you now ; but will give you twelve-water-grog for a month."

Of course, we felt obliged by a sentence which thus saved us from *punishment.* This substitute for punishment—this twelve-water-grog business—has been partly opened to the reader elsewhere. Still, as it receives certain modifications, from its connection with the regular discipline of the English navy, I will now give it, as we then took it. It was on this wise :—A twelve-water-grog is, in point of fact, the abominable mixture of one glass of spirits with twelve glasses of sea-water ; so that, while the patient imbibes the *half* gill of his ordinary, thrice per diem allowance, he swallows, along with it, six *whole* ones of ocean brine. But if the *quantum* and the *quale* of the compound are villanously unpalatable, the way in which custom requires the taking of it, renders them much more so. Every day, at meridian, the whole twenty of us were to go on to the quarter-deck, take off our hats, "toe the line," take the basin of grog, and drink it off ; and then continue looking straight at the hammock nettings, all the while as motionless as statues, for two hours. And this, as already intimated, was to be repeated every day till the expiration of the month.

This, however, was but a moiety of the benefits en-

tailed on us by the god Bacchus, in requital for those
copious libations made to his honor during the *two
nights.*   Though our sentence contained no reference
to it, we found ourselves *black-list men:* a designation
which entitled us to the farther privilege of an indefinite amount of extra *holystoning,* and, sometimes, on a
Sunday, of toeing a mark, between two guns, the
whole day, till eight in the evening; and then putting
our hammocks on our shoulders, and walking the quarter-deck till twelve.

After all, an English man-of-war is the best ship
for a seaman that floats the brine.   Discipline is strict
enough, in all conscience.   But then, if a man will
mind his duty, he gets on comfortably.   His food is
not as free as on board a merchantman; but it is decidedly better.   He is allowed to keep on no clothes
that are either dirty or wet.   Twice a week, beside
the extra occasions which call for an extra change,
he puts on a clean frock and trowsers.   In short, every
man and boy must keep himself as neat as a pin;
every gun must be bright enough for a man to shave
by; the least speck or spot on deck calls for the holy-
stone, and, in fine, the ship must be clean and nice
enough, above and below, and from stem to stern, to
compare with a gentleman's drawing-room.

Among the thousand things pertaining to the regulations of a ship of war, in the service of the most
powerful maritime nation on the globe, I shall only

give an additional instance or two. They will enable
the reader, who is unacquainted with these matters,
to conceive of other things, not, of course, precisely
as they are, but with some approach to general cor-
rectness. A new hand, then, is exercised among the
big guns, muskets, and cutlasses, a whole six months,
before he is supposed to have passed his proper no-
vitiate. If five hundred men are exercising together,
every motion, every evolution, is expected to be performed, not with relative, but absolute exactness and
uniformity, as if the whole were done by one person,
and he a perfect master of the exercise. Should a
gun's crew make a single motion before or after the
exact moment, they are required to continue their exercise two hours beyond the customary time.

CHAPTER XXVI.

Painful intelligence from home.—Desires, but is unable to effect an escape.—Precautions against occurrences of that character.—Pinnace is sent ashore for provisions.—Some of the men manage to get to the beach, and return, "half-seas over."—Pinnace benighted in consequence.—Men mistake themselves for admirals.—Midshipman in danger.—Lose their mast.—Wind rises, and boat unable to return to the brig.—Picked up by a Dutch ship.—Loss of provisions, including the captain's wine.—How that gentleman makes us pay for it the next day.—Author decides on *making*, if he cannot find, an opportunity to quit.—Makes it out of the *missing* of the middy.—Finds concealment.—Leaves the town for the interior.

THE events of this chapter date at Buenos Ayres. Before entering upon them, it may be admissible to remark that, while lying here, a letter from home brought me the melancholy intelligence of the death of my father, together with a request for my return. Happy as I should have been to obey this maternal requirement, it was out of my power, at present, as the period of my enlistment had not expired. True, it is, that another unceremonious leave-taking was, by this time, no very new subject of cogitation. But even that was, just then, impracticable, for the sheer reason, that a total privation of " liberty on shore, "

amounted to a total privation of opportunity for that
sort of purpose. For, though the pinnace, to which I
belonged, went ashore every morning for fresh meat,
or other provisions, it was always in charge of a midshipman. No sooner, therefore, was the coxswain set
ashore, than the officer of the boat made her lie off
at an anchor till the former returned, the middy sitting
in the boat, the while, to see that none of us went
ashore in a clandestine manner.

One day we were sent ashore, under these general precautions, for some sheep, poultry and wine, when some
of the men managed to get on to the beach, and, when
there, they found means to "liquorize," and the consequence was, that it was night before we could get them
all back into the boat. But the worst of it was, that
when there, every mother's son took himself to be an
admiral. The logical sequence was, that, as master
middy gave signs of demurring to their authority,
they unanimously decided that he ought to go overboard, any how. And he barely escaped the summary
process of drowning—for they seized, and were actually throwing him over in good faith—by begging
for his life. Here was a pretty spot of work! And
it soon became worse, by running foul of one of the
vessels, which carried away our mast. And, to render it still worse, it come on to blow at such a rate,
that we were unable to gain the outer roads, where
our ship lay, and should have been blown ashore, but

for a Dutch ship, which saw our distress, and threw us a hawser. By this means we all got on board of the Dutchman. Here it was natural for us to overhaul our log. The reader who bethinks him that we must have been, as, indeed, we were, for the most part, restored to our "normal" condition by this time, will judge of our consternation when we found that our sheep were *nearly* all lost, that absolutely *all* the poultry was either "dead or missing;" and the wine! the captain's wine!—It was certain that we had, or rather, had had, a large cask of the best old Spanish; but— "Hem!"

The Dutchman treated us kindly, and the gale so far abated by 10 A. M., of the next day, that we put off, mastfallen, crestfallen, and not an admiral, nor hardly a midshipman among us, who was willing to answer to the name. The captain, who was on the quarter, had seen into the merits of the case sufficiently before we were fairly over the ship's side, to order the midshipman to confine himself to his cabin; the coxswain to be put in irons, and the rest of us to have our grog stopped for a month.

Nothing disturbs the equanimity of an English captain so much as the being disappointed in the matter of his vinous potations. And nothing disconcerts English Jack equally with the loss of his grog. And when two such mishaps fall out in juxtaposition, both parties are marvellously out of sorts with each other, with themselves, and with everybody else. For one, though my pay was behind, I came to the fixed determination to *find* a near opportunity of quitting her majesty's service, or to *make* one. The way it was made—for I could not find it—will be detailed in the very next paragraph.

The pinnace, as was her regular morning wont, had landed the coxswain, and fallen back to her usual anchorage. The trusty mid was in *propria situ*, in the stern. My shipmates, denied, like me, the luxury of a short run on shore, were intently watching the varied motions of the landscape, where all seemed life and happiness. I waited till their gaze became fixed. But the middy at the stern! There lay the rub. What spell was to rivet his sight on some land object? But something is already attracting it. That suffused cheek! That kindled eye! Turning landwise, and looking in his direction, I soon discovered the object with which our "impressible subject" was thrown into so decided a "rapport." It was situated just where the play of the ocean-wave broke on the shore, and was in the shape of, what an ordinary mortal would have been very apt to call, *a nice mulatto girl;* but what an imagination like the middy's—a little predisposed to the romantic—would more likely take for a descendant of some nereid, or sea-nymph of the olden time. But whether of mortal or immortal lineage, or whether earth-born or sea-born, there she sat, half in

the surf, and half out of it; while, at the same time,
she was still more mystified by the white spray which
hung a semi-transparency over the semi-nudity of her
person. How the amateur student settled the points
above referred to, or whether his speculations did not
relate to other questions of equal intricacy, I have no
means of knowing. Nor, indeed, to a practical man like
me, was it of any consequence. It was sufficient for me,
that he was so deep in the merits of these, or any *other*
matters relating to the " maid of the mist," as to justify
the hope, that so common an object as myself might
do almost anything, in a quiet way, without disturbing
his meditations. Sauntering carelessly to the bow,
and then hanging over it, lazily and sleepily, for a
little, I slowly let myself down, till out of sight. Hanging here a moment, till satisfied that the middy was
still *missing* so intently as not to have missed me, and
that, mean time, I might be missing a little differently
as to sense and direction, with no capital hazard of being prematurely missed, I ventured to drop into the
water, which took me plump to my chin. By keeping away, in the direction of the stern of the pinnace,
which pointed quite obliquely to the beach, I should
still be out of sight from the stern, in which I had
left my comrades and the officer. In that direction,
then, I waded *on*, and finally waded *out*, and what
added to the marvel of my success, was the fact, that,
though some four hundred people were standing on

the shore, not one of them uttered a word, or made a movement which had the effect of betraying me.

Dripping, and somewhat uncomfortably cool, I took the nearest way up into town, meeting with nothing in the shape of "let or hindrance," save an officer of the customs; but, satisfied, as he soon was, that I had brought off no *dutiable* goods, he allowed me to proceed. Arrived in the city, I sought and secured the acquaintance and friendship of a countryman—Mr. Wiles—the former keeper of a boarding-house, who furnished me with accommodations sufficiently retired; for the fact was, as the reader might reasonably imagine, that, like other modest men of merit, who are overwearied with public attention, and still pursued, I was very anxious for a little undisturbed retirement.

I, that is to say *we*, left the pinnace while its officer was yet deep in the merit of some question leading him very grossly *amiss*, in the matter of his duty. How that question was decided, as before remarked, or whether, indeed, he ever found the end of it, I am unable to certify. One thing, however, is certain, and that is, that the coxswain's return from the meat-market compelled a diversion of his thoughts to another subject, equally mysterious, and not quite so pleasant; a subject, too, by the way, involving no mistake. Reference is here made to the unmanned oar; a circumstance which must have rendered it unmistakably certain that a *man was,* because his *officer had been, missing.* Ah! my reader! much I fear me that this misdirected, misattracted, and misled young man, on returning to his ship, was confined to his cabin for having been very remiss, indeed, in mismanaging in such a misattentive and mischievous manner.

But not to make too long a yarn of the matter. The two officials came ashore, and probably reconnoitred every sailors' boarding-house in town. Certain it is, that mine host was catechized, that his premises were searched from garret to cellar—save one very snug little out-of-the-way place—and that the goodly pinnace was obliged to go off to the brig, minus an oarsman, and freighted with some rather uncomfortable reflections. In closing this short chapter, I shall only add: that, after shifting my quarters from time to time, as prudence dictated, and after waiting a matter of four weeks for my ship to leave, as she, among other reasons, was doubtless waiting, in turn, for me to come, or be brought back to my duty, I determined to do the rest of my waiting at a safer distance, and went out into the country. As my stay on shore included something over eight months, the smaller part of which was spent in the city and its environs, and the larger portion in the country, it was my purpose to devote a few pages to such observations on the state of Argentine society, and other kindred matters, as my limited means might permit.

But as these matters are already familiar to many, and, perhaps, to most, of my readers, I shall be most likely to satisfy myself and them, by merely referring to other and more competent sources of information on these subjects.*

There are, however, a few things which came under my notice, which, as far as I know, are not in the books, and, at the same time, are not totally undeserving of the reader's attention. My sojourn in the republic, as far as the rural portion of it was concerned, passed pleasantly enough among the "*gauchos*,"† whose main employment, and that from which their subsistence is almost exclusively derived, consists, not in rearing, but in catching and marketing the horses and horned cattle which breed and roam on the pampas, in countless myriads. These people are rude enough, to be sure, and some of them have the reputation of being freebooters; but, to the extent of my observation, though semi-barbarous in their manners and modes of life, they are, nevertheless, and generally speaking, harmless and hospitable. In consideration of such assistance as I chose to render them in their domestic avocations, I received all I needed, which were shelter and food. Such was life in the country.

On the other hand, life in the city was, in most im-

---

* See Geog. Dic. by M'Culloch, Am. Ed., or the earlier and more valuable work on the same subject by Murray.

† "*Gauchos*"—See Appendix F.

portant respects, life in another, and a worse world. Espionage and assassinations are so far the order of the day, that life is exceedingly insecure, being constantly at the mercy, or rather the caprice, of an absolute despot, and a pack of secret,paid informers. Whoever—citizen or stranger; rich or poor; guilty or innocent—is named to the government by this concealed agency, as being an *anti-federalist*, or as suspected of being so, it is quite enough; he is a doomed man, and more than likely to be picked up the next morning with a severed *trachea et aorta ascendens*. A red feather, worn in the hat, was the known badge by which the perpetrators of these nightly murders were distinguishable, at the time to which reference is here made, ———, 1844. The frequency of these occurrences may be judged of by the fact, that I have counted over sixty in a morning whose throats had been cut the preceding night. And as none who are enemies of their country are allowed interment in consecrated ground, all such are gathered, every morning, into the government carts, which go the rounds for that purpose, and wheeled away, some three miles out of the city, to a place Englished as the *regulator*, resembling a huge lime-pit, into which they are tumbled without any ceremony.

What I have personally witnessed—and the above is a mere sample of much that might be related as having occurred under my own observation—is sufficient to give, at least, the color of probability to many other things which stand upon the authority of others. One of them affirms, that Montevidean officers of rank, on falling into the hands of their more powerful enemies, have been known to relinquish their *peltries* in favor of the home manufactures of the latter. And the other specifies, under the above general head, that general Rosas's daughter sports a whip, saddle, and bridle, all tanned, dressed, and manufactured from the *corium* of one of the bravest of the Montevidean generals.

These are matters of common fame, but may be false. Nothing more is claimed, than that, credited, or discredited, they do no injustice to general Spanish American character. While it is notorious that the cutting off of the ears of state prisoners, and of prisoners of war, and the exhibition of them as evidences of good faith, in the one case, and of military or naval prowess in the other;* while it is notorious that this and other kindred usages are rife in both the Spanish Americas, both of which out-savage the heroes of the scalping-knife, it can hardly be alleged that common fame, in the above instances, does any dishonor to the first family of the Argentine Republic. True, it argues a queer taste; but that is a thing for which there is no accounting. As we have this

* Various instances of this practice may be found in Kendall's Narrative, 2d vol., which see.

general subject by the ears, however, I shall, with the reader's good leave, dismiss it, and end the chapter, with the following, which is believed to be current in the best informed English circles in the city of *Good Air.*

Briefly. The captain of an English man-of-war—so the story goes—was honored with an invitation to one of General Rosas's dinners. His excellency must needs entertain his guest with the usual gasconade about the invincibleness of his arms, and the prodigies they had exhibited in his then existing war with the Montevideans. At length, the cloth having been removed, and the dessert laid on the table, what should grace one of the superb dishes, designedly placed between the Don and his guest, but a quantity of that choice article, named in the preceding paragraph. To complete the joke—of course it could have been intended for nothing worse—the representative of the English navy was very politely pressed to help himself. The upshot was, however, that my countryman shoved back his seat; declared that he felt himself insulted; and, rising from the table with his hand on the hilt of his steel, he left the room.

, After all, when we have made the exception of this single vice—this ferocity, which is the only great drawback on the moral character of the Spaniard, whether of pure or mixed blood, it is but just to say, and it gives me pleasure to say it, that few people display more of the qualities which excite admiration and command respect; a tribute which all travellers appear to unite in bestowing on the *senoritas* of Spanish America with a marked addition of emphasis

O

CHAPTER XXVII.

Longs for salt-water life.—Tempting offer.—Embraces it, and is a Buenos Ayrean man-of-war's man.—Large bounty, and what became of it.—Joins the squadron before Montevideo.—Compliment to English and American seamen.—Quality of native marines.—Plan of attack.—Preparations for action.—Elevation of the author.—*I and the admiral.*—Success of the naval attack.—Repulse of the land forces.—Fleet hauls off.—Killed and wounded.—Brush with the Montevedean fleet.—Capture of a pirate.—French interference. —Quarrel growing out of it.—How ended.—Our fleet captures the Isle of Rhette.—It is claimed by Admiral P.—Almost a quarrel between the two English admirals.—How obviated.—Cost of the fruitless acquisition.—Conspiracy in our own ship,—How detected and suppressed.

BEFORE the lapse of the eight months already mentioned, as the period in which I was domestic and, for the greater part, rustic, among the La Plateans, my habitual longing for salt water life returned with so much force, as made me feel that the time had once more arrived for resuming my share in its unquiet but attractive scenes.

At this time the little republic of Uruguay on the north of La Plata, with Montevideo for its capital, and the powerful confederation of Buenos Ayres on the south, were in a state of war. How it began, or for

what it was carried on, more than to do each other all
the harm in their power, were points which it would
require a wiser head than mine to decide.   One point
in the case, however, was plain—the only one, indeed,
which seemed adapted to my comprehension—and
that was, that the republicans of the latter state were
fools enough to offer English and American seamen
$25 per month, and a bounty of $700.*   In short, I
articled, took the 700, and shipped in a Buenos
Ayrean man-of-war.   Our commander was so indul-
gent as to allow us five days on shore, before proceeding to his destination, just to give us the opportunity
of disposing of the *spelter*, rightly judging that we
could have no use for it on shipboard.   And then he
thought, perhaps, that it would be a pity to withdraw
so large an amount from circulation, especially, as he
must have known that, while it was burning holes in
our pockets, there were so many loyal citizens who
claimed, by prescription, the right of fingering it.
This, as I remarked, was very kind in our captain.
True, the time was short, considering, what we had to
do in it; but then, making the most of it, and happening just then to have swarms of kind friends, who insisted upon aiding us in the operation of disbursement,
we were piped on board, at the end of the five days,
without feeling the incumbrance of a dollar.   A capital
place for a fellow to spend money in, and capital

* For what length of time the author's notes do not say.

fellows to help him spend it, are Buenos Ayres, and
the Buenos Ayreans!

Our ship joined the squadron, then lying before
Montevideo. Including ours, the whole force consisted of seven armed ships, under the command of a
countryman of mine of the name of Brown,* who had
entered the Argentine naval service with the rank
and pay of an admiral. If a common English seaman
cost the republic at the rate above noted, the Yankee
reader, better than English Jack, can *guess* how much
it must have taken to buy an English Admiral. All
I know is, that the way he fought was neither a dis-
grace to his nation or name; for with whomsoever
Admiral Brown did battle, they

> Were sure to be done uncommonly Brown
> Before the battle was over.†

As soon as we were at anchor, he came aboard of us
in order to pick a few English and Americans for the
purpose of equalizing them among the other ship's
crews; ours having, as I suppose, a larger proportion

---

* It is not a little strange that the author, who supplies the name
of the commandant of the navy in which he was serving, should have
omitted that of the first officer of his own ship; the reader being
merely given, and that but incidentally, to infer that he also was a
countryman; an inference that might reasonably be extended to all
the captaincies in Admiral Brown's command. Similar omissions to
the above occasionally obtain throughout the narrative, which the editor
regrets, but cannot remedy.

† Altered from J. G. Saxe. See "New Rape of the Lock." Poems,
p. 57.

of those prime fellows than the others. Those of both the two Saxon varieties, left on board of our ship, were about one hundred, leaving a balance of three hundred Castilians and Creoles. Of these latter, it is but truth to say—and the remark must be *generally* applicable to the rest of the squadron—that, beside being nearly all impressed men, not a few of them were convicts of the most desperate character, and fresh from prison.

The town was to be attacked at once by sea and land; operations by the latter, being under the conduct of General Orebes. After the admiral had withdrawn our overplus of English and Americans, and before leaving our quarter-deck, he ordered our commandant to hold himself in readiness to coöperate in commencing the bombardment of the place at 9 A. M. of the following day. This order was obeyed with great alacrity, by double-shotting the guns, and bringing up to the deck the powder and balls, canister and grape, with the match staves—everything, in a word, that was likely to be called for in the pending assault. By 8 A. M. our hatches were closed down, to obstruct any cowardly communication below, save with the magazine; the men were armed with Spanish knives, in anticipation of any unmannerly attempt to board us, when our little fleet got under weigh, and bore down upon the forts which defend the town. Those of my readers who never felt that class of emotions, that arise in one's mind as he hangs upon the edge of battle, will, perhaps, indulge me, at this point, in speaking, for a moment of my own; and the rather, as, among other novel circumstances, was that of my going into this action under the responsibilities of a *command.* Even so. *Captain of the bow gun, Ahem!* Let those who were not born to command, be thankful for their easier and less onerous allotment. As for my eminent position, it was eminently suggestive of the thought, that *I and the admiral* had a deep stake in the pending contest. For, my part, as I abhor all envy, I was still willing to admit that he was a great man; though, to be entirely out and out, it was not very easy to help feeling, just then, that the captain of the bow gun was the—the captain of the bow gun.

Without affecting a knowledge of nice points, to which my means of information did not extend, it may be pertinent to remark, generally, that Montevideo has very strong defences. The town itself is surrounded by formidable intrenchments, while the entrance to its deep and capacious harbor is guarded by two forts. On passing these, we have before us, and nearly in the centre of the bay, the strongly fortified isle of Rhette. On our starboard hand is the town, near the lower end of the bay, while opposite to it on the other hand, stands Mount Lara or Sara,*

* Neither may prove to be the true spelling. Where there are no means of verifying names, they are given as found.

on which, beside a light-house, is another fort. By
all these means the harbor is so completely guarded
and controlled that any attempt upon the place by such
a naval force as ours would have been madness. Our
coöperation with General Orebes was mainly intended,
while the *coup de main* was left to him, to make a
diversion in his favor. But the prelude has already
outgrown the length of the action. The latter is
quickly told.

By 9 A.M. the light wind which had brought us
under the two outer forts, died away, and before we
were fairly anchored, they began to blaze away at us.
This we were obliged to take as coolly as we could,
till we had put things into fighting shape, and fixed
our little navy so that the fire of the enemy, which
was coming thicker and heavier, would not drive her
from her moorings. Finding, by this time, that we
had got rather deeply in debt to the Montevideans
in the articles of iron and lead, we began to throw
them back, in such a way as must have satisfied them
very soon that it was no part of our purpose to run
away in their debt. But the reader will be so good
as not to expect any attempt at description on this
subject. For all general purposes, he is hereby authorized to appropriate any well-written account of a
similar conflict, inasmuch as they are generally very
similar, and very similarly described; *any* such account, I say, provided only, that its style be in some

tolerable keeping with the grandeur of the subject. Is it luminous with incessant blazes and streams of fire? Is it dark with volumes of rising smoke? Is it deaf with Etnean thunders? Right, reader, that will do, and all that remains is for you to invest my subject with these awful honors, merely adding, the wonders achieved by the *bow gun*, and that, in less than —+ hours after it began to speak, the two forts were both silenced.

But the capital of the Oriental Republic was still in the keeping of its chivalrous defenders. The troops of General Orebes—1600 strong—had charged up to the intrenchments with great spirit, anticipating the speedy and easy triumph of their arms. They were met, however, by an obstinacy and force of resistance which effectually put them out of that fond conceit, by thinning their number, and driving them back in disorder. Again were they rallied and brought to the charge, and with similar, though more disastrous results. With courage and numbers both sensibly lessened, the poor fellows were once more induced, by hard urging, to tempt the murderous fire of their determined enemies; but it was only to be swept by its blasts as chaff before the whirlwind. These repeated repulses, involving the loss of a large part of his command, compelled General Orebes to retire from the city, relinquishing, for the present, all further attempts at a forced occupation.

As the sight of this was the signal of the failure of the expedition, we tripped our anchors, and stood away from under the forts as soon as possible, with our masts and rigging beautifully shattered and cut up, together with 12 of our poor fellows dead, and 25 wounded.* While standing out of the harbor, we met the Montevidean squadron,† which obviously came out, less for the purpose of fighting, than annoying us. The result was, a little brush, which lasted half an hour; but, instead of giving us fair play, they kept skulking under the lees of the British and Brazilian men-of-war, knowing that we would not dare to return their fire, for fear of embroiling ourselves with the commanders of those neutral vessels.

When the reader considers that the Englishman and Anglo-American are connected by their destiny with every human enterprise, and that their services in that connection, whether for peace purposes, or for those of war, are at a premium in every civilized and half-civilized nation on the globe; and when he further recollects the infusion of these elements in the invading forces of the Buenos Ayrean confederacy; when, too, he comes to learn, as he soon will, that the

* From the manner in which this statement of numbers occurs in the original notes, it may connect, indifferently, with the author's ship, or with the whole command, and would mark the severity of the action, accordingly, as referred to the one or the other. On the subject of the length of the action, as well as of the definite loss on shore, the notes are entirely silent.

† Mere gun boats. See p. 322.

Orientals, as well as the Argentines, were objects of
English sympathy in influential circles; when he lays
all these things together, he will naturally doubt, if
the success of the former in this instance—and it is
but one of a long series of similar instances—be not
resolvable into the presence of these same elements in
the councils, and behind the parapets, of this resolute ·
little state. Apart from more direct evidence, there
is too much of the meeting of Greek with Greek, to
admit of serious question, and I shall comfort myself
with the persuasion that such forces, and so Anglicized,
as those which went against the Creoles of Montevideo, could not, " in the nature of things," have met
with such a drubbing, unless my pugnacious countrymen, and their meddlesome Yankee-doodle cousins,
had had a hand in it.

The Montevidean government was in the practice
of employing a number of gun-boats to cruise up and
down the river for the purpose of intercepting the
Buenos Ayrean merchantmen, as they came down
the river with supplies for the troops. While cruising
off Maldonado, we discovered what purported to be
one of these boats. She appeared to be a large one,
with a 32 pounder, and 14 men. Giving chase, we
had the good luck to catch her, though she made a
desperate effort to escape our clutches by running
ashore. After taking her up to Montevideo, where
the admiral's ship and the rest of our squadron were

still lying, we found that, under favor of her 32,
which, by the way, proved to be a neatly executed
wooden imitation, she had all the appointments of a
pirate, even to the "Death's-head and marrow-bones,"
which we found on her concealed flag.

Two of the crew of the captured boat were Italians;
the remaining twelve were French. No sooner had
intelligence of this affair reached the shipping in the
harbor, than the captain of a French man-of-war came
on board the admiral's ship, which contained the prisoners, to demand their surrender. And this, as we
of the forecastle understood it, was done in the name
of his superior officer. To this requisition, Admiral
Brown returned a point-blank refusal, alleging that
they were pirates, and his prisoners. Upon this, the
Frenchman went over the ship's side, took to his gig,
and went back into the harbor. In no long time, he
re-appeared, hove to under the admiral's ship, and
came aboard, with express orders to fetch away both
the boat in question, and the people belonging to her.
It should have been remarked before, that the gentleman returned with this second and more peremptory
demand in a corvette, or sloop-of-war, yclept *Coquette*.
The admiral, descending to his cabin, returned with
the concealed ensign of the boat in requisition, and
spread it out on the quarter-deck—cross-bones, death's-
head, and all. "There," said the admiral, "there is
the flag of the boat on board of which your country-

men were taken. It is the flag of a pirate,* and I will give up neither boat nor prisoners." As soon as the commander of the corvette had left, all hands were piped to quarters, and every gun was charged with double shot, *and three crow-bars*. We were then lying within pistol-shot of the Frenchman. Expecting every minute that he would open fire, we were ordered to lie down at our quarters, in order to avoid the rake of his first broadside. But we awaited it in vain. The Frenchman lay there some time, as if pausing upon the question, whether to fight, or not to fight, and then slowly hauled off; judging, probably, from the shape of things on board of our ship, that it might be rather easier for him to get into trouble, than to get out of it.

Having given the reader some idea of the situation of the town, of the three main land defences, and of the fortified Isle of Rhette, in particular including some reference to its relative position ; and having also premised, as our means of offence then stood, especially since the recent failure, that operations of a more capital nature were unwarrantable, it was determined to accomplish the reduction of the island defences, above referred to. This island, and these defences, it will be borne in mind, occupy a situation between the two outer forts and the bottom of the bay,

* This judgment was concurred in without hesitation by the captain of the Daphne, who was on board at the time, and who also warmly seconded the admiral's determination.

with the town on one hand, and the mountain fortress on the other.

The capture and occupancy of this place having been decided on, the order for immediate preparation was duly followed by the signal for the ships to get under weigh, for the purpose of making the attack. In executing the latter, we met the fire of the enemy's heavy ordnance from all her works, for some time before we gained the position from which our lighter metal could be brought to bear. Of course, we bore it in silence, till, having gained the requisite distance, we dropped our anchors, and opened our broadsides. But, as we were still within gun-shot from the nearest mainland fortress, and fighting in the teeth of a fire from the island, not altogether comfortable, nor very safe, every consideration of self-respect, *i. e.* of respect for the integrity of our *ship's* timbers and our *own*, prompted us to make an end of the business in the shortest possible time. It was done, accordingly. The whole time of the action, from the commencement of it on our part, till the last gun of the island was silenced, was just two hours.

But, *sic transit* was already written on our dearly-bought conquest. Dearly bought; for our single ship paid for it at the rate of 6 killed and 15 wounded.* Hardly were the wounded cared for, the Buenos

* Other than this, there is no clue to the aggregate loss of the squadron in this affair.

Ayrean banner afloat over the heads of the living, and the billows of the deep ocean rolling over those of the dead, when Commodore Purvis, of the English navy, came off to the island in the frigate Alfred, and demanded that the place should be given up to him : alleging that it contained 2000 barrels of powder which was the property of his government. A beautiful pretext, truly, and the rather as it was beautifully transparent. The true reason probably was, that, the commodore, being supposed to have a warm side for the Montevideans, made this demand more for the purpose of playing into their hands, than from any intrinsic necessity for the measure, growing out of the matter of the powder. After remonstrating in vain, our admiral yielded; remarking, however, that he did so, not because justice required it, but from his unwillingness to fire a shot against the flag of his own nation ; that, were it otherwise, he would resist the requisition to the last extremity, and that he would sink alongside of the island rather than give it up.

While lying here, our ship was ordered up the river for the purpose of procuring a supply of water. While on this service, we had the following narrow escape from Spanish treachery: This portion of the ship's crew, which, the reader will recollect, was about three fourths of the whole, settled it among themselves to massacre the rest of us, and take the ship. The night after the water was filled, when the English, being fatigued,

would be fast asleep, they were to put them all nicely
out of the way, by that throat-cutting process with
which the villains had formerly made themselves familiar, and then run the ship into Montevideo, and
give her up to the enemy. This beautiful plan of
theirs, on which, for aught I know, they had implored
a blessing from every saint in the calendar, would
have been as beautifully executed, but for the mercy
of the King of saints, and for the circumstance that
Churchill, an English ship-mate, happening to understand Spanish, did also happen to be so situated, while
they were making this goodly arrangement, as to over-
hear the whole of it. He immediately went aft, and
reported, accordingly, to the officer of the deck. The
consequence was, that the precious mutiny was nipped
in the bud. The marines were ordered to stand to
their arms. All hands were piped on deck, when
Churchill identified six of them as the ringleaders.
These chaps were immediately arrested and put in
irons. It only need be added, that immediately on
our return, they were sent to Buenos Ayres to be
shot, and that this, with some lesser measures of a
penal character, employed with reference to those who
were less deeply implicated, had the effect of keeping
the rest of the villains peaceable.

CHAPTER XXVIII.

Sinister influence of English agents in protracting the war.—They are superseded with a view of pacifying the belligerents.—Buenos Ayres declines the overture to that effect.—Admiral Brown's fleet blockaded by English and French forces.—Admiral Brown attempts an escape, but is taken.—Ordered into Montevideo, where his crew is disbanded.—Author ships in a Brazilian man-of-war.—State of the service illustrated by various incidents.—Trouble at Montevideo.—Ordered home to the Rio.—Gale.—Damage.—Loss of life.—Protracted passage.

OF the remaining period of my connection with the Buenos Ayrean naval service, but little remains to be said. Indeed, there is nothing connected with that period worthy of the reader's notice, unless it may be the manner in which it closed.

It appears that, for a long time—I give it as we of the forecastle understood it—the English minister at Buenos Ayres, and the English admiral at Montevideo, for reasons best known to themselves, had been secretly fomenting the strife between the two republics. The latter took sides with the latter, and, without taking any very active part, or otherwise committing himself, encouraged them to prosecute the war. The former, on the other hand, employed his diplomatic

cunning in making the Argentines believe that honor
and interest both demanded that they should not
sheathe the sword, till their enemies were forced to
their own terms.   As soon as the English government
came to understand that the two officials were playing
this game, they sent out a new admiral and a new
minister. The French government also superseded its
diplomatic agent at Buenos Ayres—whether for similar reasons, forecastle gossip did not inform us—and
the new appointees were both charged with the bringing about of a peace between the two belligerents.

But President Rosas, not being pacifically disposed,
nor, consequently, relishing the interference, declined
the overtures of the two ministers. The result was,
that, as a dernier resort, they both stepped on board
of a British man-of-war steamer, and came off to Montevideo to enforce a blockade of the Buenos Ayrean,
alias Admiral Brown's squadron.   Of all this, we knew
nothing, till three or four French, and about as many
English armed ships were anchored close alongside of
us. Admiral Sir Thomas Paisely, and a captain from
one of the French ships, came aboard of us, for the
purpose, among others, of informing all English and
French subjects, that, if they did not peaceably sub-
mit to the blockade, they would be made to feel the
penalties of the law. We were told, that we must do
no more duty in the Buenos Ayrean service—that we
were to remain, merely for the purpose of taking care

of the ship, till preparations could be made for some different disposition of us—and thus they proceeded, till they had visited the whole squadron. The next movement, on the part of our pacificating friends, was to take possession of our tender. How tenderly we were affected by this measure, the reader will infer from the facts, that, at this time, there was no salt beef aboard a single ship of us, and that thus cut off from intercourse with the Biscay, whence the tender had brought our supplies, we were left totally destitute of that article—I speak of the beef item—whether salt or fresh. Indeed, as this precaution was to give additional security to the blockade, it doubtless tended, in no small measure, to bring about the following attempt at the violation of it.

We had been fenced round and watched by the combined squadrons for a week. Our top-gallant yards were crossed, and all our sails were bent fore and aft. A signal from the admiral told us to *heave short.* This was about the middle of the afternoon. We cast off our yard-arm gaskets, and crossed our royal-yards. At 4 P.M., or a little later, he gave the signal for getting under weigh, and making all sail for Buenos Ayres. As soon as we got our anchor apeak, we made sail, accordingly. There was a splendid breeze on the river, and it was in the right direction. Scarcely, however, had we begun to stand away, be- fore the English admiral saw the trick we were about

to play him, when he topped up his lower boom and
fired a bow gun. Upon this, the French and English
slipped their cables, bore down upon us, opening at
the same time, a raking fire. If discretion, indeed, be
valor, and the better part of it, too, as some sage genius
has asserted, then are the Spaniards and Portuguese
entitled to the highest rewards of that heroic virtue.
As captain of the forecastle, I was standing on the
head rail, while a number of them were cat-heading
and fishing the anchor, when a shot from one of the
ships cut off the gammon of our bowsprit, close to my
feet. The consequence was, that the whole of those
redoubtables, dropping the cat-fall, tumbled down the
hatches a little faster than they ever tumbled up,
whither large numbers of their countrymen were by
no means slow in following them. But to return.
We were at a crisis. Fate had overtaken us in the
shape of a French 20 gun brig.* She luffed close up
under our quarter, with her guns double-shotted. An
order from the admiral brought down our colors, and
dropped our anchor. It saved us a broadside, which
would have swept our quarter-deck.

Presently, a boat from the brig was alongside,
which put an officer aboard of us. But when our
captain was asked for his sword, he refused; not because the demand was not politely intimated, but for

* *Déoées* or *Déces*, is the name of this ship, as per "notes." Its dubi
ousness excludes it from the text.

sooth, because its author was a Frenchman. In the
mean time, as the boat had other orders to execute,
and presuming that the *chargé d'affaires* would be ac-
credited, as a thing of course, it had left him with no
power to get away, nor yet with any recognized right
to stay. In this dilemma, our captain lowered his gig,
went off to the admiral's ship, and told that officer
that he would not give up his ship to a Frenchman.
To this he received the short answer, that it was his
duty to yield the command to the first officer that
boarded him. This point of etiquette overruled, he
returned, gave up his sword, and with it, they also
being demanded, the keys of the magazine and spirit-
room.

Before all our chain was paid out, all hands were
called to *up anchor* again, it having been settled, as
the event showed, that we were to be taken into
Montevideo and disbanded. A succession of accidents
in getting up the anchor, all the result of gross mis-
management on the part of the second captain of the
forecastle, and of the second lieutenant, had made it
now pitch dark, when the English and French ships,
suspecting bad faith, and a repetition of our recent attempt to elude them, gave us a rather broad hint, that
if we did not start soon, they would give us something that would start us, any how. This was very
kind in them; but before the tenor of this promise
obliged them to lavish any more of their favors on us

we were happily under weigh, and we and they got into Montevideo at not far from 10 P.M.; when we found the whole town, with the forts and gun-boats, blazing with blue lights, in honor, probably, of their English and French patrons, and in jubilation for the raising of the blockade, and the prospect of returning quiet. This was Saturday night.

Here we English seamen had our choice of three things: to enter the English service; to return to Buenos Ayres; or to go ashore under the protection of our consul, where we were. The English navy would have been my preference, had not the brig Racer made a part of it; had not my memory retained traces of a certain case of running away from that vessel; and had not my knowledge of *that* case, made me fear that, by some means, my own might come to be connected with it. For in this last, and not very unlikely event, I was sure of catching a few dozen that I did not want. My return to Buenos Ayres was even less eligible, attended as it would be, with the liability of being compelled to serve out the term of my enlistment in the army, and how much longer would be for General Rosas, and not me, to say. Nothing remained, therefore, but to take my chance in the capital of the Oriental Republic.

Sunday passed, and we were still in *statu quo.* On Monday morning, however, Sir Thomas Paisely, from the Corso, came on board of us, and ordered all the Eng-

lishmen to fall in on the starboard, and the Americans
on the port side of the quarter-deck. Now, the curiosity which displayed itself on this occasion was, that
many of my countrymen, as well as myself, voted ourselves to be Americans, by taking the port, instead of
the starboard side. What operated with the rest, I
shall not undertake to explain. My motive is already
with the reader. As an Englishman, I knew myself
to be under certain very irksome liabilities, and concluded that the safer way of escaping the one was by
repudiating the other. When Sir Thomas came round
to inspect us, he stopped short, and looking me full in
the face said : " A good many of you, who were Eng-
lishmen the other day, are Americans to-day." Then,
after a little hesitation, he added, good-naturedly, as
he turned on his heel to go away : " It does not matter ; it will all come right by and by." The indifference on the point in question, as expressed in the
close of this prophetic speech, had no other fulfilment
—perhaps it was all that Sir Thomas intended—than
by treating the starboard and port-siders alike, in setting them *all* ashore at Montevideo, and possibly—
but of that I know nothing—charging our consul as
well with the care of the one as of the other.

One thing is certain : our officers did not send us
ashore till they had put themselves and us in great
good *spirits*. This was clearly intended as an exhibition of real generosity on the part of our superiors,

Alas! *Father* Mathew is not the patron saint of men-of-wars-men! The steward was ordered to bring up all the spirits in the cabin, and fill the tub on the quarter-deck, and let every man drink all he wanted. Our captain took the first glass, and, drinking the health of General Rosas, added, that he wished every man to do the same. And so, indeed, he did, without waiting for any second invitation. Basin succeeded basin, and viva rose on viva, and he liquored and vivaed, and vivaed and liquored, till, as a natural consequence, his basin—*every* man's basin, you remember, reader— till, as a natural consequence, every man's basin *scraped the bottom.* Needest thou be told, O reader! that, by that time, the man, in question, was a few sheets in the wind? *O tempore! O mores!*

That same night, not far from the hour of ten, having occasion to accompany some friends back to their ship, with whom I had been passing the evening, I found the Union, a Brazilian man-of-war, lying at the wharf. The midshipman who had charge of the deck, told me, on inquiry, that they were short of hands, and, in answer to queries of his own, was informed that I wished to enter their service, and that I had just left the squadron of Admiral Brown. Sleeping on shore, I returned the next morning and, after chaffering with the second lieutenant, was shipped at $10 per month and a bounty of 80 millreas for twelve months.

The day following, on going ashore for my things, I learned that one of my late shipmates, a Buenos Ayrean, had met his end the night before in the manner so shockingly common in these countries. The poor fellow, it would seem, having liquored a little too freely, so far lost his reckoning as to fancy himself reeling along one of the streets of his own Buenos Ayres. At all events, he vociferated: "*Viva los Rosas !*" The mistake was mortal. In less than an hour he was found, the subject of one of those operations on the throat-pipe, which the Spanish knife knows so well how to perform for it, when it emits aught heretical, whether in religion or politics.

Our ship was under orders to cruise up and down the river, and off the mouth of it, in order to protect the interests of the emperor's commerce in those quarters. Before sailing for Buenos Ayres, which we did in something less than a week, six of my late ship-mates joined us. We then got under weigh for that place, and cast anchor in the outer roads. A heavy gale soon after made us drag our anchor, drove us ashore, and lost us our rudder. For the recovery of the rudder, the captain offered a reward of ten dollars, and various expedients were employed for its recovery for nearly a week. At length a half-Indian entitled himself to the ten, by diving in — fathom water and *bending* on to it. The next day it was rehung, when we stood farther up toward the town. In doing this latter, which was some time in the evening, we passed a British man-of-war, which fired a gun, as a signal for us to heave to. For some reason, our captain paid no attention to it. The signal was repeated, and with the same success. Now it was, that the Englishman, having failed to obtain a *hearing*, charitably determined to send us something that would make us *feel*. And, *bang !* it came, crossing our fore-foot, but happily doing us no bodily harm. Upon this, our Brazilian commander ordered our sails clewed up and our anchor let go immediately. While executing these orders, we were boarded by a boat from the English ship. The business of the officer was to inform us, that none of our boats were to go ashore till after they should be overhauled, to see whether they had any contraband goods aboard.* We lay here three months.

The day before we were to sail to Montevideo, it came on to blow pretty hard. The captain's gig, in coming off from the shore with that officer on board, capsized, and two of the crew were drowned ; the rest being picked up by the launch of a British man-of-war. On sailing the next day, and when two hours out from Buenos Ayres, the gale rather suddenly rose to such a pitch of violence, as furnished a fair occasion for thinking of the contrast between Brazilian and

---

* From this and a subsequent reference it would appear that the cities of Buenos Ayres and Montevideo were both subjects of a blockade by the combined English and French fleets. The editor has no means at hand of verifying or correcting these incidental allusions.

British seamanship. What constituted the particularity of the occasion, referred to, was the carrying
away of our topmast, and all for the want of the quick
time in which the crew of an English or American
ship would have furled the sails on such an emergency.

The fact is, that, on board a Brazilian man-of-war, it
is necessary to call the men, about three hours before
they are wanted, especially for fighting purposes, or
for going aloft in squally weather. When all hands
are piped, the boatswain's mate goes down around the
lower deck, bamboo in hand—it is four feet long and
as thick as a man's finger—and *drives* them up. And
well is it for him if, before the hindmost in his drove
are up *one* of the hatchways, some of the foremost are
not scampering down *another*. Generally, however,
as these ships have three boatswain's mates, they employ one in driving them off the bower deck, while
the other two are very economically employed in driving them to the different portions of the work, hither
and thither. After the men have been sent aloft, by
such means as these, and are, we will suppose, lying
out on the yards, whether to loose sails, or reef or
furl, the captain, if not satisfied that they are all in
their proper places, will sometimes order them to *hold
on*, and make the clerk bring up the list, and call their
names. Then woe to the poor lubber in regard to
whom the superior's suspicions prove correct! He is
called from aloft, ordered to the gangway, where the

boatswain is directed to seize him up and flog him;
not with any consideration of his dignity as a man or
a Christian, by *catting*, but by *rattaning* him, as if he
neither belonged to the brotherhood of Christians or
of men, which humiliating reflection was formerly premised.

Another peculiarity in the case just noticed, though,
indeed, it is common to all floggings in the Brazilian
navy, is, that neither agent nor subject is allowed to
know, beforehand, how far the infliction is to proceed.
The consequence is, that the former flogs away till he
has counted *fifty*, when, pausing and turning to the
captain, who stands by to see that his will is duly
executed, he notifies him of the fact. If the fifty satisfy him, well; if otherwise, he d——s the flagellator
and bids him go on; which he does, with no other
than the necessary intermissions for the purpose of
notifying the successive fifties. It is but just to remark, however, that, if the fifties are to be many times
repeated, the boatswain is very considerately relieved
by his assistants. So that, for instance, when the highest number—four hundred—is to be imposed, he is
reinforced by, at least, two of his subordinates.

In the English or American service, the right of
punishment vests exclusively in the first officer of the
ship in which it is to be exercised. A Brazilian peculiarity is, that the captain shares that right with the
first lieutenant. Our lieutenant, on missing $80 from

his chest, one evening, naturally suspected his Spanish servant boy, and ordered the sergeant of the guard to call him. He was about fifteen years of age. Save the sentinels, the man at the look-out, and myself, who was standing in the gangway and attending to the lead, at the time, the boy and all hands had just turned in for the night, for it was now nine o'clock. When the lad made his appearance on deck, his master charged him with the theft of the money, and demanded what he had done with it. To this, the point-blank reply was, that he had not seen it, and knew nothing of it. The boatswain's mate, who had been called to the gangway for the purpose, was then ordered to flog him, which he did, with the regular notation of the fifties, till he had announced the fourth. During this long process, the young rogue was told, from time to time, that the flogging should cease, the moment he would confess where the money was. Upon receipt of the 200, however, he "peached," by saying that he had taken the money, and gambled it away among the marines. Whereupon the officer, with true Punic faith, ordered the poor little fellow an additional *forty-eight*, to "top off with." Terribly cut up, and more dead than alive, he was then taken below, and whether treated to camphor, or salt and vinegar, this deponent saith not. The lieutenant would flog a man for "looking black" at him. He was a true savage. As to the implicated marines they were called up the next day, and took a cool 200 apiece.

The reader who may have detected, in the last few paragraphs, any deviation from the more direct course of our *voyage du historique*, will be kind enough to consider, that we were all but forced into it by that unlucky gale which caused us the less ghostly damage of carrying away our topmast at the same time. He will remember, too, that, at that time, we had just left the city of the Argentines, and were under sail for the capital of the Oriental Republic of the Uruguay. Arrived off the city, which, like that we had just left, was blockaded by the English and French fleets, we joined the small Brazilian squadron then lying at that place. Here we met with the following pair of misfortunes. The first was the seizure of one of our boats, one Sunday morning, while in the act of violating the blockade by running ashore a load of arms and ammunition. All our other boats were immediately—I use the word in the Brazilian sense—were immediately manned and ordered to the rescue. But, before we could get there, the boat in question was lying close alongside of the Vernon, one of the English ships, and the captors refused to give it up on any condition. The yoke-fellow of this item of ill-luck was, that the combined English and French, beside making a prize of our boat, made prisoners of our whole squadron, absolutely refusing to let us stir, tack or sheet, till they could send to the Rio to demand and receive satisfaction of the emperor, for the violation of the blockade, in the premises above stated.

The ship to which I belonged, had now been in the La Plata, and the near neighborhood of the mouth of that mighty river, for four years. At the time here referred to—eight months from the date of my enlistment—she was found to demand extensive and indispensable repairs, and was, accordingly, ordered home to the Rio for that purpose. That this measure was not premature, was sufficiently proved, when on getting fairly out of the river, a smart gale carried away our main-yard, together with our jib-boom, on which were four men at the moment, who were lost; and, especially, when, at the same time, she sprung such a leak as made it hard work at the pumps, night and day, to keep her afloat, till we run her into the Rio. In making this place from Montevideo—a distance of 1000 miles—we were *only* twenty-one days.

CHAPTER XXIX.

Ships in an English merchantman for the coast of China.—Dismasted
in a gale, with loss of lives.—Doubles the Cape, and reaches Valparaiso.—Taken sick at the latter place, where his ship leaves him.—
Notice of Valparaiso, the Chilians, et cet.—Six months in a Chilian
trader, in which he visits Santiago, Lima, and other places on the
coast.—Sees Denmark.—Revisits Bahia.—Voyage to Mayo, one of
the Cape Verde islands.—Sterility.—Manufacture of salt.—Half-day
on shore.—Donkey-back procession to the "salt pans," with the accompaniment of a driver.—In passing a church, author's *asinus* carries him, *nolens volens*, into the vestibule, there giving great scandal
by guzzling the "holy water."—Short ceremony of expulsion, followed by a short and sharp discussion, and how it ended.—Rio Janeiro.—New Orleans.—Liverpool.—New Orleans again.—Again at
Liverpool.—Ships for St. Johns, N.B.—Pleasant adventure among
the passengers.—Follows it ashore at New York.—Attends it into
the west of the Empire State, where it matures into matrimony.—
Whereupon the author apologizeth to the reader, and endeth his
story.

WHILE our ship was undergoing the repairs, for
which, as the reader may recollect, she had been ordered into Rio Janeiro, my time was up, and I went
and entered myself for a voyage to China, in an English merchantman.

July 18, 1845. We sailed from the Rio, and had a
very pleasant passage, till we encountered a gale off
the Falkland islands, by which we were dismasted,

with the loss of four of the people of the ship. After the gale was over, we got up a jury-mast, which brought us into one of the islands. Here, as we were unable to supply the main-mast, we got up three jury-masts, with which, under favor of Providence, we safely doubled the stormy Cape, and reached Valparaiso, where we lay three weeks, before the mast and yards were fitted, and everything *ataut* for the prosecution of our voyage. But before she was ready to sail, I was taken sick, and carried to the hospital, where my ship left me, under the care of the English consul.

My confinement, which was from a fever, lasted for seven weeks. And a matter of five weeks more, before I betook myself again to the water, afforded me an opportunity of looking round a little among the Chilians.

Valparaiso is the only city of much commercial importance in this republic. It has a population of 15,000 or 16,000, and is situated under the beetling cliffs which overhang the semi-circular bay. The only street which is worthy of the name, follows the course of the bay, is between the rocks on one hand, and the beach on the other, and is not far from three miles in length. Here are the houses of the opulent, while those of the poor are among the ravines of the hills, and the interstices of the rocks. The bay is delightful, and altogether, though it has no splendid edifices, the town is decidedly pleasant. "Santiago, the capital, is situated in a richly wooded plain, at an elevation of 2600 feet above the sea, which renders the climate agreeable and salubrious. Its aspect is irregular and picturesque. The dark tints of the fir and olive, with the lighter hues of the mimosa, mingled with steeples and houses, produce a novel and imposing effect. The houses having, in general, only one floor, and being surrounded by large gardens, the town appears completely overshadowed with foliage. Each house, in general, stands by itself, and, being strongly barricaded toward the street, forms a little fortress. They are one or two stories high, and built of unburnt brick. The streets, however, are regularly laid out, paved, and furnished with footpaths. The cathedral, several of the churches, and the director's palace, may be reckoned handsome, though they do not exhibit anything very splendid in architecture. The Alameda, a mile in length, and planted with a double row of trees, is one of the finest promenades in South America."* * * *

But for the volcanic action constantly going on in the neighboring Andes, causing frequent and ruinous earthquakes, and keeping the inhabitants in constant fear of their lives, this would be one of the most delightful countries on the globe. It is exceedingly healthy, nor is there anything desirable or valuable

* Encyclopedia of Geography.

p*

among metals, minerals, or vegetables, which it does not yield in great abundance.

The inhabitants, like those of all the Hispanio-American states, are gay, polite, hospitable, and ignorant. The ladies are darkly beautiful, exquisitely fond of music and the dance, and perform both to admiration. Here the opposite sex are at once distinguished and confounded by the broad flat hat, and the not ungraceful poncho. This is said to be the native soil of the potato, and it certainly grows here in great perfection. Wine is largely manufactured from the native grape. The *yerba*, or Paraguay tea, is also indigenous. The decoction takes the name of *matte*, and all drink it nearly scalding hot, and in profuse quantities. Among amusements, in addition to the dance already noticed, bull-fighting holds a prominent place, as it does, indeed, in all Spanish countries. The population is known only by conjecture. The more moderate estimate of 1,500,000, is believed to be the true one. But I forget the long way that this chapter is to carry us.

Shipping myself in a Chilian craft, which was employed in the coasting trade, I enjoyed the easy opportunity of extending my acquaintance with the maritime parts of the country, as also of visiting Santiago, its capital, of which I have already spoken, and Lima the chief city and seat of government of the

Peruvian republic, and various other inland portions of the two countries.

Peru, under the incas, was the largest native empire in South America. It extended more than 2,000 miles on the coast. It is believed that, in that period, the soil was more generally and successfully cultivated than since it has been under the management of its Spanish masters. The whole of the rivers appear to have been used for purposes of irrigation, and the mountains were terraced to their tops. Among the evidences of the advanced state of civilization in ancient Peru, are the remains of the royal road from Cuzco to Quito, a distance of 1,500 miles; a construction the more remarkable from the deep ravines which were bridged, and the many other obstacles which were overcome by it. Its present population is taken to be—for nobody knows—about 1,600,000, and is made up of Spaniards, Indians, and Negroes, together with the offspring of intermarriages among these various classes. The unmixed native population, however, though greatly degraded, is, by far, the most numerous. Of agriculture, there is but little, and of commerce and manufactures, less. The proverbial Potosi—now included in Bolivia or Upper Peru—is a solid mass of silver ore, 16,000 feet in height, and has a circumference of eighteen miles. The annual products of the gold and silver mines of this country have been estimated at $6,000,000.

That the ladies of Peru are fascinating, and that
they know it, and are intolerable coquettes, given to
flirtation, and not always averse to an intrigue, appears to be pretty generally conceded, even by those
whose descriptions are most favorable. Wrapping
around their faces their large loose cloaks of black
silk gauze, "they sally forth, and amuse themselves by
addressing their friends without being known by
them; mixing with the crowd to view whatever exhibition may be going forward, and, it is too likely, in
still more culpable indiscretions." Justice, too, compels the acknowledgment, that both sexes are ruinously
fond of gambling, and that household duties are subjects of the most deplorable neglect. Notwithstanding these *maculæ* in Peruvian character, it would betray a want of common fairness not to say, that it is also
courteous, generous, humane and hospitable. These
are matters of which, for the most part, I can pretend
to no personal knowledge; but of which, for obvious
reasons, it still seemed improper to omit this passing
notice.

For the same obvious reasons, I must be allowed a
word on the subject of the capital of this Ultra-Andean
republic; and the rather as, on *this* subject, I shall
only speak of what I enjoyed the opportunity of ascer-
taining from personal observation; and not any the
less my *own*, if given to the reader in the language of
a countryman. "Lima, next, to Mexico, the most

splendid city of Spanish America, is situated about
six miles in the interior from its port of Callao. It is
of a form nearly semi-circular; two miles long, and
one and a half broad; the base being washed by the
river Limac. It is surrounded by a wall of brick and
clay, twelve feet high, but capable merely of serving
for purposes of police. The houses run in straight
lines, dividing the city into a multitude of squares of
various forms and dimensions. They are built wholly
of timber, cane and unburnt brick, and are seldom
more than one, scarcely ever more than two, stories
high; but those of the rich are surrounded by porti-
coes, or open courts, inclosed by high walls and gates,
which being, as well as the interior, painted with
figures as large as life, and adorned with wooden
pillars, colored in imitation of stone, make a very gay
appearance. The plaza, or principal square, is, as in
other Spanish cities, surrounded by all the finest edifices. The viceroy's palace, however, is an old, plas-
tered, and unsightly structure of a reddish color, the
lowest story of which is strangely occupied by a row
of mean shops, above which is a gallery open to the
public. The apartments, now employed as govern
ment offices, display some vestiges of decayed magnifi-
cence. The cathedral is an elegant building, with a
stone front, and two towers of considerable height;
and the interior, particularly the great altar, is, or, at
least, was, excessively rich. Close to it is the arch-

bishop's palace, elegant, adorned with green balconies, though with the same bad taste of having little shops, among others, a drinking shop, on the ground floor. There are twenty-five convents in Lima, with churches attached to them; and fifteen nunneries. The convent of San Francisco, with its appendages, is the most extensive, and, though not so rich, is more elegant than the cathedral. An immense treasure in the precious metals was contained in these establishments; but during the revolution, great part has been abstracted, though the base materials substituted have been carefully gilded over. The population of Lima is reckoned by Caldcleugh at 70,000, of whom about 25,000 are Spaniards, 2,500 clergy, 15,000 free mulattoes, 15,000 slaves, 7,200 mestizoes, 5,200 Indians. Mr. Stephenson estimated the number at 87,000, and Mr. Proctor heard it reckoned at above 100,000; but no recent census has been taken. Callao, communicating with Lima by a very fine road, has an excellent harbor, formed by two islands. The forts by which it is defended are handsome and strong; and Callao itself is a considerable town, with 6,000 inhabitants."

In these cities—*any* Hispanio-American cities; but I now speak, more particularly, of the Chilian and Peruvian capitals—it is impossible for the most non-observing foreigner to avoid the sight of the numerous ecclesiastics, or escape the conviction that they are at once a heavy tax on the industry of the people,

and that the example of their indolence and vice
hangs as an incubus on all moral and industrial enterprise. Nothing is more obvious than that the people
hold them in 'deserved contempt for their dronish
profligacy ; nor is anything better known, at the same
time, than that the *same* people touch their hats to
them in the streets, buy their whim-whams, and send
their wives and daughters to them for confession,
where, as has been very naively said, "the big sin-
ners pardon the little ones."

Returning to Valparaiso, upon the close of the six-
months' cruise, I embarked in an Austrian vessel,
bound to Copenhagen, with a general cargo. As
nothing marked this voyage which would be likely to interest the reader, I will only say of it, that
doubling the stormy Cape twice, it was accomplished
in little more than six months. In the Albert, an
American ship, Capt. Thompson, I passed around the
Horn for the last time. She was bound to Bahia.
Here I entered the bark Cuba, Capt. Blanchard. *
* * * * * After proceeding to Rio Janeiro,
and waiting there for some time, we sailed away for
the Isle of Mayo, for a cargo of salt.

This island, with the group to which it belongs, is
claimed by the Portuguese government, though geo-
graphically connected with Africa. This group, known
as the Cape Verd Islands, is situated 80 miles from Cape
Verd, on the main land, and is composed of ten islands

Three of these, St. Jago, St. Antonio, and St. Nicholas, are large, the rest are smaller. To this latter class Fugo belongs, which, true to its name, is the seat of an active volcano. "The chief growth is cotton, which is exported to Africa; and a very fine breed of mules and asses is reared, many of which are sent to the West Indies. Goats, poultry, and turtles abound. Salt is formed in large quantities by natural evaporation, particularly in Mayo, where there is an extensive pond, into which the sea is received at high water, and the salt completely formed before next tide." From the natural sterility of these islands, and their liability to excessive drouths, the people are sometimes subjected to great distress for the means of subsistence. Most of my readers will readily recollect the famine of 1831, when of a population of 88,000,* one fourth are said to have perished.

On the Isle of Mayo, where we obtained our cargo, I saw but a single white man. He was an Englishman, and kept a grocery in the place. The face of nature is dreary and desolate. Doubtless the goats and donkeys found vegetable food *some*where. I can only say, that I saw none. With the exceptions

* For this number, as well as various other matters of a purely *statistic* character, these pages are, occasionally, indebted to the "*Encyclopedia of Geography*," together with other competent authorities. Where a quotation is properly such, it is marked accordingly; or otherwise, the substance of the author is given in the language of the narrative.

named, rocks, and sand, and salt, are the only produc-tions of the island.   The last-named of these minerals is brought from the "salt pans"—two miles from town —on the backs of the donkeys, of whom two hundred. thus employed, may sometimes be counted at once.

The only mentionable incident which occurred at this place, was the following:—On our humble and earnest application, the skipper had granted us "a day ashore," on condition that we should hire an equal number of native substitutes in the labor of taking in cargo.   Only, we were to go ashore in two parties, between whom the day was to be equally divided; in order to which, the party landing first, were to return at noon.   Mine being the forenoon division, we land-ed early, and lost no time in preparing to celebrate our half of the day.*   In order to this, it was not only settled that we were to eat and drink as many good things as our purses could procure on the island, but that we must also have a donkey-ride, and see as many of the "elephants" as our time would permit. The donkeys were engaged, accordingly, together with a boy apiece, who was to discharge the func-tion of driver.   This attendance was not all for *state;* it was equally demanded by *convenience* to ourselves, not to plead the immemorial custom of the island.

* The day in question, was July 4, 1846; but as there is no refer-ence in the memoranda to anything American in the "doings" of it, it appeared as well to let it fall out of the text into this note, where the *sans ceremonie* treatment is less likely to be a subject of animadversion.
23

For who, under an African sun, hot enough to cause
his liquefaction, would like, on an excursion of *pleasure*, too, to work his passage by plying the cudgel himself, when an additional shilling would leave him at his
ease, and, of course, more at liberty to "see things?"

We had been driven to the "salt pans" and back
again; thence, to my countryman's refectory, where
we partook of an early dinner; and thence we took
it through the town—the long, flapping ears before,
and the busy gads behind. So far the *asinade* was
neither all tragedy on the one hand, nor all farce on the
other; but about an equal mixture of both. It was
moving on with as much decorum, perhaps, as its
Oriental character demanded, till just as it neared the
little native church, when my "dapple" enacted an
interlude utterly unbefitting his own gravity, as well as
the quiet dignity of the occasion, and which, for a few
moments, threatened a catastrophe of a character decidedly tragic. As in all catholic churches, the marble or *other* stone, basin, containing the consecrated
water, stood in the vestibule of the sacred edifice, by
which we were about to pass; and, as is also catholic custom, the outer door stood open, for the reason that good
Catholics frequent the church at all hours of the day.

Such were the circumstances, when my donkey
scented the holy water, and instigated by thirst, headed
directly for the exposed entrance to it. For me, my
nautical tact was totally at fault. For, before I could

tell which rope to pull, or had time to back my main-stay, or lower my jib-boom, Long-ears had plunged his profane proboscis into the aqua sanctis, and, as the watering phrase is, was "filling in," as if, for want of water enough to moisten his glottis, he had not been able to bray the eight notes for a month. All this fell out in sight and hearing of a posse of male devotees, who chanced, at the moment, to be in and near the desecrated premises. An exclamation and a rush were simultaneous. The former, done into English, more than *implied* that the arch enemy was either *in* or *under* me; I was not quite certain which. At all events, and to make a safe case of it, they expelled us both, and with a force and suddenness, as well as with such a verbal flourish on the subject of *knives*, as left me in no doubt that, whichever of us might have been satanized in the above ejaculation, I was held responsible for the desecration and the drink. It may have been well for all of us, possibly, that my previous gleanings in the vernacular of the islanders enabled me, not only to understand, but to make myself understood on this occasion. The use made of it, after the necessary expenditure of a few vociferations for the purpose of gaining audience, was, that the game with the fighting irons they had talked about, was one that they would not have entirely in their own hands, and that they would be about as likely as anybody, to lose a little claret on the occasion.

Now, whether it was the unexpected hearing of
their own language, from so unexpected a quarter,
that induced the hesitation, or whether it was caused
by the gasconade which had gone home to their un-
derstandings, through that medium, are points of no
material consequence; but so it was, that they fairly
started back, as struck by a powerful surprise, de-
manding, as they did so, if I was not a "Portugee."
They were answered, that I was not; but this they
very courteously refused to believe. I had proved
myself to be Portuguese *enough*, that was clear. It followed, that I must be as good a *Catholic*, and, by the
most orthodox of all consequences, as innocent of any
intentional dishonor to their place of worship, as any
of themselves. Of course they had, because they
would have, the thing in their own way; and we, who
had met as enemies, parted as friends.

Aug. 10, 1846, we arrived at Rio Janiero, where we
exchanged our cargo of salt for another of coffee, and
made sail for New-Orleans, where we arrived Nov. 2.
Here, leaving Capt. Blanchard and the Cuba, I shipped
in the Albania, Capt. Craill, with a cargo of cotton,
flour, and Indian corn, bound for Liverpool. Owing
to adverse winds, especially when we were off Cape
Clear, our voyage was protracted, and attended with
considerable damage.

Jan. 23, 1847, we were in Liverpool. Having sailed
from New-Orleans Nov. 15, our passage occupied

sixty-nine days, twenty-three of which we were box-hauling about in the Channel. Here we lay twenty days. While discharging cargo, it came to pass that our poor ship happened to be caught in doing a little business in the contraband line, and that she was compelled to "walk up to the Cap'n's office and settle," to the tune of seventy-five pounds sterling. As soon as we were clear of this, and the unsmuggled part of our cargo, we got under weigh for New-Orleans once more, which was—

Feb. 12, with a load of Irish passengers. The passage was made in sixty-three days. Here I took to the Carthaginian, Capt. Isaacs, shipping only for the run to Liverpool.

April 30, found us under weigh for the above destination. When in the Gulf of Mexico, our ship sprung a leak, and it took all hands at the pumps to keep her free, till we arrived in Liverpool, which was not till the last of June.

Here lay the ship Queen, Capt. McLean, just ready to sail for New-York, with a load of passengers, and thence to St. John's, New-Brunswick, for a cargo of lumber. Wishing for reasons unimportant to the reader, to make the voyage with her, I shipped accordingly; fully intending, after its accomplishment, to revisit my native place and surviving friends, from whom I had now been separated fifteen years. It fell out otherwise. The passengers consisted, mostly, of

families from the north and south parts of my native
island, who were in quest of homes among their Yankee relations on this side of the water. Among these,
I was happy in meeting with that large and agreeable
class of people known, the world over, as "old acquaintance," and happier still in making at least *one
new one*. The consequence was—it could not be helped;
at least I thought so no long time after the first inter-
change of glances with the Caledonian maid—the consequence was, that, before we reached New-York, I
was fully made up to leave ship at that place, and follow this new adventure to one of the western coun-
ties of the Empire State. There—for thither, time,
in due process, brought us—there my story ends, and
with it, as I trust and intend, all my *ocean*, if not all
my *earthly* wanderings. I have seen many countries,
endured many hardships, escaped many dangers, and
owe a tribute of many thanks to that infinitely benign
Being who has watched over and preserved me. My
narrative, however unpretending in the manner of its
recital, claims at least the negative virtue of not having *travelled out of the record*. That it has a matrimo-
nial ending, after the manner of most works of fiction,
will not, it is hoped, detract from this its humble
merit, in the premises; as, happily for the author, imagination has as little to do with that matter, as with
any other matter of fact.

APPENDIX.

A.

As the manuscript papers afford nothing likely to prove satisfactory on the subject of convicts and the convict system, in Van Diemen's Land and the other settlements referred to, the reader is presented with the following. It is intended for Van Diemen's, but is, doubtless, applicable to the whole. It is derived from the Van Diemen's Land Almanac for 1832 :—" Van Diemen's Land being a station for the reception of offenders from Great Britain, it may, perhaps, be expected that a portion of these pages should be allotted to a subject which is very imperfectly understood at home, although of very considerable importance. There are two leading heads connected with this subject: the general state of Crown prisoners, and the incentives to good conduct with which they are presented. Upon the first point, it may be remarked, that all persons that are transported hither without reference to any previous circumstances whatever, are either placed in the public service, or are assigned to private individuals, immediately upon landing, according to their several qualifications. Those who belong to the first class, are compelled to devote the whole of their time to such occupations as are allotted them ; and in return, are fed, clothed, and lodged at the expense of the Crown. All mechanics and laborers reside in barracks, built expressly for the occasion ; but those who are employed as clerks in any of the public offices, are permitted to live elsewhere, and receive an annual pittance, varying from £10 to £18 per annum, together with a small sum for clothing. The regulations in force with respect to the whole body, effectually render their condition one of unvarying punishment; for they are not allowed the exercise either of time or talents for their own advantage, nor are they suffered to possess property, even if they have friends who would place such at their disposal. Those who are assigned to private individuals, must be *bona fide* in the service of their masters. They are not allowed to live away from his roof—must not be paid wages—not work for themselves—can go nowhere without a pass—in fact, although possessing a sort of comparative liberty, are still under the closest control imaginable. The Colonial laws against harboring prisoners are extremely severe, visiting with heavy fines all transgressors; and to which persons may very innocently render themselves liable, so various and comprehensive are the enactments. * * * * The state of persons who are sent hither for their offences should be one of punishment. They have no right to expect otherwise; yet that which is misery to one man, is thought nothing of by another;" [from which, with other considerations, the article argues in favor of discrimination in the treatment of prisoners].

With regard to the second part of this subject, or the indulgences that are open to prisoners as a reward for good conduct, they are, principally, *tickets of leave*, by which the holder is free from compulsory labor; and *emancipations*, which restore freedom, as far as regards the Colony, but do not permit the individual to leave it. But there are other intermediate steps which may be considered to partake of the nature of indulgences, such as situations in the police, &c., that are only conferred on persons of good character, but which open the road, at the end of a given period, to certain and considerable advantages. The fixed rule with regard to indulgence is undeviating good conduct, and length of service. Persons who are transported for seven years, must have resided four in the Colony before they are admissible to a ticket of leave—for fourteen, six—for life, eight. Emancipations may be hoped for, by fourteen years' men, at the end of two thirds of their sentence; by those who are for life, after having been here twelve years; but one single act that shall have brought the individual before a magistrate, so as to have a record of mis-

behavior against his name, no matter how slight its nature, there
is no saying how long, and the claim he might fancy he had, according to the rule now laid down, becomes altogether forfeited."

*   *   *   *   *

B.

THE BUMRUM, VEL BOOMERING.

To enlarge the reader's acquaintance with, and to give him,
perhaps, a juster appreciation of the native Australian skill in
handicraft matters, a printed article had been selected for this
work on the subject indicated at the head of this note. Unhap-
pily, that article has been mislaid and lost. For its details, which
were minute, as was demanded by so great a marvel, this present article can do but little more than furnish the substance of
Mr. M'Culloch's very brief account of it (see Un. Gas. Art. Australia); aided to some small extent by recollections of our lost
article, as also of verbal description, obtained some time since,
by the subject of the foregoing adventures.

The bumrum is a wooden missile; concavo-convex; curved,
and very thin. Launched by a skilful hand, it flies off in a
straight line, parallel with, and near the surface of the ground,
for the matter of fifty rods. Then it mounts high in air, per-
forming a variety of the wildest and most life-like motions. At
length it strangely begins its return; more strangely still, it falls
" within a few yards of the thrower" (M'Culloch); and most
strangely of all, it *invariably* does this—flies off horizontally;
gyrates into the heavens; then returns, and finally drops at the
feet of the projector. Though this is a savage plaything, it is
occasionally made useful by being sent among a flight of birds,
when above the farthest-reaching spear. In this case, its approach is at once so tortuous and so swift as utterly to confound
the sagacity of the game in its attempts to escape. Our adventurer advises us, however, that this masterpiece of native ingenuity finds but few, comparatively, who know how to use it;
and fewer still who are equal to its construction. The specimens

Q

possessed by his tribe were imported from other, and remote communities. A few could use, but not one of his large tribe could manufacture, a bumrum.

C.

A SIXTH CONTINENT.

" An extraordinary phenomenon, presented in the Southern Ocean, may render our settlements in New South Wales of still more eminent importance. A sixth continent is in the very act of growth before our eyes ! The Pacific is spotted with islands through the immense space of nearly fifty degrees of longitude, and as many of latitude. Every one of these islands seems to be merely a central spot for the formation of coral banks, which, by a perpetual progress, are rising from the unfathomable depths of the sea. The union of a few of these masses of rock, shapes itself into an island; the seeds of plants are carried to it by the birds, or by the waves; and from the moment that it overtops the waters, it is covered with vegetation. The new island constitutes, in its turn, a centre of growth to another circle. The great powers of nature appear to be still in peculiar activity in this region, and, to her tardier processes, she sometimes takes the assistance of the volcano and the earthquake. From the south of New Zealand to the north of the Sandwich Islands, the waters abundantly teem with those future seats of civilization. Still, the coral insect, the diminutive builder of all these mighty piles, plies his work; the ocean is intersected with myriads of these lines of foundations; and, when the rocky substructure shall have excluded the sea, then will come the dominion of man."—*Liverpool paper.*

D.

STATE OF AGRICULTURE.

" That a land enjoying one of the finest climates in the world, with a soil as good for cultivation as any one on which the sun ever shone, should remain untilled, is a subject deeply to be regretted; but thus it is. A great portion, probably nineteen-twentieths, of the whole of these islands, is uncultivated. Agriculture, with but three or four honorable exceptions, is confined principally to the native o-o, (a sort of chisel for digging the ground,) which produces little or nothing more than what is needed for home consumption, and supplies for the few ships that touch here; while the soil, that might produce exports to the amount of millions of dollars, yearly, is suffered to remain in the same state in which it has lain for untold ages."—*Missionary Herald for* 1839.

E.

FROM "GOSSIP OF SEA TRAVEL;

BY THE LATE HENRY S. CHIPMAN."

* * * "TRISTRAN is one of a group of three islands, called, on the charts, 'The Nightingale Isles;' 'Inaccessible,' and 'Nightingale,' being the names of the other two. The first mentioned —*Tristran da Cunha*—is the largest and most northerly, and is the only one of the group that is inhabited. It is nearly half-way between South America and Africa, being somewhat nearer the latter, and is, in size, about six miles square. It rises, at the northern part, to an elevation of a thousand feet, perpendicular; then commences a table-land, from the midst of which rises a conical mountain, said to be nine thousand feet above the level of the sea.

"These islands were discovered by the Portuguese, some time previous to 1648, but remained for a long time uninhabited by man; and their situation in a stormy latitude, exposed to the gales which are continually brewing in the vast expanse of surrounding water, offered but small inducement to settlers. In 1811, three Americans did, indeed, go ashore on Tristran, with the intention of remaining there some years, for the purpose of collecting the skins and oil of the seal and sea-lion, which abound on all the islands. One of them, Jonathan Lambert, is said to have proclaimed himself sovereign proprietor of the Nightingale group; but for some cause, of which I am not informed, Jonathan, in a short time, abdicated, and, together with his two subjects, left the place. Tristran at length was clutched by a tentacula of the great European polypus—a detachment of British troops, from the Cape of Good Hope, taking formal possession of it in the name of their sovereign. It was, however, soon evacuated by these, when one W. M. Glass, formerly a corporal in the Royal Artillery, landed there, accompanied by twenty-two men and three women, and made a permanent settlement. At this day the population has increased to five hundred souls. The ci-devant corporal is complimented with the title of governor, and his little colony is said to be in the most promising condition. At first, nineteen out of the twenty-two original men-settlers were, of necessity, doomed to a life of single blessedness; but, in the course of time, there grew up around the hearths of the governor and his two married subjects, a race of fine, hardy South-Sea nymphs, who, as soon as marriageable, were bestowed by his excellency to cheer the solitude of the others of his faithful and patient followers. The governor himself officiates in all ceremonies, religious, military and civil; although he is sometimes assisted in council by two of his wise men, as I infer from the following official edict, being sanctioned by the concurrence of their names:—

'We the undersigned, being three of the senior principal inhabitants of the Island of Tristran da Cunha, do hereby agree to furnish any middle-aged, respectable people, as man and wife, who are willing and capable to undertake the office of schoolmaster and mistress, with house and all necessaries for their subsistence, as well as to present them every year, at Christmas, with a tenth part of the amount of sale of our produce, so long as the schoolmaster and mistress shall conduct themselves with propriety, and choose to remain among us. And we do further agree, that any person sent to us with a certificate of good conduct and necessary qualifications, signed by the governor of the Cape of Good Hope, or by Admiral Warren, the naval commander-in-chief, shall be considered by us as eligible to the situation, and their passage to this island, paid by the master of any merchant-vessel bringing them, immediately on their arrival; the sum of passage money having been agreed upon either by the governor or admiral before mentioned.

'Signed by us, at Tristran da Cunha, this seventeenth day of January, 1834, on board His Majesty's brig, Forrester, in the presence of Commander Booth, R. N.

> W. M. GLASS, *Governor*,
> RICHARD RILEY, his × mark,
> JOHN TAYLOR, his × mark.'

"Many vessels bound to the East Indies now call at Tristran, whose little isolated peak looms up a welcome station-house to the voyager on that long and weary route. There he can obtain fresh provisions, and, what is a much greater luxury, fresh, clear water. On the north side of the island, where there is a sand-beach, and the only safe landing, a little cascade precipitates itself from the high cliffs; so that the vessels may almost come underneath to take on board this priceless beverage to many a famished mariner. Many inconveniences, however, are encountered, as well as some danger. The thick, matted sea-weed, which surrounds the island, is a sample of the former, and of the latter, those mysterious 'rollers' which of a sudden, and on the calmest days, rush reverberating upon the shore, bearing everything that falls within their scope resistlessly along with them.

"We were obliged to content ourselves with distant views of the snow-capped peak; for during six or seven days that we remained in the vicinity, there was a continual series of storms and calms, and one eternal bank of clouds hung over the island. *
* * * * *"—*Knickerbocker*, 1847.

F.

THE LASSO AND BOLAS AMONG THE GAUCHOS, &c.

"THE *gauchos*, or native peons, are the descendants of European colonists, and many of them have sprung from the best families of Spain. They are at once the most active and the most indolent of human beings; living, when not on horseback (which they generally are), in the rudest manner in mud huts. They are without agriculture, subsisting almost wholly on the flesh of oxen and game of various kinds, which they catch by means of two singular weapons, in the use of which they are extremely dexterous; the *lasso* and the *bolas*. The former, used by most natives of La Plata and Chili, is a strong platted thong of green hide, about forty feet in length, with an iron ring at one end forming a running noose; the other end being fixed by the peon on horseback to his saddle-girth. The gaucho, when about to seize an animal, whirls the noose with a portion of the thong horizontally round his head, holding the rest of the lasso coiled up in his left hand; and when near enough to the object, at a precise point of its rotation, flings off the noose, which seldom or never fails to secure the animal. If a horse, it invariably falls over the neck; if an ox, over the horns. As soon as the rider has succeeded in his aim, he suddenly turns his horse, which sets his legs in a position to resist successfully the pull of the entrapped animal. * * * * *

The bolas, used also by the Patagonian Indians, is a singular weapon carried in the girdle, and consisting of two round stones, covered with leather, each weighing about a pound. These, which are fastened to the two ends of a string, about eight feet in length, are used as a sling, one stone being kept in the hand, and the other whirled round the head till it is supposed to have acquired sufficient force, when they are together discharged at the object. The Patagonians are so expert at the management of this double-headed shot, that they will hit a mark not bigger than a shilling with both the stones at a distance of fifteen yards. It is not customary with them, however, to strike either the quanaco or the ostrich with them; but to discharge them so that the cord comes against the legs of the ostrich, or the fore-legs of the quanaco, and is twisted round them by the force and swing of the balls; so that the animal being unable to run, becomes an easy prey to the hunters." M'CULLOCH.

AUSTRALIA AND ITS GOLD.

[THE following sketches have been made since the preparation
of the foregoing narrative, and on a subject, as far as the gold
discovery is concerned, which was then unknown. In these
sketches recourse has been had to the most authentic of the pub-
lished official English documents, together with other reliable
authorities. Of the former, reference is due to the *History of
Australia* by R. M. Martin, Esq., Tallis & Co. London and New
York; of the latter, to an article in the London Times, and to
Household Words by Dickens, both of about the same date—
July of the present year, 1852. Beside an occasional paragraph
in brackets by the editor, he is obliged to use his authors with
the general understanding that abridgment is inflicted wherever
admissible, with reference to no other law than the necessity
which compels it.]

The British possessions in Austral-Asia, are Australia, or New
Holland (which contains the several colonies of New South
Wales, Port Philip, or Victoria, South Australia, and Western
Australia, or Swan River), Van Diemen's Land, New Zealand,
the Chatham, Auckland, and lesser islands—the whole compris-
ing a territorial area in the southern hemisphere nearly as large
as Europe.

In a favorable position, midway between America and Africa,
and at the extremity of Asia, they afford important capabilities
for the maintenance of British power in the East, as also for
commerce, from their contiguity to the richest and most densely
peopled portion of the globe; possessing in themselves (apart
from these considerations) a fertile soil and a salubrious clime,
they are adapted for the dwelling of millions of the Anglo-Saxon
race—and even in this early stage of their existence, with many

of their resources undeveloped, they are outlying farms, already instrumental in supplying England with augmenting quantities of grain, meat, wool, flax, tallow, timber, and other raw products, in exchange for her manufactures.

But we are to speak of Australia, remarkable for its great extent, singular conformation, and recent discovery. Less than a century ago the mere coast-line of this great "south land" was an unsolved geographical problem, as its interior is at the present moment. In the eyes of the learned, its very existence was a phenomenon; and some idea may be formed of the strange surmises entertained on the subject, from the wild hypothesis of Blumenbach, that Australia must originally have been a comet, or planetary body, which, being drawn within the sphere of attraction, fell upon this globe. Even the skilful and scientific navigators and explorers who have surveyed its coast-line and penetrated its interior, are undecided as to the cause or epoch of the formation of this vast country—whether, in a comparatively modern age, it has been left dry by the receding waters of the ocean, or extruded from the bowels of the earth by subterranean fires.

But the interest excited by this question, or by the singular animal and vegetable products of a land of contrarieties, merges into insignificance compared with that created by the extraordinary progress of British colonization *at a distance of* 15,000 *miles from the parent state.* The earliest settlement is within the recollection of the present generation. It was commenced in 1787 by the despatch to Botany Bay of a fleet laden with the refuse of our gaols and penitentiaries. For several years the convicts were on the eve of perishing by famine; but, stimulated by the hope of regaining their forfeited freedom, directed by the intelligence of their superintendents, and governed by a systematic and humane policy, these outcasts hewed down the forests, subdued the stubborn soil, and earned for themselves a home where their "sins were covered, and their iniquities remembered no more."

These pioneers prepared the way for their fellow-countrymen whom no ciime had expatriated, but who sought, at the antipodes, the means of obtaining an honorable livelihood under favor of the laws and customs of their fatherland. The result of their joint labors is now manifest in the prosperous colony of New South Wales—the proudest monument of British civilization in the 19th century.

This success led to the settlement at Hobart Town, Van Diemen's Land, in 1801-2; at Swan River, Western Australia, in 1829-30; of Adelaide, South Australia, in 1835-6; of Melbourne. Port Philip, in 1836; and of Auckland and Wellington, New Zealand, in 1840.

Australia lies between the parallels of 10° 45' and 38° 45' S. and the meridians of 112° 20' and 153° 30' E. of Greenwich. The latitudinal difference between the northern and southern extremities is 1,600 geographical miles; the greatest distance from east to west is 2,227. The area is 2,690,810 square miles, and the coast-line is nearly 8,000 nautical miles.

The proportion which Australia bears to the other divisions of the globe is thus stated :—

Divisions.	French Leagues.	Proportion.
Asia	2,200,000	17
America	2,100,000	17
Africa	1,560,000	12
Europe	501,875	4
Australia	385,000	3

[DISCOVERY.—The Chinese are supposed to have been entitled to this honor as early as the eighth century. According to French pretension, one of their navigators discovered it in 1503. With more probability, the Spanish and Portuguese discovered the north coast in 1520. Its *certain* discovery by Luis Vaes de Torres—from whom is *Torres Strait*—dates 1605. Captain Cook entered Botany Bay April, 1770.]

CLIMATE.—Excepting the marshy shores of the north-west coast, the climate of the whole country is remarkably salubrious. In New South Wales, I frequently slept in the open air without the slightest injury. It is said to be owing to the fineness of the climate that dogs do not go mad in Australia, that horses are seldom or never known to kick, that herds of wild cattle have a degree of tameness unknown on the Pampas of South America,

and that the descendants of Europeans are remarkable for an
equanimity of temper which is probably partly attributable to
the salubrity of the climate.

The air is remarkably elastic. Old persons arriving in these
colonies from Europe, find much of the hilarity of youth restored
to them. Not more than 5 or 6 sick persons will be found in
a community of 1200 or 1500. At some of the military stations,
seven years have elapsed without the loss of a man. Several
colonists are stated to be upward of 100 years of age. I saw one
woman who was said to be 125 years of age, and the singularly
horny texture of her skin seemed to confirm the statement; yet
she went about her daily work at a roadside inn.

GEOLOGY.—The mountain chain on the east coast has an axis
of granite, with occasional large masses of green stone, basalt,
and other igneous rocks. It is flanked on both sides by thick
beds of palæozoic formation, chiefly sandstone, but also containing limestone and coal.

At Port Phillip there are also igneous rocks, and on the coast
tertiary formation, resting on the edges of upturned palæozoic
beds.

In Western Australia, the Darling range consists of granite
below, covered by metamorphic rocks, and between it and the
sea is a plain, composed of tertiary beds.

In Northern Australia there is a great sandstone plateau, rising 1800 feet above the sea, and probably of palæozoic age;
whilst on the immediate shore, and round the gulf of Carpentaria,
are beds supposed to belong to the tertiary period. Similar sub-
strata are found in the central desert.

This immense island appears of diluvian rather than volcanic
origin; but different causes may have operated conjointly in its
formation. After having been left partially dry by the receding
of the mighty deep from the north to the south pole, some powerful subterranean action may have raised the crust of the globe,
in this spot, above the ocean level.

The coal formation, as yet discovered, applicable for domestic
or steam purposes, is confined chiefly to the east coast.

VEGETABLE PRODUCTIONS.—[Of the *sylva* of the country, the
editor of this work has no present data for the purpose of giving his

reader information. The prevailing growth, owing to its generally stinted character, is known under the name of *scrub*. Still there are large tracts covered with wood of the finest grain, and of the highest value known to commerce. As specimens, under the genus *eucalyptus*, our author describes the *jarrah, white gum, red gum, tuart, morrel, great blue gum, black butt, salmon-gum.* Beside these are *sandal wood, jam wood, casuarina,* and many others. [A- cargo of sandal wood, sent to Singapore for the China market, sold for £21 per ton, leaving a nett profit of £17 per ton.] A forest of the jarrah, [one of the several varieties of mahogany, and the most valuable] at a distance of eighteen miles from Perth, [the capital of W. A.,] and twenty from the sea, extends over a tract of at least 300 miles from north to south, with a known width of thirty miles from east to west. The trees are very fine, and it has been computed that this forest alone contains sufficient of this invaluable timber to build 200,000 line-of-battle ships; 20,000 navies equal to those of all Europe might, therefore, be constructed from this single forest.

FRUITS AND VEGETABLES.—In a small garden at Paramutta, I had the apple, pear, peach, nectarine, apricot, loquat, quince, cherry, plum, melon, pine-apple, figs, citron, orange, grape, mulberry, walnut, gooseberry, strawberry, raspberry and currant, all in full perfection. So abundant is the peach, that in many places, I have seen the farmers feeding their pigs with the windfalls from their teeming orchards. [The writer speaks of this fine fruit as being found in the forest, on trees grown from stones scattered by birds and bush-rangers.] The almond flourishes remarkably well, as also, in the more northern regions, the banana. The fig produces two crops in the year, grapes of every variety are in abundance, and are already dried as raisins, and extensively manufactured into wine. The olive, walnut, filbert and chestnut are in great perfection.

WHEAT, MAIZE, &c.—[Wheat averages, on good soils, from twenty to thirty bushels per acre; and our author, with his customary particularity of name and place, gives instances in which the yield per acre has gone up to eighty-five bushels. Maize yields from forty to seventy-five. The potato gives two crops in the year, and green peas are gathered in winter as well as summer.]

WOOL.—This is the great staple of the country. Its growth may be inferred from the following facts:

In 1812, there were shipped to England three bales.

In 1849, there were exported to the same market—including 19,400 bales from Van Diemen's and New Zealand—125,000 bales, averaging 280 pounds each. The present number of sheep —1850—is estimated at 13,550,000. [The number in the United States is 30,000,000.] In the next five years, the sheep walks of Australia will number 25,000,000.

ZOOLOGY AND ORNITHOLOGY.—[Referring to the former, the mammalia may be said to be mostly marsupial. The puzzle of naturalists are the *Ornithorhynchi*, *O. rufus*, and *O. fuscus*. These animals unite the body, fur, and habits of the mole, to the webbed foot and bill of the duck; are ovoviparous, and have the internal formation of a reptile. They are very shy, burrowing in the mud of rivers and swamps. Among Australian birds, passing the emu, and the several varieties of cockatoo, all noticed in the foregoing narrative, our space limits us to the particular mention of but one. This is a species of vulture, of the order *accipitres*, so fierce that, when pressed by hunger, he has been known to attack the natives themselves.]

THE ABORIGINES.—[The reader, rather than find these *miscellanea prelectiones* entirely silent on this subject, may not be displeased with the following sketch of native character; for, though taken with reference to the variety inhabiting the neighborhood of Swan River, it is, doubtless, without any flattering modification, illustrative of all the other varieties. At all events, it throws some light on the probable destiny of the native Australian; a subject on which the editor has, in the island part of the narrative, advanced what he supposes the true exposition of that sombre prospect.] In general they refuse all hard or steady work, and no wages will induce them to forego any amusement, or to settle permanently in one place. They are essentially creatures of impulse, absolutely void of any desire to better their condition, and inclined to look with contemptuous superiority on the laborious habits of their new associates. "White fellow," say they, "fool too much! Work, work—always work! Black fellow play, plenty play!" They appear. nevertheless, to be attached to the "white fellows," and are a merry, harmless, idle, good-natured race: sometimes very useful, often most provoking; on the whole, honest, but afflicted with a constitutional preference of mutton to kangaroo, which is the fertile source of compulsory labor on the roads. Schools have been established for the children, and an institution is maintained by the Wesleyan body, assisted by government, at which indefatigable and judicious efforts are made to infuse into their minds the principles of religion and social improvement. Their quickness of apprehension, as shown in the facility with which they learn reading, writing, arithmetic, &c., is said to *greatly surpass that of the white child*, and the mere experience of the schools would warrant the highest expectations of their future acquirements. But, with puberty, the inherent idleness, and the restless longings after the wild and wandering life of the bush, are developed, and the clean, bright, intelligent child, able, not merely to read, but to understand what he reads, merges into the filthy, lazy savage, gorging himself to stupidity, and basking under a gum-tree.

TRANSPORTATION FOR CRIME.—[By an Order in Council, New South Wales, or any other colony of the island, has ceased to be a penal settlement, since 1840. Van Diemen's Land and Norfolk Island are the only places to which convicts are now con·signed by the British government.]

CIVIL DIVISIONS.—*New South Wales;* settled 1787; population, 200,000; capital, *Sidney;* population, 50,000.

Victoria; settled 1836; population, 50,000; capital, *Melbourne;* population, 15,000.

South Australia; settled 1836; population, 50,000; capital, *Adelaide;* population, 15,000.

Western Australia; settled 1829; population, 5,000; capital, *Perth;* population, 1,500.

GOLD OF AUSTRALIA.—[The following accounts come down to March of the present year. It should be observed that they are *local;* so that their principal use is, not to exhibit the *full* extent of gold digging and the gold trade; but, by a few samples, to furnish us with something like a just notion of the Australian Continent as a rival of our own California.]

THE HARVEST OF GOLD.*

Three years ago, one Mr. Smith, a gentleman engaged in iron-works in Australia, made his appearance at the Government House, Sydney, with a lump of gold. He offered, for a large sum of money, to point out where he had got it, and where more was to be found in abundance. The Government, however, thinking that this might be no more than a device, and that the lump produced might, in reality, have come from California, declined to buy a gold field in the dark, but advised Mr. Smith to unfold his tale, and leave his payment to the liberality of Government. This Mr. Smith refused to do, and there the matter ended.

On the third of April, 1851, Mr. Hargraves, who had recently returned from California, addressed the Government, stating that the result of his experience in that country had led him to expect gold in Australia, that the results of his exploring had been highly satisfactory, and that for the sum of five hundred pounds he would point out the precious districts. The same answer was returned that had disposed of Mr. Smith, but with an opposite effect; for Mr. Hargraves declaring himself " satisfied to leave the remuneration for his discovery to the liberal consideration of the Government," at once named the districts, which were Lewis Ponds, Summer-Hill Creek, and Macquarie River, in Bathurst and Wellington—the present Ophir. Mr. Hargraves was directed to place himself at once in communication with the Government Surveyor.

Meantime, the news began to be whispered about. A man who appeared in Bathurst with a lump of gold worth thirty

* From Dickens' Household Words.

pounds, which he had picked up, created a great sensation, and numbers hastened to see whether they could do likewise. The Commissioner of Crown Lands became alarmed. He warned all those who had commenced their search, of the illegality of their proceedings, and made earnest application for efficient assistance, imagining that the doings in California were to be repeated in Bathurst, and that pillage and murder were to be the order of the day. The Government immediately took active measures for the maintenance of order. Troops were despatched to the gold fields, and the Inspector General of Police received a discretionary power to employ what force he thought proper.

Great was the excitement in Sydney upon the confirmation of all this intelligence. Hasty partings, deserted desks, and closed shops, multiplied in number. Every imaginable mode of conveyance was resorted to, and hundreds set off on foot.

On the fourteenth of May, the Government Surveyor reported that in communication with Mr. Hargraves, he had visited the before-mentioned districts, and after three hours' examination, "had seen quite enough :"—gold was everywhere plentiful.

A proclamation was at once issued, forbidding any person to dig without a license, setting forth divers pains and penalties for disobedience. Licenses were to be obtained upon the spot, at the rate of thirty shillings per month, liable to future alteration. No licenses were granted to any one who could not produce a certificate of discharge from his last service, or otherwise give a satisfactory account of himself; and the descriptions of such as were refused were registered. A small body of mounted police were at the same time organized, who were paid at the somewhat curious rate of three shillings and threepence per day, with rations and lodgings, when they could be procured. Fortunately, there was no attempt at disturbance, for the Governor in a despatch states, " that the rush of people, most of them armed, was so great, that had they been disposed to resist, the whole of the troops and police would have been unable to cope with them." The licenses, too, were all cheerfully paid for, either in coin or gold.

On the third of June Mr. Hargraves, who in the meantime had received a responsible appointment, underwent an examination

before the Legislative Council, when he stated that he was led
to search in the neighborhood of Bathurst, by observing the simi-
larity of the country to California. He found gold as soon as he
dismounted. He found it everywhere—he rode from the head
of the Turon River to its confluence with the Macquarie, about
one hundred miles; found gold over the whole extent; afterwards found it all along the Macquarie. Bathurst," observed
Mr. Hargraves, "is the most extraordinary place I ever saw.
Gold is actually found lying on the ground, close to the surface."
And Mr. Commissioner Green, two days afterwards, reported
that "gold was found in every pan of earth taken up."

But the most important event connected with these discoveries,
and which is without parallel in the world's history, remains to
be told.

On the sixteenth of July, the Bathurst Free Press commenced
a leader with the following passage :

"Bathurst is mad again! The delirium of golden fever has
returned with increased intensity. Men meet together, stare
stupidly at one another, and wonder what will happen next.
Everybody has a hundred times seen a hundred weight of flour.
A hundred weight of sugar is an every-day fact; but a hundred
weight of gold is a phrase scarcely known in the English language. It is beyond the range of our ordinary ideas; a sort of
physical incomprehensibility : but that it is a material existence,
our own eyes bore witness."

Now for the facts:

On Sunday, eleventh of July, it was whispered about in Sydney, that a Dr. Kerr had found a hundred weight of gold! Few
believed it. It was thought a capital joke. Monday arrived,
and all doubts were dispelled; for at mid-day a tandem drawn
by two grays drew up in front of the Free Press office. Two
immense lumps of virgin gold were displayed in the body of the
vehicle; and being freely handed round to a quickly assembled
crowd, created feelings of wonder, incredulity, and admiration,
which were increased, when a large tin box was pointed to as
containing the remainder of the hundred weight of gold. The
whole was at once lodged at the Union Bank of Australia, where
the process of weighing took place in the presence of a party of

gentlemen, including the lucky owner and the manager of the bank. The entire mass weighed about three hundred pounds, which yielded one hundred and six pounds of pure gold, valued at four thousand pounds. This magnificent mass was accidentally discovered by an educated aboriginal in the service of Dr. Kerr: who, while keeping his master's sheep, had his attention attracted to something shining on a block of quartz, and breaking off a portion with his tomahawk, this hitherto hidden treasure stared him in the face. The lump was purchased by Messrs. Thacker & Co., of Sydney, and consigned to an eminent firm in London.

Meanwhile, the Commissioner reported a gold field many miles in extent, north-east of Bathurst, adding that it would afford employment for five thousand persons, the average gain of each person being then one pound per day—while provisions, which at one time had been enormously high, owing to the cupidity of speculators, had fallen so low, that the sum of ten shillings a week was quite sufficient for one individual's subsistence. The reports from the other Commissioners were equally favorable; and it is gratifying to find that they all spoke in the highest terms of the orderly and exemplary conduct of the diggers.

Since the discoveries in the neighborhood of Sydney, there have been found, in South Australia, large tracts of country, abounding in gold, only sixteen miles from Melbourne. The most recent accounts—December 15, 1851—from these regions, are of a most astounding character. In the first week in December, nearly fifty thousand pounds value in gold was brought into Melbourne and Geelong. The amount would have been greater but for want of conveyance. "To find quartz," says the Australian and New Zealand Gazette, "is to find gold. It is found thirty-two feet from the surface in plenty. Gold is actually oozing from the earth." Nuggets of gold, from fourteen ounces to twenty-seven pounds, are to be found in abundance. A single quartz "nugget," found in Louisa creek, sold for one thousand one hundred and fifty-five pounds. The Alert was on her way home with one hundred and thirty-two thousand pounds sterling in gold, and two other vessels with similar rich cargoes.

Every town and village were becoming gradually deserted.

Those who remain behind to mind the flocks, demand such wages that farming will not long pay. Labor is in such demand, that anybody with a pair of hands can readily command thirty-five shillings per week, with board and lodging." The Government Commissioners had given in their unanimous report, that the gold fields were already so extensive as to afford remunerative employment for one hundred thousand persons. In conclusion, the last advices describe the excitement as so intense that fears were entertained that sufficient hands would not be left to get in the standing crops.

Every week the number multiplies of gold seekers' colonies planted about streams in Australia; at all, the conduct of the diggers is exemplary. Most of them cease from labor on Sunday, and spend that day as they would spend it if they were in town. The first keg of spirits taken into an Australian gold field, had its head punched out by the miners; and Government has since assisted them in the endeavor to repress the use of stronger stimulants than wine or beer. Where every member of the community possesses more or less of the great object of desire; where stolen gold could never be identified; where it would be far from easy to identify a thief who passes to and fro among communities composed entirely of chance-comers, having faces strange one to another, a little drunkenness might lead to a great deal of lawlessness and crime. There are men who will drink; and what are called by the miners "sly grogsellers," exist, and elude discovery in every gold settlement. Yet we read of one man who being drunk, had dropped the bottle which contained his gold, and are informed that he was afterwards sought out, and received due restoration of his treasure from its finder. Some settlements are much more lawless than the rest, and we have read, perhaps, more ill of Ballarat than any other; yet it is of Ballarat that we receive the following sketch from a private correspondent.

The writer, with a party of four young friends, quitted a farm near Geelong, in October, last year, to experiment as a digger at Ballarat until the harvest. One man at a gold field can do little for himself; a party of about four is requisite to make a profitable division of the labor. " With this party," our correspondent says, " I started on Thursday, October the second, for the Gold

City of Ballarat. We took with us all requisite tools; a large tarpaulin to make into a tent, and provisions to last us for two months. All this was stowed away in our own dray; and our man Tom accompanied it.

"This mode of travelling—the universal mode in Australia— is very pleasant in fine weather. We used to be up at daybreak, and start as soon as we had breakfasted. We would go on lei- surely—for bullocks won't be hurried—and get through a stage of from fifteen to twenty miles, according to the state of the roads, allowing an interval of one hour for dinner. Then we would stop for the night at some convenient camping-ground, where there was a good supply of grass, wood, and water. There our first proceedings were to make a big fire, and a great kettle of tea—a kettle, mind; then we rigged out a temporary tent, spread our beds on the ground, and went to sleep as comfortably as if we were at a first-rate hotel.

"On Monday night, having left the farm on the previous Thursday, we camped about two miles from the diggings, and ma- king a very early start, we got in sight of them a little after sunrise.

"It certainly was the most extraordinary sight I ever beheld. Imagine a valley, varying in width from one hundred to five hundred yards, enclosed on either side by high ranges of hills, thickly timbered. Through the middle of this valley there winds a rapid little stream, or 'creek,' as it is termed here. On the banks of the creek, and among the trees of the surrounding ranges were clustered tents, bark-huts formed after the native fashion with boughs and trees, and every kind of temporary hab- itation which could be put up in the course of an hour or two.

"Some idea may be formed of the number of tents and other habitations, when I say that there were then at least five thou- sand men at work within a space of about half a mile up the creek. All these had collected together in a few weeks; for it was only in the latter end of August that gold was first found in this out of the way forest valley—now the site of the City of Ballarat, as it was nicknamed by the diggers.

"We chose a place for our tent on a rather retired spot, not far from the creek; in a couple of hours our 'house,' was put

up, our stores stowed away inside it, and Tom and his team were
off on the home journey to Geelong. Leaving the others to
'set our house in order,' get in a stock of firewood, bake a damp-
per, and perform various other odd jobs attendant upon taking
up one's residence in the bush—Fred. and I set out to reconnoitre the scene of our future operations.

"The place where there was the richest deposit of gold, was
on the face of a hill which sloped gradually down from the edges
on the right hand or east side of the creek, going towards the
source. I mention these particulars, because it is worthy of
note that almost all the principal diggings have been discovered
in places similarly situated. The whole of the hill was what
geologists call an 'alluvial deposit:' consisting of various strata
of sand, gravel, large quartz boulders, and white clay, in the
order I have named them. It is in this white clay, immediately
beneath the quartz, that the gold is found. In one part of the
hill, where the discovery was first made, this layer of quartz
was visible at the surface, or 'cropped out:' in other parts, it is
to be met with at various depths, or from five to thirty feet.

"When first these diggings were discovered, there were, as
might be expected, continual disputes as to how much ground
each man should have for his operations. One party applied
to the government, which immediately appointed a commissioner,
and a whole staff of subordinates, to maintain order and enforce
certain regulations, made ostensibly for the benefit of the diggers. Of these regulations the two principal ones were, that
each person must pay thirty shillings per month for a license to
'dig, search for, and remove gold,' (I enclose you my licenses as
a curiosity :) and that no person could claim more than eight
feet square of ground to work at, at one time. In consequence
of this last regulation, the workings were concentrated in a small
part of the hill, where the gold was chiefly to be found. This
spot was perfectly riddled with holes, from eight to sixteen feet
square, separated by narrow pathways, which formed the means
of communication between each hole and the creek. A walk
about this honey-comb of holes was most amusing. The whole
place swarmed with men—some at work in the pits—others carrying down the auriferous earth to be washed in the creek—in

wheel-barrows, hand-barrows, sacks, and in tin dishes on their heads. In some of the holes I even saw men digging out bits of gold from between the stones with a table knife.

"Busy as this scene was, I think the scene at the creek was busier. Both banks, for half a mile, were lined with men, hard at work washing the earth in cradles. Each cradle employs three men; and all the cradles are placed close to one another, at intervals of not more than a yard. The noise produced by the incessant 'rock-rock,' of the cradles, was like that of an immense factory. This, together with continual hammering of a thousand picks, and the occasional crashing fall of immense trees, whose roots had been undermined by some mole of a gold digger—made a confusion of sounds of which you will find it difficult to form a just idea."

Our correspondent's party was not very fortunate in its researches at Ballarat. Having explained this to us, he continues to give his impressions of the place.

"When we arrived there, the influx of people was still going on; tents springing up at the rate of fifty per diem. This continued until the third week in September, when the number of persons on the ground was estimated at seven thousand. Strange as was the appearance of the place by day, it was still stranger at night. Before every tent was a fire; and in addition to this general illumination, there was not unfrequently a special one—the accidental burning down of some tent or other. These little conflagrations produced splendid effects; the bright glare suddenly lighting up the gloomy masses of trees, and the groups of wild-looking diggers.

"Noise, too, was a prominent feature of 'Ballarat by night.' From dusk till eleven P.M., there was a continual discharge of firearms; for almost every one brought some kind of weapon with him to the diggings. Then, there was a band which discoursed by no means eloquent music; nine tenths of the score being monopolized by the drum. In the pauses of this—which occurred, I suppose, whenever the indefatigable drummer had made his arms ache—we would hear rising from some of the tents, music of a more pleasing character. The party next ours sang hymns very correctly in four parts; and from another tent

The Last Rose of Summer', sometimes issued, played very pathetically on the flageolet.

" Sunday was always well observed at the diggings, so far as absence from work was concerned; and there was service held twice a day by different ministers. Altogether, though there were occasional fights—particularly on Sundays—there was much less disorder than one would have expected, where a large body of such men were gathered together. While we stayed, there happened only one murder and two or three robberies. You must not take the quantity of gold we got as any criterion of the amount found by other parties. Numbers made fortunes in a few weeks. One party that I knew, obtained thirty pounds weight—troy—in seven weeks; a youth of seventeen, who came out with me in the Anna Maria, received five hundred pounds as his share of six weeks' work. These are but ordinary cases. The greatest quantity known to have been taken out in one day, was sixty-three pounds weight, nearly £8,000 worth.

" On Wednesday, November fifth, we packed up, left Ballarat, and set off for Mount Alexander, where we arrived on the Saturday following. The diggings there are not confined to one spot, but extend for twelve miles up a valley. The gold is found mostly among the surface soil: some I have seen lying even among the grass. We tried first at a place where there was only one party at work; and the trial proving satisfactory, we stayed there three weeks, and obtained thirty-six ounces of gold. For a few days we did nothing; then we went over to some other diggings about five miles off. Here we went ' prospecting' for ourselves, and the first day found out a spot from which we took thirty-five ounces in one week—the last of our stay; eighteen ounces we found in a single day.

" We then started off, back to Geelong, for I was anxious to be back for the harvest. We reached home on Sunday, December 20th."

Writing on the 28th of December, our informant adds:

" This gold discovery has sent the whole country mad. There are now upwards of fifty thousand men at work at various diggings; of which I have only mentioned the two principal ones, Ballarat and Mount Alexander. Everybody who can by any means

get away, is off. It is almost impossible to obtain laborers at any
wages. Half the wheat in the country will most likely rot on
the ground for want of hands to reap it. Fortunately, we shall
be able to get in ours ourselves, for our man Tom is still with
us, and Mr. R.'s four brothers will lend us a hand. We have a
very good crop of wheat, for the first year; the barley, of which
we had an acre or two, we have already cut and thrashed, and
are going to send a load to Geelong to-morrow. I can handle
the sickle and flail pretty well for a beginner. We shall cut the
wheat next Tuesday. As soon as the harvest is over, and the
wheat thrashed out and sold, Mr. R. and I mean to make up another party and be off to the diggings. We cannot do all the
work on the farm ourselves, and hiring servants now is out of
the question. Men are asking seven shillings and sixpence a day
wages, and will only hire by the week at that rate. Things will
soon be in the same state as they are in California. All ordinary
employments will be put a stop to for a time, but there will no
doubt come a reaction in the course of a year or two."

"The contrast is very great between the orderly behavior at
the gold fields in Australia, and the disorders of California.
There are few fields, we are told, at which a miner might not
have his wife and family; if he could provide accommodation
for them, they would be as safe, and meet with just as much
respect as if they lived in their own house in town. A clergy-
man, quitting the Turon settlement, publicly returns his 'sincere
thanks to the commissioners of the Turon, and to the mining
population in general, for the many acts of kindness which he
experienced during his short residence among them. He considers it his duty,' he says, 'thus publicly to state, not only his
own personal obligations, but also the pleasure which he felt in
witnessing the general desire of all classes to promote the object
of his mission, and to profit by his humble labors;. and if,' he
says, 'he were to judge from their orderly conduct, and from
the earnest attention and apparent devotion with which they
all joined in the religious services of the Sabbath, he could not
help forming a very favorable opinion of the miners. It cannot
be denied that the great majority are sober, industrious and well-
disposed.' "

THE AUSTRALIAN GOLD DIGGINGS.

INTERESTING STATISTICS.

THE " further papers relative to the recent discovery of gold in
Australia," presented to Parliament by command of Her Majesty,
just before the close of the session, are by far the most valuable
and authentic collection of facts we have yet obtained on this important subject; and the Bluebook which contains them, is further provided with an excellent map of the southeastern portion
of the Australian continent, indicating by appropriate dabs of
gamboge the auriferous deposits which appear to speckle the
whole of that territory. We have here, therefore, a tolerably
complete history of the first six months of this singular revolution in the condition of a colony which seems destined to form
in all things an exception and a contrast to the ordinary laws
of nature.

The despatches of Mr. Latrobe, Lieutenant Governor of Victoria, convey the most vivid picture of the extent and value of
these discoveries of gold, and of their effect on the population.
Soon after the opening of the Ballarat diggings, 1,800 licenses
were issued. The ore was found pure, in irregular masses of
" great beauty," scattered in the blue clay and other superior for-
mations, and sometimes in lumps weighing seven or nine ounces.
" I witnessed," says Mr. Latrobe, " during my visit, the washing
of two tin dishes of this clay, of about 20 inches in diameter, the
yield of which was no less than eight pounds weight of pure
gold." The average produce of this spot was estimated for some
time at about 700 ounces and upwards per diem. But even this
was soon surpassed by the discoveries at Mount Alexander. The
gold raised there in December was calculated by hundred

weights, and arrived in the cities on the coast at the rate of about two tons a week. Some 20,000 persons were soon congregated in the district. Ballarat was comparatively deserted, and from the general prevalence all over the colony of the same geological formation in which gold has hitherto been found, Mr. Latrobe declares that he can " contemplate no limit to the discoveries or to the result of the opening of these fields."

Meanwhile, he adds, the whole structure of society and the whole machinery of government are dislocated. Upon the first discovery of gold in May, last year, in the Bathurst district of New South Wales, the moral effect on the laboring classes was violent, and appeared to be exaggerated; but the increased discoveries in Victoria surpassed all conceivable anticipation. In three weeks the towns of Melbourne and Geelong seemed emptied of their male inhabitants, idlers, day-laborers, shopmen, artisans, mechanics, domestic servants first; tradesmen, farmers, and clerks next; the higher classes at last; because, as employers of labor, they had no alternative but to follow where labor was to be found. It realized the fairy tale of that enchanted bird which dragged after it the peasant, the smith, the clerk, parson, and squire, as each of them tried to stop the rest. Cottages were deserted, business at a stand-still, schools closed; the ships in the harbor were abandoned, and even masters of vessels were compelled to join with the men, whom it was impossible for them to retain on board. All building contracts stopped; the survey of the country became impossible; clerks, public servants, jailers, and constables, caught the infection, and resigned their appointments. The Postmaster and Surveyor General of Victoria, apprehended a total interruption of the business of their departments. The Superintendent of the Penal Stockade announced the resignation of his constabulary. The Deputy Sheriff reported that eight men in the jail department had determined to leave, and the Colonial Surgeon feared much trouble if the attendants at the lunatic asylum should throw up their situations, for in fact that establishment was never more needed by the community. Mr. Latrobe continued to rely, with a confidence which was not altogether disappointed, on the reaction which must ensue when many of these persons would find by experience that they were utterly unfit to encounter the labor of the diggings, and that they might turn the discovery of gold to account by the increased value of their industry, or their abilities in other branches of occupation. But it became absolutely necessary to the public service forthwith to raise, by from 50 to 100 per cent. the salaries and wages of all persons employed. Thus, the wages of the police, turnkeys, letter-carriers, &c., were raised from 4s. 6d. to 7s. and 8s. a day, and the salaries of clerks about 50 per cent. The rise of wages and of prices had been even larger in private employments. Laborers rose from 5s. to 15s. and 20s. a day; on artisans' wages the increase was from 80 to 120 per cent.; men cooks got £2 and £3 a week; female servants rose 25 per cent. The quartern loaf rose in price from 5d., in December, 1850, to 1s. 4d. and even 1s. 8d., in December, 1851; meat doubled in price; bacon rose from 6d. to 2s.; and on all other articles of domestic consumption the rise was from 50 to 100 per cent. House rent, hotel charges, cartage, and boat hire, rose 50 per cent.; clothes, hardware, and furniture, 100 per cent.; saddlery was not to be got, and the price of shoeing a horse increased from 5s. to 25s. Not less than 11,000 persons had arrived by sea in the colony of Victoria in the last six months of 1851, and 2,781 from the 1st to the 17th January of this year; 8,000 licenses were issued for the month. As the vast majority of these persons arrived as consumers of general produce, and producers of no article but gold, the colony was obviously drained of all other commodities, while gold became in excess. The grand total of gold brought down under escort in the last three months of 1851, from all the diggings in Victoria, was 124,835 ounces, valued at £374,505; but it is calculated that not more than two fifths of the gold collected is forwarded by escort, so that the real amount found would be more than double this sum. The total amount known to have been exported down to the 8th of January, 1852, from Victoria, is upwards of 220,000 ounces; and the quantity shipped from Sydney is 142,975 ounces. When it is remembered that all these effects have been produced in little more than six months from the first discovery of the gold down to the date of the latest despatches, and that the scene of action is in an almost unexplored region of that portion of the globe most remote from Europe and from civilization, they will certainly be ranked among the most curious and surprising phenomena in the history of mankind. We shall shortly revert to the subject, in order to take into consideration the measures taken, or to be taken, by the home authorities, on the receipt of this intelligence. Those measures consist chiefly in an immediate increase of the military and naval forces in the colony, for, as matters now stand, a well-armed pirate, who should anchor in Hobson's Bay, would have no difficulty in laying the capital of Victoria under contribution to any amount; and even the maintenance of peace and order in the town depends mainly on the good-will of the respectable inhabitants. The second object is the promotion of emigration in the form most calculated to provide for the general wants of the community; and the last is the question of establishing a local mint and assay office, in order to legalize the transactions in gold, by introducing a regular standard of fineness. Those subjects have been attentively considered by Her Majesty's government, and in part provided for by Sir John Pakington, whose last despatches to Sir Charles Fitzroy and Mr. Latrobe are also before us: but whatever may be the measures taken, it is impossible not to apprehend that the influx of loose emigration from all countries, the sudden overthrow of the ordinary standard of value in the colony, and the consequent suspension of the usual and necessary occupations of many classes of society, will, for some time to come, be attended with very serious inconvenience.

THE GOLD FIELDS OF VICTORIA, AUSTRALIA.*

SINCE the first discovery of the wonderfully prolific gold mines of this colony, a continuous discussion has gone on as to the actual extent of the treasures they have poured upon us; and all sorts of vague calculations and wild estimates have been promulgated, varying in their results to an extent quite startling to those who really value sound statistical information. The amount shipped—the amount brought down by the government escort

* From the Melbourne Argus, March 4.

—the amount passing through the banks, or purchased by individual brokers, have each and all been made the groundwork of estimates of the actual yield, and with a variety in the ultimate conclusions which would be amusing if it were not a matter of national importance that is at issue.

A few weeks ago we ventured to throw together such few data as we thought important in arriving at an accurate estimate, and the opinions arrived at, avowedly founded, as in part they were, upon mere conjecture, have since proved to have been so near the truth, that we think it very well worth while once more to recur to the subject—once more to collate and compare such facts as may lead to a tolerably sound opinion, on the part of the community, as to the real value of the treasure which we have lately discovered at our feet.

In proceeding to endeavor fairly to estimate the extent of the golden harvest already reaped, we will first show how erroneous has been the opinion very generally held, that the great bulk of the gold has been conveyed to market through the agency of the government escort. In our last estimate, we calculated the amount which had arrived by private hand at one third of that which had travelled by the means expressly provided for it, and we calculated it at that in accordance with the opinions of many gentlemen of high authority in such matters, but with a strong impression on our own part that any such proportion was less than the reality. This impression is now borne out by the following facts.

The notice in the *Government Gazette*, announcing the establishment of an armed escort, bears date the 30th of September, 1851. On the following day, the first gold transmitted by this mode of conveyance arrived in Geelong, then the head-quarters of the gold mines of Victoria. The following is a list of successive arrivals from that date to the present, the quantities conveyed to Melbourne and Geelong, being added together :

AMOUNT BY ESCORT.

		Ounces.			Ounces.
Oct. 1	. .	96	Dec. 31 . .		11,174
" 9	. . .	1,239	Jan. 7 . . .		10,998

				Ounces.						Ounces.
Oct.	15	.	.	1,998	Jan.	15	.	.		14,598
"	22	.	. .	2,708	"	22	.	. .		12,050
"	29	.	.	2,830	"	29	.	.		16,087
Nov.	5	.	. .	4,721	Feb.	5	.	. .		11,876
"	12	.	.	8,474	"	11	.	.		11,115
"	19	.	. .	10,138	"	19	.	. .		11,202
"	26	.	. .	12,106	"	26	.	.		21,916
Dec.	3	.	. .	16,669						
"	10	.	.	26,656	Total by escort,					284,364
"	17	.	. .	19,492	Val. at £3 per oz.,					£703,092
"	24	.	.	10,851						

And now let us look at the amount of gold which has actually reached the markets, and about the existence of which there can be no possible doubt, the whole having either been already shipped, or being now lodged in known places.

At the beginning of this month, the amount of gold actually shipped and entered through the Custom House, consisted of 455,061 ounces, valued at £1,865,183, or nearly twice the amount arrived by escort.

We subjoin the list of vessels conveying gold, and the amount shipped respectively by each:

1851.

	Oz.	dwt.	gr.
Oct. 20—Shamrock, for Sydney . . .	1,547	15	0
Nov. 6—Coquette, for Sydney	788	6	4
19—Shamrock, for Sydney . . .	2,652	10	0
Dec. 6—Hero, for London	26,734	0	0
15—Dorset, for Hobart Town . .	583	5	0
22—Melbourne, for London . . .	60,586	0	0
24—Shamrock, for Sydney . . .	24,938	0	0
29—Favorite, for Sydney . . .	744	6	12
30—Himalaya, for London . . .	26,547	5	0

1852.

	Oz.	dwt.	gr.
Jan. 6—Hirondelle, for Sydney . . .	1,708	0	1
7—Swordfish, for Hobart Town . .	900	0	0
8—Phebe, for Sydney	2,504	0	0
15—Brilliant, for London . . .	55,077	1	14
15—Thomas and Henry, for Launceston .	1,000	1	1

1852.		Oz.	dwt.	gr.
Jan. 16—Sarah Ann, for London	. . .	14,044	6	0
20—Susanne, for Hamburg	. .	8,411	0	0
26—Shamrock, for Sydney	. , .	26,821	8	0
29—Statesman, for London	. . .	52,545	0	9
29—May Queen, for London	. . ,	389	0	0
Feb. 3—Dart, for Sydney .	. . . .	1,876	0	0
4—Christabel, for London	. . ;	54	0	0
4—Cape Horn, for Sydney	. . .	1,525	0	0
5—Favorite, for Sydney	. . .	3,205	6	0
6—Helen, for London	. . . .	1,286	0	0
6—Cornelius, for London	. . .	795	0	0
10—Aberfoyle, for London .	. . .	40,272	0	0
11—Prince of Wales, for Sydney	. .	5,109	0	0
20—Clara, for Sydney	. . . .	1,848	0	0
25—Enchanter, for London	. . .	29,354	0	0
25—Shamrock, for Sydney .	. . .	34,578	0	0
27—Syria, for London	. . . .	11,503	0	0
28—Northumberland, for London	. .	16,900	0	0
28—Don Juan, for Sydney	. . .	3,585	0	0
	Total,	455,061	10	8

In addition to which, we have the amounts lying in the treasury not yet applied for by the diggers or their agents, and the amounts in the hands of the various banks here and at Geelong. We have been favored with the requisite information in each case, and we now add together the various amounts:

	Ounces.
Amount of gold shipped to the evening of 2d March,	455,061
Amount lying in the treasury at the same date,	33,030
Amount at Union Bank in Melbourne and Geelong,	20,354
Am't at Bank of Australasia in Melbourne and Geelong,	29,826
Amount at Bank of New South Wales,	10,999
Total,	549,270
Value at £3 per ounce,	£1,647,810

We now have to leave the beaten path of ascertained facts, and having shown by the return of gold actually shipped or safely lodged in the banks and treasury, that the amount brought down by private hand, very much exceeds that transmitted by escort, we must resort, in an endeavor to form some estimate of the total amount as yet realized, to something very little better than conjecture. We beg of our readers, particularly those at a distance, to remark distinctly the line of demarkation which separates our facts from our estimates arrived at without that solid foundation.

Any attempt to estimate the quantity of gold held by private hands in the two great markets is one of pure guess work. In our last calculations, of the 19th of November and 20th December, we stated it at 8,000 ounces; but since then so common an article of merchandise has gold become, and so ordinarily do we see it handed about in its little washleather bags, that considering the numbers of returned diggers now in the two great towns, we think that we may safely triple the amount we have named, and consider 24,000 ounces now held exclusive of that at the banks and treasury as a very moderate estimate.

Again, the amount held by the diggers and buyers along the roads, and at the gold field, cannot be arrived at by access to any very reliable data. On the 20th of December, we calculated the number of diggers on the roads and on the ground at 20,000, and allowed them four ounces of gold dust each. The diggers now at Mount Alexander cannot be less than twice that number, or 40,000; but as the dry weather has lately very much diminished their individual success, we will only allow them one half as much per man as in our last estimate, or two ounces each.

The total yield of the Victoria gold fields will thus stand as follows:

	Ounces.
Amount actually shipped to the 2d of March,	455,061
Amount held in the banks and treasury,	94,209
Estimated amount in private hands in the towns,	24,000
Estimated amount in the hands of diggers and others on the road and at the mines,	80,000
Total,	653,270

—Or, 54,489 lbs. 2 oz.; 544 cwt. 89 lbs. 2 oz.; 27 tons 4 cwt.
89 lbs. 2 oz.—Total value sterling, £1,959,810.

And even here, we exclude all gold conveyed by private hands
to adjacent colonies, which has not been passed at the customs,
although, if these amounts were attainable, we have no doubt
that they would prove to be very great in the aggregate.

As we have stated before, the first large discovery of gold in
this colony was announced on the 29th of September; so that
the above most astonishing results have been achieved within a
trifle over five months. When the energies of the diggers are
set free again by the arrival of the rainy season, we believe that
through the industry of the vast number of people now assembled on the ground, an amount of gold will be sent into the
market, infinitely greater and more astounding than anything
we have yet seen.

LATEST FROM THE AUSTRALIAN MINES:

[Condensed from the London Times, the London Chronicle, and
the London News, of Sept. 2d to the 29th:

The total quantity of gold exported from Sydney, to May 13th,
was $7,000,000.

To May 22d, there had been exported from Port Phillip, over
$11,000,000; or between 32 and 33 tons.

At Melbourne, within less than a month, ending June 26th,
the weekly diggings had risen, from a little over 31,000 ounces, to
105,000. From California, as well as from the sister colonies
and elsewhere, emigrants were daily arriving by hundreds.

The specimens of quartz, exhibited at Sydney, are described
as "studded with gold in all directions." Some quartz, it was
reported, had yielded 88 ounces of gold to the ton.

A scientific gentleman, who has made extensive researches in
the auriferous districts of that country, declares, to the Colonial
Secretary, his opinion, that gold exists over an area of 16,000
square miles.]

LIFE OF NAPOLEON BONAPARTE,
Emperor of France.

BY J. G. LOCKHART.

With Steel Portrait, 392 pp. 12mo., Muslin. Price $1 25.

> "The lightning may flash and the loud thunder rattle,
> He heeds not, he hears not, he's free from all pain ;
> He has slept his last sleep, he has fought his last battle,
> No sound can awake him to glory again."

He was the greatest actor the world has known since the time of Cæsar. He sported with crowns and sceptres as the baubles of a child. He rode triumphantly to power over the ruins of the thrones with which he strewed his pathway. Vast armies melted away like wax before him. He moved over the earth as a meteor traverses the sky, astonishing and startling all by the suddenness and brilliancy of his career. Here was his greatness. The earth will feel his power till its last cycle shall have been run.

THE LIFE
OF
THE EMPRESS JOSEPHINE,
First Wife of Napoleon.

BY P. C. HEADLEY.

With Steel Portrait, 383 pp., 12mo., Muslin. Price $1 25.

> "Like the lily,
> That once was mistress of the field and flowers here,
> I'll hang my head and perish."

Josephine, for the times in which she lived, was a model of female character ; and if this volume shall make the study of it more general, it will so far extend the admiration of the pure and beautiful, in contrast with all the forms of corruption humanity could present in a period of bloody Revolution. The Empress was a greater personage than Napoleon in the elements of *moral* grandeur, and retained her sovereignty in the *hearts* of the people, while he ruled by the unrivaled splendor of his genius.

Sold by all Booksellers. Mailed, *post-paid*, to any address, upon receipt of price.

C. M. SAXTON, MILLER & Co., Publishers,
25 Park Row, New York.

CPSIA information can be obtained
at www.ICGtesting.com
Printed in the USA
BVHW030800221022
649807BV00003B/24